DANGEROUS INSTINCTS

MARY ELLEN O'TOOLE, PH.D., retired from the FBI in 2009. She continues to teach at the FBI National Academy and lives in Stafford, Virginia.

ALISA BOWMAN is a professional writer and collaborator. She lives in Emmaus, Pennsylvania.

Praise for *Dangerous Instincts*

"Mary Ellen O'Toole is my hero! In *Dangerous Instincts* she offers sound advice and fascinating examples gleaned from her long career in the Behavioral Analysis Unit of the FBI. This book will save many lives—including, quite possibly, your own. Whether the knowledge you find herein saves you from a con man, a rapist, a thief, a killer, or just a miserable marriage, this is a classic, valuable book."
> —Ann Rule, author of *The Stranger Beside Me*
> and *Don't Look Behind You*

"A masterful and compelling primer on survival in a world in which people are not always what we think them to be. Dr. O'Toole's deep understanding of the nature and implications of psychopathy . . . is particularly impressive, and shared by only a few other criminal investigators. This is an important and well-written book on topics of concern to everyone. A great read, highly recommended."
> —Robert Hare, Ph.D., author of *Without Conscience*

"Whether you are a fan of the television profiler, fancy yourself a good judge of character, or just want to protect yourself and your family in the post-9/11 world, *Dangerous Instincts* will provide the skills you need and should be on the top of your must-read list."
> —Paul Babiak, Ph.D., author of *Snakes in Suits:*
> *When Psychopaths Go to Work*

"As a writer of serial killer fiction, I rely on my observations of human behavior to craft my characters. But for Mary Ellen O'Toole, such interpretations are not an offshoot of her talents—they go to the heart of her long career as an FBI profiler. *Dangerous Instincts* is a bible to keep on your shelf—to be read annually. Its lessons are that important."
> —Alan Jacobson, national bestselling author of *Inmate 1577*

DANGEROUS INSTINCTS

Use an FBI Profiler's Tactics to Avoid Unsafe Situations

Mary Ellen O'Toole, Ph.D.
and Alisa Bowman

A PLUME BOOK

PLUME
Published by the Penguin Group
Penguin Group (USA) Inc., 375 Hudson Street, New York, New York 10014, U.S.A. • Penguin
Group (Canada), 90 Eglinton Avenue East, Suite 700, Toronto, Ontario, Canada M4P 2Y3 (a divi-
sion of Pearson Penguin Canada Inc.) • Penguin Books Ltd., 80 Strand, London WC2R 0RL,
England • Penguin Ireland, 25 St. Stephen's Green, Dublin 2, Ireland (a division of Penguin Books
Ltd.) • Penguin Group (Australia), 250 Camberwell Road, Camberwell, Victoria 3124, Australia (a
division of Pearson Australia Group Pty. Ltd.) • Penguin Books India Pvt. Ltd., 11 Community
Centre, Panchsheel Park, New Delhi – 110 017, India • Penguin Books (NZ), 67 Apollo Drive,
Rosedale, Auckland 0632, New Zealand (a division of Pearson New Zealand Ltd.) • Penguin Books
(South Africa) (Pty.) Ltd., 24 Sturdee Avenue, Rosebank, Johannesburg 2196, South Africa

Penguin Books Ltd., Registered Offices: 80 Strand, London WC2R 0RL, England

Published by Plume, a member of Penguin Group (USA) Inc. Previously published in a Hudson
Street Press edition.

First Plume Printing, October 2012
10 9 8 7 6 5 4 3 2

Ⓟ REGISTERED TRADEMARK—MARCA REGISTRADA

The Library of Congress has catalogued the Hudson Street Press edition as follows:

O'Toole, Mary Ellen.
  Dangerous instincts : how gut feelings lead us astray / Mary Ellen O'Toole and Alisa Bowman.
  p. cm.
  Includes bibliographical references and index.
  ISBN 978-1-59463-083-5 (hc.)
  ISBN 978-0-452-29852-1 (pbk.)
  1. Criminal behavior, Prediction of. 2. Criminal psychology. I. Bowman, Alisa. II. Title.
  HV8073.5.O86 2011
  364.3—dc22   2011015663

Printed in the United States of America

PUBLISHER'S NOTE
Penguin is committed to publishing works of quality and integrity. In that spirit, we are proud to
offer this book to our readers; however, the story, the experiences, and the words are the authors'
alone. The views expressed in this book are those of the authors and not those of Penguin or the
FBI. Some names and identifying characteristics have been changed to protect the privacy of individuals involved.

While the author has made every effort to provide accurate telephone numbers, Internet addresses, and other contact information at the time of publication, neither the publisher nor the
author assumes any responsibility for errors, or for changes that occur after publication. Further,
publisher does not have any control over and does not assume any responsibility for author or
third-party Web sites or their content.

The writing of *Dangerous Instincts* was a journey for me; my co-author, Alisa Bowman; and our literary agent, Michael Harriot, who brought us all together in the belief that we would click, and we did. We were three people committed to this effort who believed that this book could and would make a difference in other people's lives—to keep them safer and to help them make better life-changing decisions. During the time we spent writing and fine-tuning this book, we each suffered enormous personal losses. Alisa lost her grandmother, Elmina; Mike lost his mother, Laura; and I lost my sister, Ann. I know they would all be proud of *Dangerous Instincts* and its power to change people's lives. Therefore it is to them that we dedicate this book. We thank them for being the grandmother, mother, and sister they were, and the memory they will always be.

Ann O'Toole Caster

Elmina Elvia Bauman

Laura Harriot

Contents

Acknowledgments

We were thrilled when Caroline Sutton and her team at Hudson Street Press expressed such strong enthusiasm for this book. From the moment we walked in Caroline's office for our first meeting, we knew we were about to join forces with the best possible support team any author could have. In particular, we're grateful for Meghan Stevenson's skilled editing. She helped sharpen the copy, better focus the book, and remove extraneous details that could have bogged down the reading. She not only edited the book; she applied its lessons to her daily life. She couldn't have been any more committed to the cause. We're also thankful that Elizabeth Keenan and Courtney Nobile shepherded us through the publicity process and so expertly helped to get the word out. And we of course were delighted that Hudson Street as a whole provided us with so much support and worked tirelessly to make this book a success.

Michael Harriot, our literary agent at Folio, realized that Mary Ellen should write a book long before Mary Ellen did. He also realized that we would make a great team. He's an excellent matchmaker. This project truly would never have happened if it were not for his ideas and guidance.

We also thank the many gracious people who so generously allowed us to tell their stories in this book so that others might learn from them.

Mary Ellen

I have many people to thank who, because of their support and belief in me, allowed me to accept this wonderful opportunity to write a book about my passion—human behavior. Sadly some of these special people are no longer here, but their influence in my life is present every day. They include my mother, Isabelle Murphy O'Toole, and my aunts and uncles: Ann, Tom, John, and Alice Murphy. They all had a part in raising me. I had my own little village, and I know I am the better for it.

I want to thank my incredible family. Thank you to my sister, Ann O'Toole Caster, and my brother, Michael Regan O'Toole. We were parentless for most of our lives, but we remained a strong and supportive family unit for one another. I would not be who I am today if it were not for my siblings and their families: Andy, Tom, Peter, and Emily Caster; and Nancy, Megan, Olivia, Harlowe, and Mary Beth O'Toole.

Meeting Dr. Robert Hare remains the highlight of my twenty-eight-year FBI career. I tell the story this way: When I first met Dr. Hare at a conference in Seattle, I felt like I was meeting my Dr. Sigmund Freud. I still do. I am so grateful for his professional guidance and help, all the teaching and research he shared with me, and his confidence and trust in me to "spread the word" about psychopathy and its impact on society. To Dr. Hare and his wonderful wife, Averil, I say thank you so much. I am honored to have you as two of my dearest friends.

For years, I have had the privilege of working side by side with some of the most amazing and talented behaviorists in the world—men and women who were willing to share their expertise and support me in developing my own: Alice Casey, FBI Behavioral Analysis Unit (BAU); Marie Dyson, FBI BAU (retired); Matt Logan, Ph.D., Royal Canadian Mounted Police, Behavioral Sciences Unit (BSU) (retired); Tom Neer, FBI BAU (retired); Anthony Pinizzotto, Ph.D., FBI BSU (retired); Robert Ressler, FBI BSU (retired); Sharon Smith, Ph.D., FBI BSU (retired); Mark Safarik, FBI BAU (retired); Ronald Tunkel, ATF BAU.

My very dear friend Special Agent Ann Todd, of the FBI's National Press Office, taught me so much about how to work with the media and how to improve my communication skills in a venue that can be quite brutal. Her support, guidance, and faith in me helped me to get through some tough times and some very challenging interviews. She was so excited about the prospect of me writing this book and told me it would be a success. That was the encouragement I needed.

To my friend the renowned author Alan Jacobson, I want to say thank you. You told me to go for it when I called you and said I was scared and uncertain about whether I had what it took to write a book.

I want to thank all the agencies that over the years gave me the opportunity and privilege to work with their officers, detectives, and prosecutors on such important cases. I also want to say to all the FBI profile coordinators located in FBI field offices throughout the United States that it was an honor to work with you. You brought me into cases that allowed me to broaden my understanding of human behavior and to be impressed every day with the incredible work that you tirelessly do.

To the Texas Tower Heroes, the surviving victims and family members I lovingly call "My Austin Group," thank you for sharing all your time, your information, and mostly yourselves so I could understand what really happened on that hot August day in 1966 on top of the University of Texas tower. Charles Whitman started the carnage, but you ended it and walked into history with your astonishing courage and bravery.

I lost my beloved dog Buddy toward the end of our writing this book. Buddy would wait so patiently during the many hours that my coauthor kept me on the phone, and he kept me company as I edited many pages of this book. Buddy would listen for the sound of the desk lamp as I clicked it off for the day, and he would jump up because he knew it was time for us to take our long walk along the Potomac River. It's not the same without him.

Mike Harriot and Alisa seemed to know there was a book here. I was not so sure about it. They believed in the project and they believed in me. They were so wonderful to work with. I remain in awe of Alisa's talents every day, and I will always be grateful to Mike for putting our team together. He had a vision and he was right.

Alisa

When I first met Mary Ellen, she asked me, "Do you keep your doors locked?" I said, "We lock them at night." She asked, "But not during the day?" She looked at me quizzically, in the way people sometimes look when they know something that you don't. I came home that day and started locking my doors 24-7. This often meant that I accidentally locked out my husband, because he was not used to taking a key with him when he took out the trash. There were also many nights when, due to what I was writing about in this book, I was too scared to be home alone. Oh, and I heard strange noises. And, yes, I had nightmares. I thank him for graciously putting up with me.

He and our daughter, Kaarina, generously shared me with this book. The writing deadline happened to coincide with the winter holidays. I thank them both for forgiving me.

I am also thankful for the many people who listened with rapt attention as I talked about this book. Your questions helped me figure out what did and did not belong in its pages.

I would never have become the writer I am today if it were not for my parents, Marilyn and Don Bauman, who have read every word I have ever written, even the dreadfully boring reports I wrote in high school and college. My great aunt (now deceased) always told me I was brilliant and that I could become anything. I think of her whenever I feel as if I'm staring at a brick wall that I can't scale, and it helps. My high school journalism teacher, Anna Hayden, planted a love of words in my soul. Various writers and mentors talked me into staying in the business many times when I thought about quitting. They know who they are. My literary agent, Michael Harriot, discovered me and told me that I was more valuable than I realized.

And Mary Ellen O'Toole was not only a joy to work with but also had an incredible book inside of her. I'm honored to have had the opportunity to work on it.

Introduction

Not long after I retired from the FBI, I hired Paul, a carpenter, to replace the drywall in my bathroom. He'd originally been referred to me by a close friend, someone who'd known him for some time.

Paul was decorated with tattoos from head to foot, and he wore his hair in a ponytail. I knew that there were plenty of people—perhaps you are one of them—who would think that Paul looked scary.

My friend had also told me that Paul had been a member of a gang many years before. This piece of information concerned me, so I asked Paul about it.

He did not attempt to hide his past. He talked about it openly. "I threw down the colors," he said, implying that he no longer lived that lifestyle.

After talking for a while, I could tell, based on how he'd answered my questions and the referral from my friend, that Paul was a conscientious, hard worker. He was a true craftsman. I could tell from his behavior that he was really a gentle soul. I didn't want to exclude him just because of something he might have been involved in twenty years ago. I based my decision to hire him on the behavior and the personality of the man he is today. I gave him the benefit of the doubt. I hired him to replace the drywall in my bathroom.

When he showed up for work, however, Paul brought along his cousin

Jack. The friend who'd recommended Paul had not mentioned a cousin. Paul had not told me about his cousin. I had not interviewed Jack before, and I had no references for him. I knew absolutely nothing about him.

Normally I did not allow people into my house before asking them a few questions. It comes with the job.

I'd spent more than fourteen years with the FBI's Behavioral Analysis Unit (BAU). The BAU—the focus of the hit television crime drama *Criminal Minds*—consults with law enforcement all over the world to help it understand and solve some of the most violent and complex crimes ever committed.

I'd interviewed some of the world's most prolific serial killers. I'd walked through their lairs. I'd seen what they'd done to their victims. I'd glimpsed the worst examples of man's inhumanity to man.

I've seen what can happen when someone lets the wrong person through her front door.

Should I break this safety rule just this once and allow this other person into my home?

Paul introduced us. We talked briefly. Jack seemed likable, polite, and certainly nonthreatening.

I knew that Paul wanted to mentor someone in the business. I knew he wanted to pass on his master craftsman's skills. We'd talked about this before, and I'd thought it was a nice thing for Paul to want to do.

And since Jack was his cousin, I assumed Paul knew Jack well—well enough to know whether it was a good idea to bring him into the home of an FBI agent. I let them in. Paul supervised Jack the entire time. Neither one gave me any cause for concern. They replaced my drywall, and then they left.

I could see that Paul took great care with his work. He did a quality job. As a result, I hired Paul several times after that. Sometimes Jack came with him. Sometimes he didn't.

I later heard that Jack had been arrested for attempting to hire a contract killer to murder his girlfriend. Then I heard that he'd tried to take out contracts on additional people from his jail cell.

And I'd opened my door and allowed him into my home, even though I had not checked him out, because my gut instinct had told me that he was safe.

Danger Is Not Instinctual

Of all people, I know not to trust gut feelings. Based on what I saw and experienced on the job as an FBI behavioral analyst, I know that you can't decide whether a person or a situation is dangerous based only on whether you feel fearful.

In my work as an FBI agent and an FBI profiler for many years, I've interviewed countless victims who told me that they "never saw it coming." Their feelings did not alert them that danger was in their midst. The instincts and intuition they thought they could trust had let them down and caused them, at times, to willingly walk into harm's way. Over and over again, I saw people unwittingly bring the same sorts of issues and problems into their lives. They:

- didn't know how to get people to open up, do what they wanted, or provide the information they sought
- did not seem to have the ability to recognize the risks they were about to walk into
- consistently made poor decisions that resulted in years of regret
- were not able to recognize individuals who posed a real threat to them or their family

Dangerous Instincts teaches you how to go beyond the gut feelings that get so many people into trouble. In this book you'll find a simple analytical process that will help you to more accurately detect danger, deceit, evasiveness, and more. You'll learn about dangerous behavior, risky situations, high-risk decision making, interpersonal communication, and even psychopaths—individuals without consciences who are stunningly callous and lacking in empathy for others. This book shows you how to peel back human behavior in an illustrative way so you can use that information to make better decisions, size up people more accurately, assess potentially threatening situations, minimize threats in your everyday life, and conduct better "interviews" with people in everyday life situations—both at work and at home.

Do You Go with Your Gut?

We tend to trust our bodily sensations: hair pricking on the backs of our necks, shivers down our spines, racing heartbeats, and sinking gut feelings. We've been taught to read such sensations as signs of trouble and their absence as signs of safety. Yet over and over again, I've seen gut feelings lead people to ignore very rational signs that all is *not* okay and to instead open the door to danger.

It's these gut sensations that cause smart people to do seemingly unwise things, to engage in risky behaviors that earn them the kind of fame no one wants. They become the victims of identity theft, phishing schemes, bad investments, and physical harm. They suffer needless regret and heartache.

Their false security about their ability to judge someone's personality and intentions causes them to trust the very people they should not—con men, pedophiles, serial rapists, murderers, stalkers, spouse abusers, and psychopaths.

Indeed it was very likely just these sorts of "dangerous instincts" that caused investors to trust Bernie Madoff with their money. It's tempting to think that you would not have been tricked by Madoff—that something in your gut would have alerted you that he was up to no good. But are you sure about that? Madoff swindled many highly educated, powerful people over a period of ten to twenty years. Did all of those people ignore their gut instincts when they agreed to those investments? Did they sense fear, trickery, suspicion, and uncertainty, and then push them aside?

Their behavior would suggest otherwise. They followed through with investing their money with him. These investors were not naive. They were not of low intelligence. They were not lacking in common sense.

Investors trusted Madoff precisely because he knew how to manipulate their gut feelings. He disarmed them with his charm. He impressed them with his career accomplishments. He lulled them with glowing recommendations from other investors who were also unknowingly being conned. He was incredibly successful, wealthy, and respected. He had been in business for years. He knew people in high places, and he himself was at the top.

Madoff knew how to make investors feel good about him and about his scheme. He created a sanctuary of false safety. People trusted him. They liked him.

As a result, they gave him their money.

We all like to think of ourselves as smarter and less naive than the typical crime victim. We like to think that we somehow possess instincts that would alert us when a dangerous person is in our midst.

I've found, however, that few if any of us have instincts that are so accurate and perceptive that we should ever rely on them when making important decisions, especially when those decisions involve our safety or the safety of our families, workplaces, or finances.

In reality, our instincts lead us to read people incorrectly. They cause us to overlook or ignore the dangerousness of some people and situations. They cause us to make poor and, at times, unwise and unsafe decisions about whom to trust to:

- manage our money
- watch our children
- clean or repair our homes
- lock up our businesses at night
- work at our companies
- friend us on Facebook
- share our information on Twitter
- help us pass the time as we sit in an airport or wait for a train
- give us or our children a ride
- date and marry

Do You Really Know Your Neighbors?

Frequently when I lecture, someone will raise a hand and claim to be a phenomenally good judge of personality and to have flawless instincts.

Perhaps you feel the same way.

That's why I want you to think about these questions:

1. How do you know that others around you are not dangerous? For instance, how do you decide who to rent a room to, whether it's okay to allow your child to sleep over at a neighbor's house, or whether to give your neighbor the key to yours?

2. How safe is it to allow your child to drive with another teen or parents from the neighborhood?

3. How do you know that your next-door neighbor isn't a dangerous psychopath, a sex offender, or an arsonist?

4. Based on your gut feelings, which of those three types of criminals (arsonist, psychopath, or sex offender) do you think would be worse to have living next door?

If you are like most people, then you probably don't put much thought into whether it's safe for your child to sleep at a neighbor's home or whether it's safe to invite those neighbors to your home for dinner. That's because your instincts tell you that your neighbor is trustworthy, and your instincts tell you this because your neighbor does normal things that other normal, well-adjusted people do. For instance, he's probably married and has kids. He might walk his dog each morning or grow vegetables in a backyard garden. Maybe he dresses up in a suit, gets in a car, and goes to work every day. He probably looks normal, too, and so do his house and yard. The grass is well groomed. The shutters are freshly painted. There's a basketball hoop over the garage door.

He's friendly and polite. He waves when he sees you. He asks you about your day and about your kids. He tells you about his. He makes eye contact. He shakes your hand. He smiles. He's even done generous favors for you, like shovel your sidewalks and driveway when you've been out of town.

All of those seemingly normal characteristics are precisely why park ranger David Parker Ray easily blended into his Elephant Butte Lake neighborhood in New Mexico. His neighbors described him as a "regular guy." None had any idea that he was a sexual sadist who was using a small trailer in his backyard as a torture chamber. It was there that he repeatedly shocked, beat, and terrorized an unknown number of women over a period of many years.

His neighbors thought he was a normal guy and, after I interviewed David Parker Ray, I could understand why. He took my hand and cupped it in both of his. He said, "How are you? It's nice to meet you." He politely answered my questions. He cracked jokes. He was charming and gracious. He seemed as if he was a sixty-year-old man who respected and admired women. I had to continually tell myself, "Don't forget what you know, Mary Ellen. You just came from that toy box." (The "toy box" was David's term for the room where he stored his whips, chains, pulleys, straps, clamps, blades, saws, sex toys, and other devices that he used to torture women. It's where he kept women for hours and days as he tortured them, became sexually aroused, and recorded all his deviant sexual behavior so he could watch it and enjoy it later on.)

I knew what David had done and I knew what David was—a criminal sexual sadist. He was sexually aroused by the victim's response to his infliction of physical and emotional pain. He had kidnapped his victims, drugged them, and kept them in his home and in the toy box for his sexual pleasure.

"It might not seem as if this man is capable of doing that," I reminded myself. "But you know that a victim was found running out of his home, naked, wearing only a chain around her neck and telling police she had been physically tortured, repeatedly, by Ray and a female friend for several days following his kidnapping her."

Indeed, outside his toy box David Parker Ray did not seem anything other than perfectly normal. Inside it, he was anything but.

Our upbringings and our media consumption have trained us to believe numerous myths that cause us to overlook the David Parker Rays in our midst. One of these myths is that of the straggly haired stranger. This is the guy who roams the world, committing heinous crimes, never gets caught, and just keeps on getting away with his horrible behavior. The myth of the straggly haired stranger is one of several I will explore in this book—myths that cause many of us to let our guard down at precisely the wrong moment and to keep it up when we otherwise don't have to.

For instance, you'll learn the following:

• That our instincts often lead us to trust people based on superficial details—details that generally have little to do with true normalcy. In fact, dangerous people can be masters at appearing normal.
They dress nicely and keep their houses presentable. They usually
don't look out of place. They don't seem threatening, and our under-
lying belief is that if we are nice to them they will be nice to us.

• We generally distrust people based on superficial details too.
This is why we often assume that straggly haired strangers—especially
the ones who are socially inept, off-putting, and shifty eyed—pose the
greatest threat to us. In reality, some of the most dangerous of people
fit right in. They can be outgoing, charming, and exceptionally good
at making eye contact and putting us at ease.

In reality, you can't tell whether one of your neighbors is a sex offender, psychopath, or arsonist just by giving him or her the once-over.
You also can't tell—based on the type of car he or she owns—if your
neighbor is a responsible driver who does not text while behind the wheel
or has serious anger-management issues that result in frequent road rage.
Knowing that your neighbor is married or has children tells you, for instance, nothing about the massive gun collection in his home, one he
keeps loaded and ready to be used at a moment's notice. You don't know
if those guns are stored where curious children can access them, or if he
uses them to threaten his family when he has had too much to drink after
a bad day at the office.

I'm guessing that there's a lot you don't know about your neighbors,
but by the end of this book you'll realize what you don't know, why those
details are important, and how to fill in those blanks.

As for what's worse, a sex offender, an arsonist, or a psychopath—it
depends. A psychopath might be a violent serial killer. That's scary. I
wouldn't want someone like that living next door to me! Yet not all psychopaths are violent. In fact, most are not. A sex offender could be a serial rapist or someone with fantasies about abducting and holding
adolescent children. For instance, it could be someone like John Es-

posito, the man who abducted ten-year-old Katie Beers—a child he knew because he was friendly with her family—and for sixteen days confined her in a two-by-three-foot bunker he'd built in his suburban home. Or the sex offender might be someone who was convicted of statutory rape because he'd had sex with a consenting sixteen-year-old when he was eighteen. There's a big difference between those two extremes. The arsonist could be someone like John Leonard Orr, a fire captain and one of the most highly regarded arson investigators in California, who was convicted of setting deadly fires in crowded, public places. Or it could be someone who played with matches when he was twelve, accidentally burned down a family shed, and ended up being labeled an arsonist even though he never set another fire.

"Psychopath," "arsonist," and "sex offender" are all labels. To truly understand whether someone is dangerous, you must look behind the label and study that person's behavior. This book will show you how.

What Profilers Know

I am always asked, "What does a profiler do? How do you analyze behavior? What do you look for?"

TV programs like *Criminal Minds* and *CSI*, along with hundreds of Hollywood movies and books, attempt to capture the essence of the profiler's "process," but they get it wrong a lot of the time. Profiling is not magic. Profilers do not walk into a room, glance at the suit someone is wearing, and proclaim, "You're the killer. I can tell by your body language and that one book on your bookshelf."

No, we're not psychic or mind readers and we don't rely on crystal balls. Instead we are observers of behavior. We take into account what we observe at a crime scene and also consider the behaviors that are absent from a crime scene. We add that to other pertinent information, like forensics (blood-spatter patterns, ballistics, and wound pathology), autopsy reports, investigative reports, and more. We use that information to develop a "criminal investigative analysis" (a profile), investigative and interview strategies, and strategies for the prosecution during court procedures.

For years, as an FBI profiler, I studied human behavior—the behavior of the offender, the behavior of the victim, and the behavior of other people who surrounded both.

It wasn't until after I'd retired that I realized what I'd learned as a profiler could be very useful to others. That is what this book is about. It captures the process of an FBI profiler and applies that process to everyday life. It teaches you how to read behavior so you can assess the dangerousness of situations; make the kinds of decisions that, though all of us make them regularly, have a far-reaching impact on our lives; and effectively communicate with people, especially when strong interviewing skills are essential.

You will probably never find yourself in a position where you have to track down a dangerous criminal. It is not likely you will ever interview a serial killer, a kidnapper, a bank robber, a politician who has taken thousands in bribes, or the victim of a violent crime.

You will, however, be able to learn from a profiler's expertise and apply that expertise to your life. For instance, some of the communication skills I successfully relied on in hundreds of interviews with dangerous criminals can make a big difference in the success of your interpersonal communication with the people around you—family, friends, colleagues, and even strangers.

Normally information about how to stay safe focuses on what to do if you are, for example, tossed into the trunk of a car or abducted at knife- or gunpoint—both of which are incredibly rare situations that the vast majority of people will never find themselves in. Here you will learn how to make the kinds of serious and stressful decisions that confront all of us, all the time. Decisions like the following:

- whether to hand your car keys over to your teen or allow him or her to catch a ride from a friend
- how to respond when a coworker spreads lies about you and tries to malign you at work or on the Internet
- who to hire to manage your finances, fix your computer, babysit your child, or clean your home
- whether it's a good idea to place a personal ad online, what it

should say, and how you will screen the people who respond to it
- what to do when a friend or family member asks to move in with you
- how to handle a bullying incident at your child's school
- how to respond when your college-age daughter accidentally lets it slip that her boyfriend might have anger-management issues

Think about the important decisions you make. Can you trust your housekeeper with a key to your home? Is it safe to let your child's coach give him a ride home from practice? Should you make this financial investment with someone recommended to you? Is it okay to bring the guy you are dating home with you for the night? Should you give your Social Security number and other sensitive information to this financial adviser? Should you confront that neighbor about a problem you are having with him?

Such decisions and how you handle them can pose serious, long-term ramifications. They can result in lost sleep and worry. And in some cases the wrong decision, the wrong actions, or the wrong communication style can put you in a situation where the consequences are stunning and might even result in death or dire legal, financial, or career problems.

Wouldn't you like to know that you are making the best and safest decision in such cases? Wouldn't you want to know how to see signs of danger and do something about it? Wouldn't you like to be able to spot problem behavior before it's too late to respond?

Dangerous Instincts will help you to do all of that and more.

The Secret of SMART Decision Making

While at the FBI, I used a logical, step-by-step process to make important decisions. I used it when deciding how to interview suspects, when doing threat and dangerousness assessments of individuals, and when creating investigative and interview strategies that would lead to the identification of a suspect or cause one to open up and talk about his crimes. This process, however, works for *all* important decisions and can be used by any person. You don't need a background in psychology or criminology to use it.

This book will teach you this process. I call it SMART, an acronym that stands for "sound method of assessing and recognizing trouble." You'll learn more about it in chapter 2. For now, know that this process will show you how to assess other people for signs of potentially dangerous behavioral characteristics. You'll find out how to get people to open up and give you the information you seek—even people like stonewalling spouses, cagey job applicants, and threatening neighbors. You'll even find out how to tell if someone is lying or being evasive—and what to do about it.

Dangerous Instincts will help you minimize your decision-making risk and be safer overall. You will feel more confident and self-assured that you have weighed all your options, done a thorough risk assessment, and made the smartest decision possible.

DANGEROUS
INSTINCTS

Chapter 1

Test Your Instincts

Would you date a rapist? Would you get into a drunk driver's car? Would you ask a thief to invest your money? Would you allow your child to sleep over at a pedophile's house? Would you let a serial killer into your home? Would you ignore behavior that warns that someone will likely shoot up a school, college classroom, or a workplace?

Most people answer all of those questions with a loud and confident "No!" I'm guessing you would as well. Like most people, you might assume that you would sense if someone were about to con or hurt you. Perhaps you think that you would get an "all is not right" sensation in your gut, heart, or somewhere else.

Unless you are highly unusual, however, you probably wouldn't sense such danger at all. If more people could sense deceit or danger, a lot fewer people would become victims of violent crime, identity theft, pyramid schemes, and investment fraud.

When I talk with people about the unfortunate events that have taken place over their lives, I hear expressions like "It just came out of nowhere," "I never saw that one coming," and "I can't believe something like this could have happened to me."

Such expressions are telling. They mean that these folks were not forewarned by any gut feelings at all. They did not sense fear. They did not sense deceit. They did not have a premonition of something bad about to happen.

Their instincts and intuition let them down. Have yours let you down too? Later in this book, we'll walk through some of the decisions you've made in the past, and we'll analyze them to see what type of an assessment process you used, how well it's working for you, and whether it can be improved upon.

For now, let's have a little fun. Consider the scenarios in the following pages. Think carefully about what you would do in each. How would you assess the situation? What information would you factor into your decision? What information would you deem not important? Then consult the answer that follows each question to find out just how dangerous your instincts really are.

The Test

1. Jane is widowed and in her early fifties. It's been a few years since her spouse passed away and now she is ready to meet someone. Her friends, however, do not know any bachelors her age, and she's been unable to meet any at church or through her various hobbies. Her friends have been telling her to try online dating. She's resisted for a long time, assuming that she would only meet undesirable men that way. She's also been a little embarrassed to think she might have to resort to this in order to meet a man. And she's wondered if there's something wrong with her that she can't meet someone the old-fashioned way. Maybe she's too old, not attractive anymore, or too set in her ways?

Having exhausted her other options, Jane decides to give online dating a try. She joins an online dating site and reads a bunch of ads on it. Most of the descriptions seem like outright lies or just pathetic. She is about ready to give up hope when she comes across this ad placed by Kevin, a fifty-eight-year-old man:

I am looking for that special someone who will love and care for me and always be there for me as I will be there for her. I'm not into play-

ing games. I'm financially independent and recently retired from run-
ning my own company for many years. I've traveled the world. I am
physically fit and good-looking. I'm ready to settle down with the per-
fect soul mate. I will treat you with respect, kindness, caring, under-
standing, trust, honesty, compassion, love, and joy.

**What, if anything, can Jane tell from this ad that will help her
to determine whether to get in touch with Kevin? What types of
questions might she ask him to determine whether he's someone
she would like to date? And what should she tell him about herself?**

Should Jane hop on this one quick before someone else snatches up
this great catch of a guy? I'm not so sure about that. Before I get into why
I think Jane should be wary of this gentleman, let's take a closer look at
the potential pros and cons of this decision. On the positive side, Kevin
might be the perfect catch, someone who will serve as a wonderful com-
panion for Jane. But I'm a retired FBI profiler who chased bad guys for
most of my career, so of course one of the first thoughts that pops into my
head is that Kevin could also be a serial killer, rapist, or con man. Con
artists have been known to comb dating sites in search of victims. For
instance, William Michael Barber (also known as the Don Juan of Con)
allegedly lured several of his victims via Internet dating sites. He married
them, cleaned out their bank accounts, and then fled.

Romance fraud is one of the top five ruses used by Internet scam artists. In such "sweetheart scams" the con artist usually claims to live in another country. He might tell you that he is blown away by your photo and
feels a strong bond and can't wait to meet you in person. Alas, he doesn't
have enough money for airfare. Will you send him money for a ticket?

Can you see where this is headed?

But even if Kevin isn't a murderer or a con man, he might have a
drinking problem, mental-health issues, or serious anger-management
problems. Jane would not want to take on those kinds of problems. He
might be someone who gets involved in one dead-end relationship after
another. He may have stalked or harassed other women who broke up
with him. If he's *not* the perfect catch, it's a waste of Jane's time and might

prevent her from finding the right man. More important, dating him could lead to emotional pain and suffering, financial loss, or even physical harm.

Because of all of this, Jane will want to be very careful. If she misreads him and fails to spot danger signs ahead of time, the potential risk to her is quite high. Now let's take a closer look at what Kevin wrote in his ad:

• *I am looking for that special someone who will love and care for me and always be there for me as I will be there for her.* This is what he's looking for. He wants a woman who will always be there for him. So far, so good, although the word "always" should give Jane pause. This could be a sign that Kevin might see the world in black-and-white terms—a world of absolutes—which could suggest a certain amount of rigidness. He writes that he wants someone who would love and care for him. That's asking for a lot. In return, he "will be there for her." That sounds a little inequitable—as if he's not offering as much as he's asking for. He could be using linguistic flattery to lure a woman into having contact with him. His words could be more se-ductive than truthful.

• *I'm not into playing games.* Whenever someone offers unsolic-ited information about what they are *not*, it stands out as a red flag. When I see the phrase "I'm not into playing games," I wonder if someone has accused him of playing games in the past. Otherwise, why bring it up?

It's similar to someone saying, "I don't want to hurt your feelings but . . ." In other words, they don't want to hurt my feelings but are going to go ahead and do it anyway. These kinds of phrases are indica-tors of deception. They don't necessarily guarantee that someone is trying to deceive you, but they are indicators that they might be. Such phrases should make you pause so you can consider the other person's true motives.

• *I'm financially independent and recently retired from running my own company for many years.* He's implying that he is financially stable. This might be a good thing for Jane.

• *I've traveled the world.* He's worldly. This is possibly another plus in Kevin's favor.

• *I am physically fit and good-looking.* Although this might sound like a plus, I would counsel Jane to think about the kind of person who would boast about being good-looking. Whether he's easy on the eyes or not, most nonnarcissistic people do not describe themselves as "good-looking." Does Jane want to date someone who is self-absorbed? More important, does she want to date someone who might be dangerous? Psychopaths tend to be narcissistic and grandiose—they are precisely the type of people who would brag about owning their own companies, of being good-looking, and of traveling the world.

• *I'm ready to settle down with the perfect soul mate.* This line initially might make Kevin seem like a man who is ready to commit. I, however, would counsel Jane to take a closer look at the word "perfect." No woman is perfect. Is he searching for something that is not real? Will he hold Jane up to standards that she can't possibly meet? It's likely, especially when you add the word "perfect" to the word "always" from a few sentences before.

Now let's consider the term "soul mate." A friend of mine often says, "Soul mates are like unicorns. Neither one exists." I subscribe to that notion. If Kevin is looking for a unicorn, he's setting himself—and Jane—up for disappointment. Jane is only human after all.

He also might be using this phrase and others because he wants to impress women and persuade them to lower their guard. If this man is a psychopath, then he will say anything about himself—true or not—if he thinks it will help him achieve his goal. He will have read that women want a "soul mate," so he will use that term as a lure. It may have helped him to lure women in the past.

• *I will treat you with respect, kindness, caring, understanding, trust, honesty, compassion, love, and joy.* This line certainly makes Kevin sound like a great guy. After all, who wouldn't want to be treated this way? That's precisely why I would counsel Jane to be wary. There are too many positive nouns in this sentence. It's over the top. It's a little too good to be true.

Let's assume for a moment that I'm overanalyzing the ad and that this Kevin is a good guy who just wants to meet a good woman. Maybe, for argument's sake, Kevin asked his granddaughter for help with the ad, and that's why it has so many flowery and over-the-top descriptions.

Even if that's the case, Jane has no way of knowing, from the ad alone, what Kevin is really like. If I were Jane's life coach, I would recommend that she e-mail Kevin a number of open-ended questions that will help her to learn more about him and determine what kind of person he is:

- How do you feel about online dating and the type of people you meet?
- What are your biggest concerns about meeting someone online?
- What do you think are the risks?
- When you've had good dating experiences, how did those experiences go?
- When you've had bad dating experiences, what made those experiences bad?

In his answers, she will want to look for verification that what he said in the ad is true. Here are a few things she could look for and what they mean:

- *He blames all his past failed relationships on the women involved.* He might not be as understanding as he claims to be.

- *He writes numerous "I" and "me" statements.* He could be too self-absorbed for Jane's tastes.

- *He evades her questions.* Rather than directly answering, he says, "Let me get back to you on that" or "I don't know about that but . . ." Or he might pretend he never got the question at all, or he might change the topic. Any of this might mean that there's something he'd rather Jane didn't know.

• *He responds defensively.* He asks, "Why would you ask me something like that?" This, too, could mean that the question has hit a nerve and that he's got something to hide.

• *He continually talks about how great he is.* He might be trying to overcompensate for something Jane might perceive as a negative. He also might be incredibly arrogant and self-centered.

• *He is fearless and disregards any risks.* He might be the type of person who would not be able to understand the feelings of others. If he is a thrill seeker who does not think through his decisions, he might be too willing to take risks involving Jane, her life, her money, her investments, and her feelings, and that could create serious problems for her.

You'll learn more about how to interview people and interpret the answers they provide in chapter 8.

2. Dr. James works in human resources at a major university and will be part of a team interviewing potential candidates for an associate professor position in the English department. He is concerned about the incidents of school and campus shootings, as well as other incidents of workplace violence, throughout the country. What information do you think will be important for Dr. James when he and his team interview an applicant to ensure that the person does not one day threaten violence or act out violently at the university?

Did this question stump you? It stumps most people. And it does because most people assume either that people who are likely to become violent in the workplace have a certain look about them—they are easy to spot—or that it's impossible to spot someone who is likely to become violent until the day that person acts out. They assume that violent people snap, and there's no predicting who will snap and who won't until the day it happens.

Neither of these assumptions is true. People who commit workplace violence don't dress a certain way, have a specific hairstyle, or share any other visual characteristic. They are not necessarily all loners with poor social skills who live alone in a disheveled home with a cat. (This stereotype gives a bad name to those of us who live alone, own a cat, and are very happy and a risk to no one!)

A good interviewer, however, can spot someone who is likely to commit workplace violence.

For example, people who are predisposed to workplace violence are likely to have anger issues, a preoccupation with violence, and are "injustice collectors" (more on injustice collectors on page 186). That means they are easily offended, and they do not forgive or forget. They ruminate about real or imagined insults and blame others for their failures.[1] Of course, Dr. James can't ask, "Are you an injustice collector?" during an interview, but he can ask the following questions:

- How do you feel about the tenure process? What do you think the university administration should take into account when granting or not granting tenure?
- In the past, when management hasn't handled things to your liking, what have you done?
- What type of coworkers have you had problems with in the past and how have you resolved those problems?
- What type of feedback, both negative and positive have you received in your prior positions, and how did you address the negative feedback?

As he listens to a candidate answer these questions, Dr. James will be looking for information that the candidate might accidentally leak out. For instance, does the candidate blame others for conflicts and criticism or take ownership of his other mistakes? Someone who blames others might, at best, not be a joy to work with. At worst, he could be an injustice collector who harbors violent fantasies, resents others for their success, broods about perceived mistreatment at work, and who one day decides to act out violently against his bosses and coworkers.

Dr. James will also want to listen for times when the candidate might have disagreed with a policy and then just ignored it and broke the rules. That could be a red flag. You'll learn more about how to screen people for threatening violent behavior later in this book.

> **3. A new family has moved into Shannon's neighborhood. They have a son about her son's age, and the children have hit it off. Shannon briefly met the new family on the day they moved in. They seemed pleasant and normal enough. Their son, Kyle, wants her son, Max, to sleep over for the night. What types of things should Shannon make sure she knows before agreeing to allow her son to spend the night?**

In my experience, I saw more people willing to let their children go with others they don't know well than to lend their cars to a good friend. If you are a parent and you are being honest with yourself, then you can probably think of times when you've allowed your child to sleep over at another child's house without a second thought. You may have done it without even meeting the other child's parents.

Or if you did know the parents and you did ask some questions, chances are the questions centered on basic things like what time they put the kids to bed and whether dinner would be served.

You did so because your instincts told you that these neighbors were safe, and they probably caused you to think so for these reasons:

- You assume that dangerous people don't have spouses and children, and that they either live alone or live in someone else's neighborhood.
- You assume that no parent could ever hurt a child. You think all parents possess an instinctual empathy that causes them to want to protect any child.
- You assume that people who look normal *are* normal, and your neighbors all look normal.

- Your children attend the same school, and you assume the school would have spotted something and done something about it if there were a problem.

Yet all of these reasons are false, and you'll learn more about why later in this book. Even if Shannon's new neighbors are not pedophiles or murderers, there are still many questions that she has not yet considered:

- Are there loaded guns in the house and, if so, is it possible for the children to access them?
- Does this couple own porn or violent videos that Shannon doesn't want her son to see?
- Does either parent drink excessively or do drugs, including abusing over-the-counter drugs?
- Is either parent verbally or physically abusive?
- Do any members of the family have anger-management issues?
- Does anyone in the family engage in sexually inappropriate behavior?
- Are there animals in the house? If so, are they child-friendly?
- Are hazardous substances like cleaning fluids, pest-control chemicals, and flammables kept out of reach and safely stored?
- Is either parent careless about smoking, cooking, baking, or the proper use of space heaters and likely to accidentally start a fire?
- Do they lock their doors at night?
- Are there other children in the home? If so, what is their disposition? Are any of them likely to bully, abuse, or threaten Shannon's son?
- Who else comes into the home? Who else has access to the children?
- Does either parent have criminal records and for what? Do they associate with people who have criminal records and, if so, for what?

- Have these new neighbors had problems with families in neighborhoods where they've previously lived?

Are you thinking, "Who could ask such questions? My neighbors would think I'm a paranoid freak if I asked such things!" You have a point. These are not the kinds of questions that Shannon can ask in rapid fire while standing on her neighbor's front porch. They could be interpreted as offensive, and the neighbors might become defensive. If they had something to hide, they would make sure to hide it.

I would counsel Shannon to explain that this is not a good night for a sleepover. This is a stalling tactic, designed to provide Shannon with more time to gather important information. Shannon should definitely go on-line and check to see if these neighbors are registered sex offenders and whether there have been any police reports that mention their names. For instance, if they have a dangerous dog that has bitten someone, there will probably be a police report on the incident or their addresses might be listed on a dangerous-dog registry. Shannon will be able to find any of this publicly available information on the Internet. While she's at it, she might Google the names of all the family members, just to see what comes up. Is either parent writing a blog? If so, what is it about? Are they on Facebook, Myspace, or another social networking site? If so, what types of things do they post?

Do you think this is excessive? Consider that Phillip Garrido, the man accused of kidnapping and holding Jaycee Dugard for eighteen years, was a registered sex offender. His neighbors thought he was an okay guy. One of them spotted a young girl in Garrido's backyard soon after Dugard's disappearance, but he thought nothing of it. Had that neighbor checked up on Garrido and discovered that Garrido was a registered sex offender who was barred by law from spending time with children, he might have thought to call the police.

But let's say everything checks out: Shannon's neighbors are not registered sex offenders, they have a squeaky-clean police record, and a Google search reveals nothing out of the ordinary. Does the absence of information mean that problem behavior is absent? Not necessarily.

Next she might meet with her neighbors in different social settings.

She might visit them for a chat. While in their home, she might see objects that will allow her to ask important questions in a polite way. For instance, if she sees mounted deer heads, she could ask, "Do you hunt?" The answer to that question will allow her to politely ask other questions that help her to determine whether there are guns in the house and where and how they are stored.

She might also have the neighbors over for dinner, during which she can more easily ask many questions and listen carefully to the information they provide. She might, for instance, observe the mother and father. How do they interact? Does the father seem to control the mother and tell her what to do and say? Do they fight a little too openly, as if aggressive arguing is commonplace for them? Do they drink too much? Do they trash everyone they know? How do they treat their children? Are they domineering? Are they on top of things? Or do they ignore their kids?

Over time, as Shannon gets to know this family better, she'll be able to make a better decision about whether it's safe for her child to sleep in their home.

> **4. A telephone repairman comes to your door. He's dressed in a uniform. He shows you his identification and tells you he is working on lines that were damaged during a recent storm. He tells you his work will be limited to the outside, but he will need access to your phone line inside the house at some point. He is believable, seems trustworthy, his story makes sense, and he is polite and professional. How do you decide whether to let him in?**

Perhaps you've let such a person into your home before. Maybe it was someone who wanted to test your water. Maybe it was a salesperson who wanted to give you a free estimate for replacing your windows. Maybe it was a census worker. Whoever it was, you did a quick once-over and assumed that the person did not look dangerous. Anyway, he or she would not be there very long.

You were fortunate.

Several women in the Midwest who opened their doors to Anthony

Joe LaRette were not. He was dressed in a telephone repairman's uniform. Because of this, these women did not perceive him as a threat. They let him into their homes. Then he sexually assaulted and/or murdered them.

Dangerous people are quite adept at seeming harmless and at spinning lies that lead you to trust them. Based on what I've witnessed during my career with the FBI, I can tell you this with conviction: We can't tell if someone is dangerous just by giving them a quick look up and down. I'm trained to detect psychopathic traits in people. Even I wouldn't trust myself to be able to tell—just by looking at someone—if it was safe to let a stranger inside. Psychopathy, the most dangerous of personality disorders, cannot be assessed simply by looking at someone. Most of the time, neither can other types of dangerousness.

You might be thinking that people like Anthony Joe LaRette are rare. That's true. The likelihood of you opening your door to a serial killer is roughly one in 8.7 million. You are more likely to get struck by lightning.

It is more likely, however, that you might be facing someone who is casing your home (in order to burglarize it later) or who has intentions of scamming you.

I recommend that you consider the following before making a decision to open the door:

- Are you expecting someone?
- How easy would it be for the person on the other side of the door to overpower you and force his or her way in? (Note: It's a lot easier for someone to push his or her way in than most people think.)
- Are you alone? If you are not alone, would someone be able to get help or fend off a potential attacker? Is there someone home who is even more vulnerable than you are, making it even more important to not allow a stranger into your home?
- Can you verify the identity of the person on the other side of the door without making yourself vulnerable to an attack?

Can you see who it is through a window or peephole, or talk
to the person through the door? Can you call the company to
make sure the service person is there legitimately, on company business?

• Does he have anything on him or in his hands that could be
used as a weapon against you?

You might say that these are all basic precautions, yet I see people
ignore them every day. I have neighbors, for instance, who never lock
their doors—day or night. And I know many parents who assume that
their latchkey children know better than to open the door whenever
someone knocks and no adults are home. I can't tell you how many grieving parents I have comforted who told me, "But she knows not to open
the door. I told her never to open the door to a stranger." In my experience, children always open the door.

Later in this book, you'll create your own assessment process for de-
tecting trouble at the front door. For now, however, if you are not expecting someone, you are vulnerable, and you cannot verify the identity of the
person at the door, I would recommend not answering the door at all.
Anyone with a legitimate reason to be there will leave a note or follow up
with a phone call. Although this might seem rude, consider that your
safety is more important than whether the company gets the job done
that day.

**5. Larry is one of many professionals who commutes to work
in the D.C. area, where drivers can only travel in the commuter
lane—and avoid the worst of the rush-hour traffic—if they have a
passenger in their car. For this reason, "slugging" has become a
common practice. Sluggers gather at park and ride lots and catch
rides with other commuters, usually people they've just met.
Larry is such a slugger.**

**Larry's wife doesn't like that he does this. She worries that it
is dangerous and has warned him that he's eventually going to get
into a serial killer's car. Larry has assured her that slugging is
perfectly safe. No one has ever been murdered as a result of it.**

"Serial killers might prey on hitchhikers and prostitutes, but they don't prey on commuters," he tells her. "Anyway, I can fight off anyone. No one is going to overpower me."

Today Larry has a choice between two drivers. One is a woman in a Mercedes. He peers in her window. He sees a child's car seat in the back. The driver is alone. She's dressed in a professional pants suit and seems friendly. It looks like she's got the AC going, and it's a hot day.

The other driver is a man in an old sedan that is missing its hubcaps. He's dressed in jeans and a T-shirt. He has two other passengers. The windows are down. Larry can't tell for sure, but he suspects that this car does not have AC.

Larry decides to go with the woman. He figures the ride will be a lot more pleasant, that few Mercedes-driving mothers are dangerous, and that he could overpower her if it became necessary.

What is wrong with Larry's decision?

Did you just do a set of mental calculations, trying to figure out which car would be safer for Larry? Maybe, like Larry, you thought the woman in the Mercedes was the best bet for the following reasons:

- She's a woman and therefore less of a physical threat.
- She has kids (based on the car seat in the back).
- She's in a luxury car.

Or maybe you thought the other car was a safer bet because the presence of other passengers would provide safety in numbers.

Both decisions, however, are flawed.

First let's talk about the woman in the Mercedes. Beyond taking into account how it might perform in an accident, the type of car means very little in terms of personal safety. So does the presence of the child's car seat.

The fact that she's a woman could possibly make her slightly safer than the other driver, but not for the reasons that you or my hypothetical Larry probably think. If he thinks he can fight her off because he's bigger than she is, he's wrong. If she has a gun, his body size and physical strength will mean very little. She's safer than the other driver because women are three times less likely to die in car accidents than men are. According to the 2009 Traffic Safety Culture Index, men are also more likely to speed, run red lights, tailgate, and drive while fatigued.

But none of this means it's safe to get in her car. I'll elaborate on why in a couple of paragraphs.

First let's consider the other car. The problem with assuming safety in numbers is this: You don't know if the other passengers are innocent commuters like Larry or if they are accomplices planning to work with the driver in order to steal from or even murder Larry. Even if the driver is harmless, you don't know if all the passengers are, too, and vice versa.

But Larry's biggest lapse in judgment is this: He thinks he can look at a driver and tell if he or she is safe. He can't. Even I can't do that, and I'm trained to assess whether someone is a psychopath!

I'm guessing you might not believe me, so let me tell you a story. Colleen Stan also thought she could tell whether someone was dangerous. As she hitchhiked her way from Eugene, Oregon, to Westwood, California, she checked out each person who offered her a ride, trying to calculate the likelihood that the driver might be dangerous. She even passed up two rides because something seemed off about the drivers.

But when a Dodge Colt stopped and she saw a man, woman, and baby inside, she relaxed. They looked like a clean-cut, friendly family. She got in.

The driver was Cameron Hooker. He drove to a remote location, pulled out a knife, threatened to slash Colleen's throat, and then handcuffed, blindfolded, bound, and gagged her. He kept her as a sex slave for the next seven years—torturing her and keeping her locked in small box stored under his bed.

You just can't tell whether someone is dangerous by looking at them or at the type of car they drive or at what's in that car.

It would be exceedingly unlikely for Larry to step inside the car of a serial sexual sadist, but not for him to get in the car with someone who is a high-risk driver. You cannot look at someone and evaluate whether they are a skilled driver. You also cannot look at someone and tell whether they:

- text and drive or practice other dangerous or distracting driving behaviors
- have insurance that's up to date
- have drugs in the car that could get pinned on you if discovered by the police
- are operating a reliable vehicle, with airbags, seat belts and other safety features that are working properly
- have a neurological condition such as Alzheimer's disease that could impair their response time in breaking, swerving to avoid an accident, or taking other actions needed to drive a car safely
- drank alcohol or took drugs—legal or illegal—that morning
- have a bad driving record or prior incidents of aggressive driving or receiving multiple tickets or warnings
- own the car they are in

It doesn't matter how strong of a guy Larry is. If he steps into a car with a bad driver and that driver gets into a terrible accident, Larry is going to get hurt. These potential consequences of slugging won't make the front page of the newspaper, but they can have a serious and lasting negative impact on a person and their family's life.

Larry doesn't know any of these things about either driver. He never even thought of them. That means Larry doesn't have enough information to make a safe decision. More important, his ability to get those answers while standing in the middle of a park and ride lot are slim to none. Larry's wife is correct: Slugging could be dangerous. Eventually there is a good chance it will get him into trouble.

    6. Mary works in corporate security for a major bank. She is deciding what the bank should do about Caroline Miller, a twenty-one-year-old teller who has worked at the bank for one year. Caroline's supervisor and a consultant from human resources are worried that Caroline's twenty-four-year-old husband, Jim Miller, may attempt to come into the bank to threaten or hurt his wife.

    In the past, Caroline has come to work with bruises and cuts,

and she's explained them away by saying that she fell or was in a car accident. Now, however, Caroline has filed for divorce, and she has told the HR consultant that her husband is abusive.

According to Caroline, Jim has threatened to come to the bank and confront another employee, Peter Jones, because he thinks Caroline is having an affair with him. Since their separation, Jim and Caroline have been seen, by one of her coworkers, sitting in their car and arguing.

Within the last month, Caroline applied for a bank loan in order to purchase a new motorcycle. The loan was declined because of a poor credit rating.

When Caroline initially applied for her position with the bank, Jim also submitted an application for employment and was interviewed but not hired. His employment record was incomplete, and during the interview he admitted that he had a prior felony conviction for possession of drugs and illegal possession of a firearm. He explained that the conviction was a huge misunderstanding and that he was pursuing legal means to have his record "expunged." The woman who interviewed Jim for employment described him as being charming but egotistical. During the interview, the way Jim looked at her made her so uncomfortable that she had to look away. His eyes were like a snake's. It unnerved her.

About nine months ago, an unidentified man robbed the branch of the bank where Caroline works, pointing a gun at her and demanding all the money from her drawer. She complied. The same person is believed to be responsible for at least two other robberies at different banks in the area.

What do you think is going on here? What else does Mary need to know in order to make a decision about how to resolve the situation? Are these isolated events? Or do they all tie together?

I have used this scenario when I train corporate security and human resources personnel. It usually stumps most of the people in the room.

Some people might reason that Jim's charm, incomplete employment record, and attempt to explain away his criminal record as a "misunderstanding" are signs that he might be a psychopath.

I usually have a few people in the room who suspect that Jim might have been the person who robbed the bank.

Never, however, has anyone come up with the following questions for Mary to consider:

1. Is Caroline really a domestic abuse victim? Are the signs of domestic abuse a ruse to distract bank employees from something else?
2. If Jim robbed the bank, did Caroline hand over the money because she was scared or did she do it because she was complicit in his scheme?
3. What was really going on in the car when the coworker saw Jim and Caroline? Were they really fighting over the divorce? Was he making threats that she has not told the bank about? Is his violence escalating?
4. Will he come back to the bank and kill his wife and others because he is paranoid and jealous and suspects Caroline of having an affair?

We've been conditioned to sympathize with and trust people who appear like victims. For instance, a few years ago, when a woman accused three Duke University lacrosse players of rape, most people vehemently took the alleged victim's side. When I heard about the details of that case, however, I was pretty sure that the woman's story was fabricated. False allegations of rape are extremely rare, but this woman said and did several things that caused me to doubt her story.

When I mentioned this to some of my family or friends, they told me that I did not know what I was talking about. Some even became angry with me, saying things like "Who would ever lie about something like that?" The alleged victim's story, however, was eventually proven false, and the lacrosse players were vindicated.

Our natural inclination is to put ourselves in someone else's shoes. We forget, however, that other people do not necessarily wear the same types of shoes we do. They do not necessarily share our behavior, personality, and values. Just because you or I would never falsely accuse someone else of a serious crime like rape doesn't mean that no one else would do such a thing. The same is true in this bank scenario. Looks can be deceiving, and things are not always what they appear to be. If Mary trusts her instinct to protect Caroline, without considering all the facts, she and others at the bank, including customers, might very well end up victims themselves.

7. Graham writes a motivational blog that offers career and life tips. For several months, he's been getting a lot of mail from Lisa, who describes herself as "his biggest fan." This admirer e-mails Graham positive comments once every other week, like clockwork. Graham tries to interact with all his fans and to answer every single e-mail. That way they will continue to come back and tell others about his blog. For this reason, Graham has been responding to Lisa with a quick e-mail that says, "Thank you for reading!" or "Thanks for your kind words!"

Over time Graham has learned that Lisa lives overseas and that she reads his blog because she is currently unemployed and searching for a new job.

Recently Graham posted a photo of himself. That day Lisa e-mailed the following:

> *I am, of course, your biggest fan, but I would like to offer you a constructive critique. You need to wear your blue suit when you have your photo taken. It goes with your eyes. I suggest wearing it with your red tie, for contrast. You also should cut your hair shorter. This will make you look more self-confident and more polished, like the sexy man I know you to be.*

Graham doesn't know what to make of this. Initially he was annoyed, thinking, "How dare she tell me how to dress and cut my hair?" He doesn't respond right away, however, because he can't think of what to write.

A few days go by. Graham gets busy and forgets about the e-mail.

A week later he gets this e-mail from Lisa:

Why didn't you respond to my e-mail? I need to hear from you. I'm not trying to harass you, but I just cannot believe you would be so insensitive and irresponsible as to not respond to your e-mails like this.

A few hours later, he gets yet another e-mail from Lisa. It says:

You apparently are not the person I thought you were. In fact, you seem to have some real flaws in your character. You are obviously very immature, arrogant, and way too self-absorbed. You don't understand the importance of responding immediately to the very people who made this amateur blog even halfway enjoyable. I am done with you, and I intend to make sure you know exactly what I mean. You should not be in a position to influence other people through your worthless blog and advice. I really do hate you.

Then Graham logs on to Facebook, where he finds that Lisa has written several statements on his wall that demonize and insult him.

What about this exchange should give Graham cause for concern? What about it should cause Graham to rest easy?

Do you think that Lisa is a harmless fan? After all, she's a woman who lives overseas. How much of a threat could she possibly pose to Graham? Perhaps Graham should just e-mail a quick "sorry," set the record straight, explain that there's been a misunderstanding, that he's really a good person, and that he was just busy?

Or do you think that Lisa is the kind of Internet nuisance who should be put in her place? Perhaps Graham should fire off an angry e-mail that teaches her some politeness and manners? Perhaps Graham should share Lisa's e-mail address with all of his friends and have them respond with some derogatory comments of their own?

Or do you think Lisa is dangerous and that Graham should send her a curt e-mail asking her to not contact him ever again?

All of these tactics are the opposite of what Graham should do.

In reality, Lisa's gender has little to do with the potential threat she poses to Graham. That she lives overseas *might* be cause for relief, assuming she really does live overseas.

Indeed, Graham may falsely assume he knows more about Lisa than he really does. He's relying on what she's told him, but he doesn't know if any of that information is truthful or factual. Graham is underestimating Internet fabrication, which happens all the time. For all Graham knows, Lisa lives near him and has been following him around for weeks and months without him noticing her. That she knows he owns a blue suit and a red tie suggests as much.

For that matter, Graham can't even know for sure if Lisa is really a woman. It's possible that her entire Internet persona has been fabricated. She might really be a teenage Internet troll who finds enjoyment in wasting people's time online. She might be a convicted felon. For all Graham knows, she might even be his next-door neighbor.

Lisa is behaving like a cyberstalker, and it's very likely that she is one. Three details give this away: She's described herself as Graham's "biggest fan," which puts Graham up on a pedestal. She's sexualized Graham. Then, when she didn't get the response she wanted, she went from adulation to demonization, and her behavior appears to be escalating.

Many people think of cyberstalkers as mere annoyances. Yet cyberstalkers can be potentially very dangerous. These stalkers tend to target victims through Internet chat rooms, discussion boards, social networking sites, blogs, and e-mail. They've been known to steal their victims' identities, send viruses to their victims' computers, bully their victims online, and defame and malign their victims' reputations.

Lisa might physically lash out at Graham's family, too. Often the person most at risk in a stalking case isn't the person being stalked. Rather it's the person or people the stalker sees standing in the way between them and their target.

Not all stalkers escalate to violent behavior. Many of them are only a constant yet annoying presence in someone's life. Lisa's recent e-mail, however, is cause for concern. She's gone from e-mailing once every other week to several times in one week, and the tone and content of the e-mails have dramatically changed as well. This could be a sign that Lisa's behavior is becoming worse, more threatening, and that she might eventually turn physically violent or destructive in other ways. For instance, Lisa has already tried to damage Graham's reputation online. She might show up at his place of employment or even his residence.

If Graham continues to communicate with Lisa in *any* way, he'll only encourage her advances. Negative communication is still communication. If he argues with her, he'll incite her, causing her to become even more obsessed. If he's nice, he'll still increase her obsession. And if he asks her to leave him alone, she won't.

His best strategy is to mitigate or reduce the risk that Lisa will evolve from a nuisance into someone who is set on harming him physically, emotionally, financially, or professionally. He will want to cut off all contact and save copies of all communication from her. If Lisa escalates—by contacting him by phone, leaving handwritten notes at his home, threatening him, mailing him gifts, increasing the frequency of her contact, contacting him by multiple methods (phone, text, e-mail, fax), or revealing that she's somehow gathered more personal information about him—he should contact an intervening resource for help. He might consult law enforcement for a restraining order, or a lawyer, private investigator, or legal consultant. If Lisa begins marring his reputation online, he might consult a firm that specializes in repairing online reputations. He also might contact his Internet service provider and see if they will take up the cause.

———

How did you do? Did you get a perfect score? Or did you call some of them right and some of them wrong? Most people, if they are being honest, tell me that they guessed correctly on some, and not so correctly on others. You might be the same. That's because gut feelings can be right sometimes—and they can be wrong a lot more often. When it comes to your personal safety and well-being, however, wouldn't you want to use a method that has a better track record? By the end of this book, you will know that method, and you will be able to put it to work for you in your life.

CHAPTER 1 RAP SHEET

- You can't tell if people are dangerous just by looking at them.
- You can't always take people at their word.
- Dangerous people are good at blending in.
- If you ask the right questions, you can learn how someone is likely to behave by listening to his or her answers.
- You can't walk a mile in a dangerous person's shoes because dangerous people wear a different kind of shoe—one that doesn't fit you.

Chapter 2

The Dangers of Relying on Instincts and Intuition

My coauthor knows a woman who believes that all her problems stem from bad luck. She's a single mother who earns not much more than the minimum wage. Her car doesn't always start and her babysitters don't always show up, preventing her from getting to work. She's lost quite a few jobs because of undependable cars and babysitters.

These job losses have led to her not paying bills on time, which has led to her phone, power, or Internet being cut off. She's been evicted from apartments.

If you met this woman and listened to her tale of woe, you would probably think, "The poor thing. She just can't get a break. One person should not have so much bad luck. Life really isn't fair. I really feel sorry for her."

In reality, though, this woman probably isn't any less lucky than you are or I am. Her problems don't stem from bad luck. They stem from decisions that resulted in a lifelong trickle effect.

Let's take a closer look at some of her decisions and the resulting consequences:

- She got angry and decided to take it out on another student.
  Consequently she was expelled from college.

- She decided to have unprotected intercourse with a man she did not know very well. Consequently she got pregnant, even though she did not have the financial resources or lifestyle to support a baby.
- She decided to take advantage of various people in her life—demanding they give her money and other types of support. Consequently, friends, family members, and even Good Samaritan acquaintances stopped supporting her.
- She became angry with the father of her child for not giving her enough money, so she decided to teach him a lesson. She went to court and severed his paternal rights. Consequently he was no longer available to watch their child while she was at work—causing her to rely on a string of undependable babysitters. Eventually she lost her jobs.

If this woman learned how to accurately assess people and situations for danger and to make thoughtful, analytical decisions rather than impulsive, emotion-driven ones, she'd feel in control of her life and she would stop feeling like a victim of bad luck.

Why Luck Is Dangerous

"Luck" is a nebulous term that means different things to different people. It's not something you can define or quantify. How can you know whether your luck is any worse or better than anyone else's? How can you know if it's getting better or worse? How can you come up with strategies to change it?

Perhaps most problematic is the way people use the concept of luck as a way to avoid taking ownership of their lives. If you see every outcome as a result of luck, you have no motivation to change your decision-making process. Flawed assessment and decision-making processes are what tend to get many people into trouble and bring them disappointment, resentment, failure, and severe negative consequences.

Throughout this book, you will learn an analytical process that will help you to go beyond luck. As a result, you will feel more in control of your life and less like a victim of bad luck.

Why Intuition Is Dangerous

Many books encourage people to trust their intuition; they claim that fear will guide you away from danger and that your sense of happiness will bring good fortune.

According to such books, we are all supposed to have a magical inner radar that allows us to acquire knowledge without thinking or reasoning. For instance, highly intuitive people are thought to be able to feel out whether a person is dangerous. They are supposed to be able to foresee, before they step on board, whether a plane will go down. They are thought to be able to sense danger before danger happens. They are almost psychic.

Yet there is little science to back any of this up. Do you believe in intuition? Do you rely on it when making decisions?

Let's for a moment assume that you answered yes and that intuition plays a huge role in how your conduct your life. If so, I'd like you to think about a few additional questions.

- Do you believe in your powers of intuition so much that you would trust them to tell when to pull a parachute cord after jumping from an airplane, even if you never skydived before?
- Do you believe in intuition so much that you would put your entire life's savings on a number on a roulette wheel that gave you a good feeling?
- Do you believe in it so much that you would trust it to help you drive a car while blindfolded?
- If your son, daughter, brother, or sister told you they were going to abandon their life and family to move across the world to follow a religious charlatan, would you accept the explanation that they "just feel good about him"?

- Would you willingly step foot into the lions' enclosure at a
  zoo and use your intuition to decide the best way to interact
  with these dangerous wild animals?

I'm guessing that you would not want to rely on your powers of intuition to do any of these things.

In high-risk situations—situations that could have dire long-term consequences including physical harm or death—it seems reckless to rely on
intuition, doesn't it? It sure does to me.

Like luck, intuition is not quantifiable. It's not measurable either.
There is no known way to hone or improve it. And we don't even know
where it is. Do you feel intuition in your stomach? Your chest? Your head?

Our intuitive read on a given person or situation will be influenced by
a range of variables such as our upbringing, culture, and religion. How
well rested we are and even whether we are under the influence of drugs
or alcohol will affect how we feel about people and situations. Even if you
have intuition, your ability to feel out a situation will be dulled by some
of the following factors:

- Stress
- Fear
- Lack of experience
- Drugs or alcohol
- Fatigue
- Emotional and/or psychological needs and problems

Note that in a high-risk situation, you will likely be feeling plenty of
stress and fear, and you will probably be out of your element too. When
you are under stress, your emotions and sensations tend to be even less
trustworthy than when you are relaxed. Many people tell me that they
have decided against doing something based on a bad feeling they had in
their gut. What I've wondered is this: Was that bad feeling a sign that they
should not buy the car or take the job, or just a sign that they were nervous or scared? Were they really relying on this mysterious thing known
as intuition, or were they simply caving under the pressure of stress?

Think back over your life and about the many different decisions you've made—and especially about the ones you *felt* your way through. How many serious relationships did you get into because you felt a strong connection to someone, only to later realize the person was a jerk? How many business transactions have you made because you had a "good feeling" about something, only to learn later you'd just lost your shirt? How often have you trusted someone because you liked him or her, only to have this person abuse that trust or otherwise hurt you?

If these are things that tend to happen over and over again in your life, your powers of intuition may not be as strong as you believe.

When making important decisions about safety and well-being, do you really want to be relying on something that has proven in the past to be faulty? Do you really want to rely solely on intuition—which can be affected by fatigue, stress, arrogance, ignorance, emotional attraction, and physical or psychological needs—rather than use analytical reasoning, which involves the same process no matter what?

Why Instincts Are Dangerous

Although some people use the two terms interchangeably, "instincts" are not the same thing as "intuition."

Scientists define instincts as inborn behavioral patterns that we exhibit in response to a specific stimulus. For instance, salmon have a spawning instinct that leads them to swim upstream to lay their eggs. Similarly, many birds instinctually fly south in the winter. They do so even though they've never been taught to do it. They are born knowing to do it.

It's obvious that human babies are born with some instincts, because they do many things that no one taught them to do. For instance, they cry when they are hungry or pull away from something that is painful.

Even as adults we engage in more instinctual behavior than we realize, and some of this behavior can harm us more than it helps.

For instance, we have a survival instinct that causes us to fear death and situations that could lead to it. Yet this survival instinct is not necessarily going to keep us out of harm's way. It doesn't prevent danger, and it doesn't teach us how to react to it. Our survival instinct says, "Yes, I want to live!" But it doesn't tell us precisely how to stay alive.

Your survival instinct will probably kick in, for example, if you are ever to find yourself on fire. That instinct, however, will not necessarily tell you what to do to put out the fire. If anything, your natural inclination might be to run. That's why we teach children to stop, drop, and roll. If they haven't been trained via constant repetition and practice, most people will not drop and roll when they are on fire. They will run, which does not put out the fire and may even make it worse.

This is why businesses and schools have earthquake and fire drills—to help people practice the correct response over and over again so that it becomes ingrained.

Let's look at another situation where survival instincts might kick in but not necessarily tell us what to do. Have you ever started to skid after hitting an icy patch on the road, seen a big fat tree ahead and reflexively hit the brake? What happened? Did you end up hitting the tree? Chances are you did.

Indeed, the correct way to steer out of a skid goes against our survival instinct. Our instincts scream, "Hit the brake! Hit the brake!" because we want the car to stop to avoid hitting the tree, but braking won't slow a car when its tires are moving over ice. Rather, it causes the tires to lose traction. End result: You lose control of the car and can't steer out of the skid.

The correct way to steer out of a skid is to turn the wheel in the direction you want to go—away from the tree—and to gently accelerate to encourage the tires to grip the road.

It goes against your body's natural inclinations. This is referred to as being counterintuitive.

Here are a few other situations in which our survival instinct can cause us to do the opposite of what we need to do to be safe:

- Do you remember when John F. Kennedy Jr. crashed his plane into the Atlantic? He was trying to land his plane in the dark. It was foggy, and he could not see the horizon. Therefore he couldn't tell just by looking whether his plane was parallel or perpendicular to the ocean. The plane's instruments told him that it was in a nosedive, but

Kennedy's inner ear told him that the plane was horizontal. He trusted his inner ear and his eyes, and he brought the plane into a nosedive into the ocean. As pilot Eric Nolte wrote of the incident, "Our feelings, indulged without examination, will kill us."

• I lived in San Francisco for many years, so I can tell you first-hand how strong the urge to run outside is after the shaking of an earthquake starts. Yet during the severe earthquakes, people died when they ran outside and were killed by falling debris. The greatest dangers are objects just outside a structure, such as a utility pole or something else that could fall. If you are indoors, the best strategy may not be to run outside but rather to get underneath something sturdy that will cushion you from falling debris, such as a bed or a doorframe.

• Think about what people often do when caught in a riptide. Most people feel an urge to swim against the tide, which allows the tide to pull them farther and farther into the ocean. They eventually get tired and drown. The right thing to do is swim, not away from, but parallel to the current until you escape it, but your instincts won't tell you to do that.

• Sadly, I've seen that in cases of school violence, students' instinct is to hide under their desks rather than to run out of the building. Their survival instincts are telling them two things: "Hide" and

The Dangerous Truth

Many people tell me that they would scream bloody murder if someone attempted to assault or kidnap them. What I've learned from interviewing the victims of violent crime, however, is that your natural reaction to a threat is not necessarily predictable. Some people are mute through an entire encounter. Their fear incapacitates them. Others have told me that they kicked and screamed, cried uncontrollably, or repeatedly asked the offender, "Who are you and why are you doing this?" I've learned that different people react to fear in different ways and that your reaction is unpredictable unless you plan and practice in advance.

"Put something solid between me and the threat." Yet desks do not provide adequate protection from flying bullets, and students who hide under desks or tables become stationary targets.

The Dangers of Instinctlike Habits

Survival instincts are inborn. You don't learn them. They are present from the day you take your first breath.

You can, however, repeatedly practice a behavior until it becomes habitual and as a result instinctlike. For instance, in the FBI we never pick up spent casings during shooting practice because we don't want to habitually bend down and start picking up spent casings in the middle of a real shoot-out, when even the slightest hesitation could get us killed. If we picked up the casings over and over again during practice, that's exactly what we would do in a real-life situation. That's why we practice, practice, and practice the reaction we want to have during an actual shoot-out.

We also practice shooting to hit a target in the torso or head. We don't practice shooting at the kneecaps or the arms. What do you think is going to happen during a real-life shoot-out? We're going to aim for the heart or head—without thinking about it.

The Dangerous Truth

Some home owners like to have a handgun for protection. Initially this might seem like a smart decision. But if you do not train yourself to use a handgun for that specific purpose, then you can't know precisely what you will do if you are ever in the position of facing down an intruder. It's likely that the intruder will be much more skilled at handling and shooting a gun than you are. If you are walking into a face-off for the very first time in your life, your risk of physical harm is very high. If you want to keep a gun in the home, I highly recommend becoming familiar with the gun by doing frequent target practice.

In real life, we automatically default to what we've trained ourselves to do. We lean on instinctlike habits.

And these instinctlike habits can be acquired, trained, and strengthened. The problem, of course, is that you can't practice for every single situation in life before it happens. You might be able to rely on learned instincts in some situations. For instance, if you are a lifeguard, you will probably be able to rescue a drowning victim based on your learned instincts. If you are a lawyer, you can probably negotiate based on learned instincts. And as a profiler who has studied human behavior, I probably make more than a few decisions based on learned instincts.

That's because in each case the person has trained for the situation over and over again, so that their brain and body can operate on autopilot whenever they find themselves in it.

Your ability to think critically also depends on how much practice you've had in making the same sort of decision. But what do you do when you are in a situation that puts you out of your area of practice? If you rely only on untrained, unrehearsed, or raw instincts that you have not honed for that situation, how can you possibly react correctly?

The Dangers of Rigid Rules

If you live in a city or a neighborhood where there is noted criminal activity, you have likely picked up a few tactics that help you to stay safe in that setting. Those tactics have probably worked for you too. Most of them probably involve minimizing contact with people you don't know. For instance, you might be wary whenever a stranger asks you a question or takes an unusual interest in you.

But the complete avoidance of strangers is not really a strategy. It's a lifestyle, and it's what people resort to when they don't know how to do risk assessments. Some strangers are not a threat to you. You may avoid them, however, because you don't have a process in place that helps you to sort out the harmful strangers from the harmless ones. You may default to an interpersonal style of distancing yourself and of being unfriendly and uncommunicative toward anyone you don't know. If you only have one tool in your assessment toolbox, that's the one you will use all the time.

For instance, let's say there's a knock at your front door. How do you decide whether to open the door? You might say that you have a policy: You never open the door when you are not expecting someone. This strategy might have kept you safe in the past, and it's certainly prevented annoying solicitors from getting a piece of your time. But what if the person on the other side of the door is your neighbor, knocking to tell you that the house two doors down is on fire? What if the person on the other side of the door is a motorist who is there to tell you that she thinks she just hit your dog, who is still alive but in dire need of veterinary care? What if the person on the other side of the door is a police officer who is there to tell you about some burglaries in the neighborhood and offer some advice on how you can avoid being a victim? Wouldn't you want to answer your door? Can you see how it would be helpful to have an assessment process that helps you quickly determine when to open the door and when not to?

More important, strangers are not the only people who pose a threat to you. If staying away from strangers is your primary safety strategy, how will you stay safe around all the other people in your life who are not strangers to you? How will you protect your best interests at work, in romantic relationships, and with the various people you hire (housekeepers, contractors, lawn servicers, and so on)? What happens when you find yourself in a situation that falls outside your rigid safety rules? How will you protect yourself?

As you will soon learn, strangers generally pose less of a potential threat to you than others closer to you who you probably openly allow into your comfort zone. It's just as important—if not more important—to be able to assess the threat of people close to you as it is to be able to assess the threat of strangers.

For all of these reasons and more, it's important to have an assessment process you can use to protect yourself physically, emotionally, psychologically, financially, professionally, and legally no matter where you find yourself and no matter who you find yourself with. Without a well-honed and well-practiced assessment process in place, you will find yourself relying on instincts and intuition whenever you are in an unfamiliar situation.

Once you learn how to make your own risk assessments, your life will not be so limiting. Rather than feeling paranoid and overly protective, you will realize the power you have to be in charge of your life, your circumstances, and relationships. Decision making will not be so overwhelming, stressful, and uncertain. While life will continue to be challenging, you can anticipate and manage these challenges in a much more effective way.

The SMART Model

In this book you will learn a decision-making and risk-assessment process that does not rely on instinct or intuition. Rather, it relies on experience, practice, and training.

When you make decisions based on instinct or intuition, you *feel* your way through, basing your decisions on gut feelings and emotions. When you make decisions based on the SMART model, you *think* them through. Yes, there might be some emotion and feeling involved. There will be times when you have no other choice than to make a decision despite the fear, sadness, frustration, or other emotion you might be experiencing.

But you will not be making decisions *because* of your emotions. You will learn how to keep feelings of helplessness, confusion, and desperation from nudging you into decisions that could potentially result in calamity. Instead you will make decisions by using an analytical assessment process that is always the same no matter what emotion you might be experiencing.

I call this process the SMART model. As mentioned, it's SMART because it's a:

S = sound
M = method of
A = assessing and
R = recognizing
T = trouble

This method will help you to determine the risk involved in making a decision and avoid making decisions that you will come to regret. It will help you to overcome the weaknesses that could cloud your judgment—weaknesses like inherent biases, stress you might be under, strong emotions, pressure from others, or skills you currently lack. How many times have you felt overwhelmed, desperate, or lost but had to make a decision anyway? The SMART model will be particularly helpful in situations where there is a lot of emotion.

This process will also help you to determine the true risk that any given situation poses. You will know, based on the SMART model, whether the given situation really is safe or whether there are unseen or unanticipated threats that should cause you concern. And you will also be able to assess the risk in trusting other people—with your heart, money, children, livelihood, reputation, or life. Finally, the SMART model will help you determine the best way to interview someone, so you can persuade them to open up and provide you with the information you need to make your decision or to resolve a conflict or problem.

Whenever faced with a dilemma, our goal is for you to ask yourself, "Am I making a SMART decision?" Later on you'll learn how. In the next few chapters, however, let's first look more closely at why this model is so important.

CHAPTER 2 RAP SHEET

- You do not have to feel that you are a victim of bad luck or random circumstances. By learning how to make SMART decisions, you can change your circumstances for the better.
- You probably regret decisions that you made spontaneously, impulsively, and based on your emotions. You are less likely to regret decisions that are thoughtful, careful, and made with your long-term future in mind.
- Many people who believe in intuition in theory would never rely on it during a life-or-death situation because they intuitively know just how unreliable it is.

- Your survival instinct might guide you to safety some of the time, but it's just as likely to guide you into danger.
- You can train your instincts to react to some situations, but you cannot train them to react to all situations.
- The SMART model is a "sound method of assessing and recognizing trouble."

Chapter 3

Personality: It's What Makes People Tick

'd been working a child-abduction case for months, and I suspected that Tom, a close friend of the victim's mother, might have had something to do with the child's disappearance. Tom had proven difficult to deal with. When I'd tried to ask him questions about the child's disappearance, he'd been uncooperative and suspicious of where the investigation was headed. He was arrogant and confrontational, and he seemed to have a side of himself that he kept secret.

I knew that Tom didn't like me, but I wanted to know more about him and the kind of person he was. So I'd been talking to a number of his friends and acquaintances, and Tom didn't like that. I asked one of them, Allan, if he wouldn't mind coming to the FBI office to talk with me. He agreed.

Tom drove Allan to the office and waited outside for him to finish.

When Allan walked into the interview room, he seemed uncomfortable and nervous. I thought his nervousness was odd. He was not a suspect in the case, and I'm a low-key interviewer. I'm not the type of person who gets someone to talk by pushing my weight around and making threats. Instead I usually get people to open up by being sincere, serious, nonjudgmental, and by listening intently to what they are saying. (More on why this approach works in chapter 8.) I've interviewed many, many people, and my presence doesn't usually make them nervous. In fact, most people open up to me and tell me things they would never tell someone else.

I took a look at Allan. He was dressed casually but had too much clothing on for the mild California weather.

"Are you wired? Do you have a tape recorder on you?" I asked. This was not usually my opening line.

"Yes," he said. He sheepishly pulled a tape recorder from under his shirt and handed it to me.

When I walked out of the interview room that day, the other agents marveled. "Are you psychic?"

The answer to that question is no. I'm not psychic. I suspected that Allan might attempt to tape the interview. And as you keep reading this chapter, you'll understand how I came to that conclusion.

It's Not Mind Reading

What happened with Allan that day was a made-for-TV moment. On television shows such as *Criminal Minds* and *The Mentalist*, the investigators seem to have the ability to read minds and predict human behavior. In one episode of *The Mentalist*, for instance, Patrick Jane (a former psychic con man who now serves as a police consultant) walks into a room and notices that a man in a suit is patting his jacket pocket a few too many times.

He asks to see the drugs the man has hidden in his pocket.

Apparently, according to this show, anyone who pats their jacket pocket must have drugs in it.

It's not that simple.

And while real-life behavioral analysts like me may—at times—seem to be able to read minds or see into the future, we can't. What we are really doing is reading people's behavior for insights into their personality. Once we understand someone's personality, we have a really good idea of what that person is likely to do in a given situation.

For instance, in the example of my interview with Allan, I already knew that Tom was dominant and controlling. I also knew that Tom was extremely concerned about what might be said during the interview. And I knew that Tom was not a rule follower. It's a crime to tape an FBI interview without consent, but that's not the sort of thing that would concern Tom.

It is, however, the kind of thing that would concern Allan, who was a rule follower, for the most part. I knew that Allan had the type of personality that could easily be persuaded to do something. He was intimidated by Tom. Tom had told Allan that he was being harassed by the FBI, and Allan had believed him. Allan was naive, and I was concerned that he was being used by Tom and didn't even realize it.

Allan was willing to commit a federal crime because his friend had told him to do it, but it made him uncomfortable—and it showed. Also he was dressed in an outfit that would have allowed him to hide something.

I'm not psychic, and I can't read minds. I just happened to do a good assessment based on my knowledge of Tom and Allan and what I knew about their behavior and personalities.

Why Feelings Are Unreliable Assessment Tools

When most people try to get a read on someone—whether it's a potential date, employee, babysitter, or stranger—they usually rely on how they feel. If they have a good feeling when they are around the person, they put them in a "positive" category. If they have a bad feeling, they sort them into a "negative" category.

This is where we get the expression "feeling someone out." It's also where we get the expressions "we just click," "we have great chemistry," "I have a good feeling about this one," and "there's just something about him."

The problem with this is that we tend to feel good about people based on superficial characteristics that have very little to do with how innocent or dangerous they really are. The clothes someone wears, the smile on their face, or the warmth of their hug can all make us feel good about a person—even if that person is about to con or hurt us.

As it turns out, it's really easy to manipulate feelings, and dangerous people know how to do just that. They know how to disarm you, get you to feel comfortable, and create the sense that the two of you have a special bond. They do it through impression management. They compliment you, pay attention to you, and spin lies that allow you to believe that the two of you have something in common. That's why they are so successful at conning and manipulating people.

Several other factors can throw off your feelings, too, making them more reliable assessment tools in some situations and a lot less reliable in others. Your feelings can change depending on your internal state. Stress changes how you feel. Alcohol and various medications (both prescription and over-the-counter) will change how you feel. A good night's sleep will change how you feel.

Have you ever gone to bed thinking that your spouse was a despicable human being, only to wake the next morning wondering what you were so angry about the night before? Indeed lack of sleep tends to make us feel more negative. So can stress. And alcohol and some medications can do the opposite, causing us to feel good about people who would usually cause us to have our guard up.

Your feelings about someone can change from moment to moment and day to day. Yet the person in question has not changed at all. You might feel better, but the person in question might be just as dangerous as ever.

Relying on feelings to read people can also cause you to miss or ignore important information that would contradict whatever feelings you have. For instance, early in a new relationship, your feelings of affection for someone could cause you to overlook any number of dangerous details, such as a man's controlling nature or a woman's constant need for attention.

For these reasons, feeling someone out is not an accurate way to assess whether they are a good fit for your company, a good caregiver for your child, or even a good friend or lover.

Why Personality Is So Important

Your personality is the motor that drives all your behavior, decisions, and choices. It conditions how you view the world, how you view others, and how you think others view you. It determines how you cope with stressors and situations. It affects how you act and react to what's going on around you and how you interact with others. It's who you are.

Once you understand someone's personality, you can do a much better job of predicting how that person will react in various situations. You'll be more effective and successful in dealing with others because you will begin to understand their behavior. You will know what makes them tick.

For instance, students tend to threaten violence quite often, but fortunately most of those threats will never be carried out. Still, the seriousness of the threat cannot be determined solely by words. A student may say, "I am going to shoot up the school," but one student might just be saying it, while another may very well do it. That's why I'm often called in to sort out the seriousness of the threat and help determine if a student really will bring a gun to school or set off a bomb. I do this by finding out as much as I can about the student who made the threat, including his unique biological, psychological, and social factors. (This is known as the biopsychosocial model.) I look into his family life, his social life, his academic life, and more. I find out everything I can about his behavior over time. That gives me a sense of his personality, and it helps me to determine whether he is likely to act out in a violent or threatening way.

It's for this reason that signs in airports caution you not to joke about bringing bombs or unauthorized items onto an airplane. The folks in Homeland Security take every single one of those statements seriously because they know nothing about the personalities behind them. You might be a harmless person who says a dumb thing because you are in the middle of a very stressful moment, but the folks in Homeland Security don't know whether you are a harmless, frustrated passenger or a mission-oriented terrorist who just leaked his intentions.

Homeland Security officials can't get a read on your personality just from the outfit you happened to wear to the airport that day or by the expression on your face. If the only words they hear come out of your mouth are, "I want this plane to go down," they are going to take that very seriously.

To be able to tease out whether someone could be dangerous, you must have insight into that person's personality, and you'll gain those insights by observing and learning about that person's behavior over time.

The more you practice reading people, the better you'll get at it and the more accurate your assessments of various people will become. Unlike intuition—which cannot be trained or tested—this step-by-step process of reading behavior and assessing personality can be honed and improved. This is in large part what I did as an FBI profiler. There were no smoke and mirrors. It came down to observing and interpreting behavior, and then understanding the personality that produced that behavior.

You'll learn more about how to read someone else's behavior and know more about their personality later in this book. For now, though, I'd like to go into a few misconceptions about personality.

Myth 1: Adults can have significant changes in their personalities.

More than a hundred years ago, a man named Phineas Gage was in a railroad accident during which an iron rod punctured his cheek and was driven into the frontal lobe of his brain.

Amazingly, he survived the accident and went on to live twelve more years, but he was forever changed. The spike had damaged the part of his brain responsible for weighing future consequences. The iron rod changed the once smart and likable Gage into an impulsive, hostile, and volatile man.

There are only a few things that will cause a radical change in personality. Having an iron rod puncture your frontal lobe is one of them. Others include diseases, trauma, and medications that affect that same area of the brain.

Barring those circumstances, most adults' personalities don't change all that much. As Albert Einstein once famously said, "Women marry men hoping they will change. Men marry women hoping they will not. So each is inevitably disappointed."

The problem with marrying someone with the expectation that he will change is this: Your personality is pretty much formed by your late twenties. Sometime after age thirty, it becomes less and less likely to change and you will take that personality with you into old age.

Personality development is a very complex, dynamic, and interactive process. One's personality is determined by both genetics (nature) and environment. The latter is commonly referred to as the "nurture" part of the equation. Indicators of a person's personality traits begin to emerge at an early age. Then the personality continues to develop and evolve until it becomes hardwired. After that, it's questionable whether a change in one's personality is possible. Researchers from the University of California, Riverside, compared teachers' personality ratings of 2,400 elementary school children from the 1960s with videotaped interviews of those same individuals forty years later. They found that many personality attributes both remained unchanged and affected their behavior as adults. For instance, children with "verbally fluent" personalities (defined as unrestrained talkativeness) spoke fluently, displayed a high degree of intelligence, and were interested in intellectual matters as adults. Children with low verbal fluency tended to give up when faced with obstacles and had an awkward interpersonal style as adults.[2]

Once the personality becomes hardwired, significant changes are not likely. If someone is emotionally distant at age thirty, chances are he will still be emotionally distant years from now too. If your adult friend has always been self-centered and self-focused, it is likely that she will continue to be.

Yes, you can communicate and compromise, and people can successfully modify specific behaviors. They can stop smoking, for instance, or overcome a fear of heights (acrophobia) or a fear of dogs (cynophobia). But those are not hardwired personality traits. Rather, they are acquired fears (phobias) or addictions that can respond to therapy, especially cognitive behavioral therapies.

Adult personality traits, such as extroversion and introversion, do not tend to change, or at least do not change with any significance. So if you marry someone who is reserved, quiet, and low-key—someone who requires less social interaction with others—it's not likely that you will be able to turn that person into someone who is permanently the life of the party and who is energized by involvement with others. Likewise, an adult who is described as disagreeable—always seeing life's glass as half-empty, and with little interest in the well-being of others—is not likely to permanently morph into someone who is compassionate or less antagonistic or who has an overall optimistic or positive view of the world. If you marry someone whose outlook on life is negative despite all the good things that happen to him or her, who is impersonal, suspicious, and lacking in empathy, you will likely live the rest of your life in great frustration and hurt or eventually get divorced.

That's why it's so important to understand a person's personality before allowing a relationship with them to become too intimate. You can never fully get into someone's head, but you can gain insights into their personality by observing their behavior in a variety of situations and over a period of time. The key is to look for a pattern of behavior. The more you observe the person, the better. From time to time, we all engage in behavior that is selfish, strange, and even out of character. Maybe, for instance, you are essentially calm and easygoing but quick to become angry when tired. If someone observes you only when you are fatigued, he might come away with the false notion that you have a short fuse. But if that person sees you in many situations, over a period of time, he or she will have a more accurate view of your personality.

Myth 2: You can leave your personality at the door.

Supervisors often ask employees to leave their personalities at the door, to walk into the conference room, for example, without their conflicts or differences. But employees can't leave their personality at the door any more easily than they can leave a body part at the door. Their personality is who they are. It influences how they communicate, how they interact with others, and how they believe others see them and judge them. It's what makes them unique as a person. An employee who is quick to anger and impulsive cannot change those personality traits just by walking out of one room and into another. Personality is hardwired.

The only ways to prevent someone's seriously problematic personality from showing up at a meeting are either to not invite that person to the meeting or to not hire such a person in the first place.

Myth 3: Some people have Jekyll-and-Hyde personalities.

In Robert Louis Stevenson's novella *The Strange Case of Dr. Jekyll and Mr. Hyde*, Dr. Jekyll takes drugs that release his evil side and slowly turn him into the violent and unstable Mr. Hyde. In real life, many people seem to believe that such seismic personality shifts are possible, even without the magic potion. That's why, when someone commits a horrible act of violence, friends, relatives, and loved ones will remark, "I never saw that side of him" or "He just snapped."

For instance, very few battered spouses ever say, "I knew he was going to abuse me from the moment I first laid eyes on him." If they knew that, they wouldn't have dated and eventually married these men. So when the boyfriend or husband becomes abusive, they frequently see it as a change in personality from good to bad. They will remark, "He's not the person I married" or "Something changed in him."

Yes, normal people do lose their tempers and get angry from time to time. Yes, sometimes when people are under enormous pressure they behave in ways that are aberrant for them. And, yes, certain diseases can erode parts of the brain that are responsible for helping people determine the difference between right and wrong—causing huge shifts in their behavior as a result.

But I am not talking about those sorts of situations here. I'm talking about regular people, who do not "snap" at all. In such people, the potential to act out violently is always there. It's just not noticed, recognized, or interpreted correctly. In such cases, what usually happens is one, or both, of the following:

1. People who are dangerous, abusive, or threatening frequently manifest behaviors that are engaging, charming, and nonthreatening. Someone who is prone to violence, angry outbursts, and aggressiveness, for instance, doesn't usually behave in a concerning way all day long. So loved ones, coworkers, and friends often see what they want

to see and ignore what they don't want to see or what they don't know how to interpret. A woman who is dating a man who is abusive might initially ignore and explain away his jealousy, thinking, "He loves me so much." When that jealousy results in physical abuse, however, she incorrectly thinks he's become a different man.

2. Dangerous people can be very good at impression management and at hiding the concerning aspects of their personalities. A wife abuser, for instance, will turn on the charm early in the relationship, until he knows he's got the woman lured in. Then slowly, over time, he'll reveal his true nature.

Impression management may be one reason why Colonel Russell Williams of the Royal Canadian Air Force was able to escape detection for so many years. He pled guilty to eighty-eight charges, including two counts of first-degree murder. The crimes took place over several years. They started with voyeurism and progressed to breaking into homes, stealing lingerie, and masturbating on women's beds. From there, he progressed to sexually assaulting women and then to rape and murder. His crimes were extreme, but Williams was so adept at seeming normal that no one suspected he could ever be capable of such behavior. He lived a double life. In one part of his life, he was a highly respected and successful air force commander. In another, he was a sexual deviant and a predator.

Myth 4: Quiet people have no personality.

Sometimes, when describing someone else, a person will say, "He has no personality" or "She has zero personality." Unless the person they are describing is no longer in the land of the living, this just isn't the case. There is no such thing as having no personality. We all have a personality.

What people really mean is that the person is shy, reserved, introverted, and not particularly social.

Another mistake people tend to make is to link shyness either with dangerousness or harmlessness. For instance, they might decide that someone who is very shy and socially awkward must be "weird" and therefore "creepy." Or they might think that someone who is a little reticent is "sensitive" and "deep" and therefore "harmless." Yet being outgoing or reserved has no correlation with how dangerous or harmless a person is. Both extroverts and introverts are equally capable of behaving dangerously.

Myth 5: A mood disorder is more concerning than a personality disorder.

A Hollywood celebrity was much in the news as this book was being written. In one story, sources remarked that it was good news that this person didn't have bipolar disorder but rather seemed to *only* have a *common* personality disorder.

What the media didn't quite understand as it reported this story is that a mood disorder, such as bipolar disease, can be very successfully managed with medications and therapy. Many personality disorders are less successfully treated by standard therapies, and certain types of personality disorders can be more problematic than most mood disorders. Although some personality disorders might respond positively to standard therapies, others do not.

Myth 6: You can have a "nice" or "good" personality.

Whenever I hear someone describe a person as "nice" or "good," I always think, "What a cop-out." That description tells me nothing about the personality. It is vanilla; it says nothing about the person's unique makeup. When I hear someone describe a person as "nice," it tells me that the describer is a fencer, someone who doesn't want to say anything negative because they are afraid of being seen as judgmental. They also might not know the person all that well or worry that what they say will get back to this "nice" person. No one is just nice or good. People's personalities are far more complex and dynamic than a one-word adjective can cover. When I ask what someone is like, I want to know about the patterns of behavior he exhibits in interactions with others, his view of the world, his perception of himself, and his perception of how others view him.

CHAPTER 3 RAP SHEET

- You can't read people's minds, but you can—by observing their behavior and listening to what they say—get a read on their personalities. Doing so will allow you to predict how they might react in a given situation.
- Your feelings about someone can be easily manipulated by flattery, impression management, and more. For these reasons, feelings or gut instincts are usually not an accurate way to gauge the dangerousness or trustworthiness of another person.
- Once you understand someone's personality, you can more accurately anticipate, and even predict, how that person will react in various situations.

Chapter 4

What Makes People Dangerous

I watched Gary Leon Ridgway—better known as the Green River Killer—walk down the prison hallway and into the interview room. He thrust his chest out, swayed his shoulders, and walked with an incredible swagger for a guy who was handcuffed and flanked by highly trained and physically fit guards. The men and women in Gary's tactical detail were larger than him and they outnumbered him.

Yet Gary did not walk like a subdued convict. No, if anything, he walked and acted as if this tactical team was really his protective detail. It was as if—in Gary's mind—he was a VIP and these people were sent to follow him around for his protection.

Gary did not walk with shame. No, everything about him seemed to be saying, "I'm Gary Ridgway, and I am proud to be the Green River Killer."

Gary had spent more than two decades kidnapping women off the streets of Seattle, Washington, then killing and burying them in cluster graves in nearby areas. Now he had agreed to plead guilty to these murders and to be interviewed by law enforcement in exchange for not being executed. Part of the agreement involved him assisting the King County Sheriff's Office to identify and locate the bodies of what turned out to be his forty-eight victims.

I joined a team of awesome detectives and incredible interviewers who met with Gary over six months. We couldn't just take Gary's word for what he had done. Serial sexual killers are notorious for bragging about how many people they've murdered. We wanted to find the bodies of his victims so families could finally know what had happened to their loved ones and who was responsible for their deaths. We also needed to know the full extent of Gary Ridgway's damage.

Gary was difficult to interview. He was not consistent with his information, and he was more helpful on some days than others. Sometimes he was interactive and responsive, but on other days, getting information out of Gary was like pulling teeth. One day he would confess to killing a young woman. The next he'd deny it. To pin him down, we had to know every detail about every victim that we suspected he murdered.

It was my role to interview Gary about his personality, family, upbringing, and crime from a behavioral perspective. Using my understanding of psychopathy (a subject you'll learn more about later in this chapter), I crafted a number of questions designed to sort through Gary's lies and evasiveness and to determine whether he felt any remorse for his victims or the crimes he had committed.

On the first day, I walked into the interview room and sat next to him. He turned his head to stare at me. I looked back at him. He was a normal-looking sixty-year-old man with glasses. He was in good shape, with strong, muscled arms. He was polite, quiet, and smiled appropriately. He was actually nice. I expected that he would be.

"Gary, I don't have a lot of time," I said. "I need to get up to Canada to work on this other serial murder case, but there's one thing I'd really like to find out before I go. I want to study only the best serial killers. How good of a serial killer are you? Where would you put yourself on a scale comparing yourself to other serial killers?"

His responses implied that he thought he would be at the top. He thought he was one of the best, if not *the* best serial killer. This is something you might expect a star athlete, renowned scientist, or movie star to say. But a serial killer?

On another occasion he commented that the video camera being used to record all the interviews was not focused on his face, as it should be. Gary appeared to really like being videotaped. It allowed him to be the center of attention and talk about what he loved doing. He believed being taped would make him more famous, and it did.

He openly talked to me and other investigators about his necrophiliac behavior (having sex with the women's lifeless bodies) as if it were completely normal.

I asked Gary if he felt remorse for his victims and his crimes. He responded that he felt bad about them. "What does feeling bad feel like for you?" I asked. If you or I had committed the types of crimes Gary had, we would probably answer such a question by saying that we felt horrible about taking these women's lives and ruining the lives of their loved ones. Gary, however, could not articulate what "feeling bad" meant to him. I pressed him. Eventually he explained that he felt bad about the evidence that was left at the scenes.

Whenever I tell these stories about Gary, people are incredulous. "How can someone be so proud of such violent behavior?" they ask. Most people can't wrap their minds around it.

And that's just it. They can't possibly instinctually understand the personality of a serial sexual killer because it is the complete opposite of their own. They believe someone like this has to be crazy, evil, or a monster, but those are only labels and have no investigative value. Such words have no clinical meaning.

Gary is a serial sexual killer. He killed women for sexual reasons. He liked it, and he was good at it. He had sex with the bodies of dead women because it was sexually gratifying to him. This pathological behavior made Gary feel powerful and omnipotent, and he craved those feelings.

Because I'd spent my career studying and interviewing people just like him, I understood Gary's personality. I knew, before I ever walked into that interview room, what would happen if I told Gary that I was in a hurry to investigate another series of crimes committed by another serial sexual killer that Gary was aware of due to news reports. I knew Gary would be annoyed if I acted like another killer was more successful, more interesting, and more notorious. He would attempt to impress me and get me to understand his point of view.

I knew that killing was probably the one thing that Gary was most proud of. It was the one thing he was exceptionally good at.

He wasn't particularly successful in a lot of areas of his life, but he was one of the most prolific sexual predators ever recorded in the United States. His crimes spanned more than three decades.

Gary hunted human beings. He conned, manipulated, strangled, and murdered one woman after another. He stole their belongings and had sex with their lifeless bodies. Killing was a passion for him. He enjoyed it. He found it exciting and thrilling, and it gave him a sense of power and control. It's what got him out of bed in the morning, and it put him to sleep at night.

He called his encounters with these women "dates."

Gary thought of the women he killed as possessions, and their bodies were a treasured collection for him—a collection that he drove past and visited often.

Gary had kept all of this secret for more than twenty-five years. He'd

The Dangerous Truth

Serial sexual predators like Gary Ridgway are able to lure their victims through impression management and by taking steps to look and behave as normally as possible. Gary hunted street-smart prostitutes who had worked the same strip for years. These were women who understood street survival, and they were aware that there was a killer operating in their neighborhood. They were cognizant that there was danger out there, yet he was able to convince them—through charm and using props he kept in the car with him—that he was not a threat. There were times when he even took his young son with him as he hunted for prostitutes. Those who got into his car saw his son as a sign of safety. They assumed a father with a small boy could not be a serial murderer. In reality, however, a father who is callous enough to take a small child with him while he cruises the strip for a prostitute might also be callous enough to commit murder. That Gary had his son in the car with him said more about how dangerous and mission-oriented he was than about how harmless he might be.

never had the opportunity to talk about the one thing he was most ac-complished at and proud of—until these interviews.

So for nearly six months, as these interviews were going on, he boasted about his murderous exploits.

You Can't Walk a Mile in a Criminal's Shoes

It's my hope that by the end of this chapter you will come to understand what motivates dangerous criminals like Gary. It's important to understand the motivations and personalities of people whose behavior is so extreme. Behavior falls along a continuum. Your behavior and the behavior of your friends and family might fall more toward the opposite, more law-abiding end of the continuum. Still, if you understand extremely dangerous behavior, you'll have a framework to use and understand human behavior in general, and yours specifically.

Serial sexual killers like Gary are rare, and they generally prey on highly vulnerable people who live high-risk lifestyles—people like prostitutes, runaways, and the homeless. In my work with the FBI, these victims were particularly compelling for me. Their lives and lifestyles were hard for them to maintain. Most had families who loved them dearly and wanted them home. Their vulnerabilities were often brought about by hardships in life they couldn't avoid, and the vulnerabilities of their lifestyles exposed them to dangerous people such as Gary.

You probably don't live that kind of lifestyle, so the likelihood of you ever meeting someone like Gary is quite small. But chances are you *will* meet a psychopath (more on what a psychopath is in just a few pages). In addition to psychopaths, you will probably, over the course of your life, meet many people who could be dangerous to you in other ways. It's important to be able to assess people's dangerousness. That way you can avoid people who are likely to hurt you financially, psychologically, emotionally, physically, professionally, legally, and in other ways. In this chapter you will learn to dispel fourteen myths that tend to get in the way of spotting dangerous behaviors.

What Blinds You to Danger

Your instincts and intuition are clouded by your own perceptions—based on your own personality and experiences—of what is normal behavior and what is not. You would never con or harm someone, so your gut feelings lead you to believe that your friends, coworkers, and neighbors—who all seem as normal as you—wouldn't either.

But your friends, coworkers, and neighbors aren't you, and they don't share your personality traits and characteristics, your background, your family influence, and more. What stresses them out, worries them, excites them, or saddens them is different from what stresses you out, worries you, excites you, or saddens you.

Your personality isn't the only thing that may bias you and influence your judgment when trying to get inside the head of a potentially dangerous individual. Years of misinformation—fed to you by TV crime dramas, news reports, self-defense courses, and forwarded e-mails—have probably made your ability to judge people even less trustworthy. For instance, on many popular TV programs, most of the psychopathic serial sexual killers start their killing sprees after a life stressor has caused them to "snap" and thus act out in a very aggressive way. As you'll learn later in this chapter, this is rarely the case. This kind of behavior evolves over time. It is not the result of snapping in the course of a twenty-four-hour period.

Television dramas are not the only sources of misinformation. Some of these myths about dangerous people have even been spread by individuals who call themselves experts in psychopathy and serial murder but who are not experts at all. I can't tell you how often I've cringed as I've listened to a television reporter interview someone who claims to be an expert but who has little to no on-the-job training when it comes to dealing with dangerous people, especially psychopaths. In one sentence these so-called experts call someone a psychopathic killer and in the very next refer to them as "a monster" or as having "snapped." Those are giveaways that the person being interviewed knows little to nothing about psychopaths.

In the following pages, we'll take a closer look at some of this misinformation and how it clouds your judgment when deciding whether to put your trust in someone else, be it a friend, romantic partner, employee, coworker, business partner, or hired help. Let's start with myths about psychopaths.

The Dangerous Truth

Many people think that serial sexual killers prefer a specific type of victim and that they will not deviate from that preference. For instance, people often assumed that Ted Bundy, a notorious serial sexual killer operating during the 1970s and early 1980s, preferred to murder women with brown hair parted down the middle. However, when, following his conviction, he was asked about his victim-selection process and victim preference, Bundy replied that hair parted down the middle was simply the style in the seventies. He wasn't necessarily picking victims because of their hairstyle. He was picking victims that he deemed worthy enough (attractive, middle or up per middle class, educated, and so on) to be killed by him.

In reality, the victim selection process that a serial killer uses can be a lot more complex and a lot less rigid than most people think. For Gary Ridgway, it revolved around the victim who was most accessible. Gary was infatuated with prostitutes. He picked women up on a regular basis to have sex with them. He would "date" the same woman over and over, and he would not murder every prostitute he picked up. Their ages varied, they came from different racial and cultural backgrounds, but he picked them because of their lifestyle.

I believe that Gary's choice of victims was the result of his desire to hunt a lot of victims to satiate his paraphiliac interests and predatory instincts. His victims were women who would engage in a wide variety of sexual behaviors in exchange for money. Gary knew that other people they interacted with would be considered suspects in their disappearances. He also knew that these women did not maintain regular schedules and that because of their erratic patterns they could be missing for days, weeks, or months before their families would realize it and report them missing. This gave Gary the opportunity to put a great deal of time and distance between him and his victims.

What Makes a Psychopath Tick?

The word "psychopath" is probably one of the most misunderstood words in the English language, and it is often used to describe people who are not psychopaths at all.

Psychopaths are classically referred to as people without a conscience. It's likely that in your lifetime you will encounter a psychopath and not realize it. He or she might be a neighbor, acquaintance, coworker, friend, or love interest. It might be someone you meet casually, such as a store clerk or a cab driver. It might be the person who works in the next cubicle. It might even be a family member.

My colleague and dear friend Robert D. Hare, Ph.D.—considered the world's foremost expert in psychopathy—estimates that 1 percent of the general population and 10 percent of the prison population is psychopathic. Psychopaths exist in all cultures and races and have existed over time and throughout history.

Although psychopathy is more common in men, psychopaths can be male or female. They can be married and have children. They can be quite smart or of average intelligence. They are not out of touch with reality and they know right from wrong. They look as normal as we do. They can blend in well with the society in which they are living. Most psychopaths are not violent, but because of their cluster of very specific personality traits and characteristics, they live life on the edge. They con and manipulate people. They take risks but take no responsibility for their actions. They lie pathologically, have a profound lack of empathy for others, and are stunningly callous in their interactions with people, even those who should be close to them. They live a life where rules are for the unwashed masses and not for someone as special as they are. They take what they want, when they want it. They are parasitic users of people regardless of the consequences to their victims, and they possess a re-markable ability to walk away from the havoc they wreak with a skip in their step, a smile on their face, and a dark predatory look in their eyes as they spot their next victim.

Psychopathy is a devastating personality disorder (an enduring pat-tern of thoughts and behaviors that differs from cultural expectations; is pervasive, inflexible, and stable over time; and leads to distress or impairment). It includes a cluster of the following traits, characteristics, and behaviors:

- Glib, superficial charm
- Grandiose sense of self-worth
- Pathological lying
- Cunning and manipulative
- Lack of remorse or guilt
- Shallow emotions
- Callousness and lack of empathy
- Failure to accept responsibility for one's actions
- Stimulation seeking
- Parasitic orientation
- Lack of realistic goals
- Impulsivity
- Irresponsibility
- Poor behavior controls
- Juvenile delinquency
- Early behavior problems
- Criminal versatility[3]

You might recognize some of these traits in yourself or someone you know. That doesn't mean that you are a psychopath. Someone is considered a psychopath when these traits and characteristics are consistently present in every aspect of the person's life, throughout his or her life.

Psychopathy is not an either/or disorder but rather is dimensional. It's a pattern. It emerges at a young age and it becomes fixed. You don't turn psychopathy on and off at will. And psychopaths don't believe there is anything wrong with them, so they don't seek out counseling unless it is in their best interest. For example, in a prison setting many psychopaths will only participate in therapy groups in order to make a better appearance before the parole board.

Not all psychopaths share equal amounts of every single trait, but it is the affective traits that distinguish this personality disorder from all the others: lack of remorse or guilt, shallow emotions, callous lack of empathy for others, and failure to accept responsibility. This lack of remorse and empathy is what allows psychopathic serial sexual killers to sleep next to their wives after having just killed someone. It's also what allows white-collar offenders to risk and lose the retirement savings of their clients and then put all the blame on their clients for agreeing to the investment in the first place. It's what allows certain types of sex offenders to kidnap, sexually assault, and murder children, and then play games of cat and mouse with law enforcement. It's what causes these sex offenders to become empowered by the excitement and thrill of what they just did and at being so clever at getting away with it. It's what allows some politicians or religious or world leaders to egregiously abuse their power and destroy other people around them, especially when their reign of power is coming to an end.

A psychopath feels about as guilty about destroying your peace of mind, reputation, financial livelihood, and life as you do when you blow your nose into a tissue and toss it in the trash. After you discard the tissue, do you worry about it? Do you think about it? Does it bother you that it's there in the trash, feeling discarded and used?

No, it doesn't. And psychopaths feel as emotionally attached to their victims as you feel to that tissue.

It's their lack of remorse and their callous lack of empathy that makes psychopaths so dangerous. For instance, pedophilia is a paraphiliac behavior that is defined as involving fantasies about, sexual attraction to, and illegal sexual interaction with a child or children. Not all pedophiles are psychopaths, and the nonpsychopathic pedophiles can feel remorse and guilt for their behavior. A psychopathic pedophile, however, is someone who is sexually attracted to children, victimizes children, and feels no remorse about this behavior. They will take greater risks to access a child in order to make the crime more exciting, will disregard the consequences of their behavior, will not accept responsibility even when caught, and are more likely to recidivate if the opportunity presents itself.

An arsonist sets fires for a variety of reasons. If someone is hurt or killed, some arsonists are capable of feeling remorse and/or guilt. A psychopathic arsonist, however, would feel no remorse or guilt about property damage or lost lives due to the fires he sets. His concerns would be for himself, about not wanting to be caught or to go to prison.

The psychopathic pedophile and arsonist are also more likely to incorporate thrill and excitement into their crimes to make them even more satisfying for them. They will even modify their behaviors so each time they commit a crime they get better and better at it in order to evade detection and apprehension.

Because of this, when a psychopath engages in criminal behavior he can be one of the most dangerous of criminals.

Psychopaths also have shallow or prototypical emotions. They have learned to pretend, sometimes with precision, how to emulate emotions they see in others around them. Superficially, psychopaths can attempt to show emotions by crying or saying the right words, like "I love you." The emotional landscape of a psychopath, however, lacks depth and breadth. It is barren.[4]

Because of this, psychopaths have to mime feelings and make them up. Asking a psychopath what remorse or guilt feels like is like asking a man what it feels like to be pregnant. It is an experience they have never had. In order to answer the question, they can only resort to what others have told them about this experience and what they have observed in people around them. They cannot speak from personal experience. Psychopaths can describe feelings, but they have no personal experience with them. Their description is based on what they have observed in others, but when you dig a little deeper, you will find that they have a very difficult time describing emotions in an appropriate context, which can frustrate them or even make them angry.

You might assume that, due to their lack of emotion, psychopaths may come off as odd and robotic. Although some do, many are extremely good at impression management. They might not know what remorse *feels* like, but they know what it looks like. They watch TV and observe the people around them. This is why some of them break down and cry in the courtroom. Are they crying because they really feel remorse about what they've done? I doubt it. I've seen killers turn on the tears when they thought they would help them accomplish a goal, and then turn them right back off again. They are actors who know how to pretend to be remorseful because it makes them appear like the people around them.

For instance, Dennis Rader, known as the BTK killer (Bind Torture Kill killer), calmly and dispassionately detailed every aspect of his murders in one of his initial courtroom appearances, and he did so without shedding a tear. He related how the members of the Otero family— including two children—did not die right away when he strangled them. "I had never strangled anyone before, so I really didn't know how much pressure you had to put on a person or how long it would take," he said.

He referred to his victims as "projects." He seemed detached and aloof.

After that day, his attorneys must have explained to him that a little remorse might help him when it came to sentencing. The next time he came to court he appeared, when it was in his best interest, to display more emotion.

However, psychopaths can become angry. For instance, several times when I asked Gary Ridgway about souvenirs he took from his victims, he narrowed his eyes. They became cold and reptilian. I realized that these were the eyes his victims would have seen when he was killing them. Gary was angry that I seemed to think of him as an average serial killer who would take souvenirs. He saw himself as better than that, denied taking souvenirs, and was quite annoyed that I didn't believe him.

Psychopaths are also predatory and manipulative. They don't think the rules apply to them. They are grandiose thrill seekers who take no responsibility for their behavior and have a view of the world in which they dominate and can take whatever they want, when they want it.

"Living on the edge" is a phrase frequently used to describe the psychopathic lifestyle. If they are involved in criminal behavior, their crimes will most likely have a certain quality to them that satisfies their need for thrill and sensation, even if it puts them at a greater risk of being caught. For example, Gary Ridgway drove around with a dead body in his car. This is very high-risk behavior. If he got stopped for a traffic violation or was involved in an accident and the body was found, he would have immediately been arrested and charged.

The Dangerous Truth

Some people think that they can spot a psychopath when he or she walks into the room. But you just can't look at someone and tell whether they have traits of psychopathy. If you meet a psychopath casually, you won't realize what he is. If you know one more intimately, you will eventually feel used and manipulated. You will realize how insignificant you and your feelings are to him. His grandiosity will be apparent in every aspect of his life. You will get worn out dealing with him, and he will blame you for why the marriage or relationship fails. It will never be his fault. You will absolutely know something is wrong, but you may blame it on yourself, seek therapy, try harder, and constantly be afraid.

Myth 1: You are either a psychopath or you aren't.

To assess for psychopathy, we use a clinical instrument called the Psychopathy Checklist-Revised (PCL-R). It consists of twenty items, each scored on a scale of 0–2. This assessment must be done by a highly trained professional. Researched and designed by Dr. Robert Hare, the PCL-R is considered the gold standard for the assessment of this personality disorder.

A person must score 30 out of a possible 40 to be assessed as a psychopath. However, a score in the mid to high twenties indicates that an individual manifests many of the traits and characteristics. Not all psychopaths share equal amounts of every trait in the psychopathic cluster, and some psychopaths score higher on some traits than others. Labeling someone a psychopath is a very serious matter and should not be done casually or recklessly. It has tremendous implications, so the diagnosis should only be made after a proper assessment.

Dr. Hare compares psychopathy to blood pressure. Like blood pressure, everyone has some traits of psychopathy, but some people test much higher in certain traits than others. It's the affective traits of psychopathy (lack of empathy, lack of remorse, and shallow emotions) that are the hallmarks of this disorder.

Myth 2: The words "sociopath" and "psychopath" are interchangeable.

People toss the terms "sociopath" and "psychopath" around on TV as if they mean the same thing, but they don't. The empirical research suggests that there is a neurological difference between psychopaths and nonpsychopaths, and this neurological difference is manifested by the traits and characteristics I listed earlier. Ongoing research suggests there are four types of psychopaths. The type of psychopath someone is depends on how that person manifests the traits and characteristics of the disorder.

"Sociopath," on the other hand, is a term generally used to refer to individuals who have grown up in an environment where being criminally antisocial is the norm. It is a learned behavior. A sociopath's emotional deficits are more likely to be the result of their environment. They may not be neurological. For example, people who grow up with gang violence or some other type of organized crime environment may learn the importance of being antisocial (breaking the law) as a way of life. But they are still capable of feeling a greater range of more normal emotions in some areas of their life, for example, with families and loved ones.

Myth 3: Psychopaths are psychotic.

Usually, when people call someone "a psycho" they really mean "crazy," or out of touch with reality. Psychopaths are not crazy—even if some of the crimes they commit are bizarre and heinous.

For instance, Gary Ridgway was not hearing voices when he revisited the dumpsites and had postmortem sex with the prostitutes he killed. Gary would pull maggots off their vaginal areas. He would break the women's leg bones so he could shove their stiffened legs apart. This is pathological behavior, but it was also the behavior of a man who was completely in touch with reality.

What Gary did may very well be bizarre, but it was not a result of psychosis or impaired judgment. People who are psychotic are out of touch with reality because they suffer from a debilitating mental illness. They can hallucinate and hear voices that tell them to do things that are strange or even illegal.

Gary Ridgway did not hallucinate or hear voices. He had no trouble holding down a job. He blended in with his community and projected a normal persona. He was married, with children and grandchildren. He shopped and ate at neighborhood restaurants, went on vacations, and interacted with other normal people all the time. He did not live a life of erratic, aberrant, or unpredictable behavior. This is why he flew under law enforcement's radar screen for so many years. He maintained a facade of normalcy.

Gary was methodical and calculated. He killed because he enjoyed it, not because he was out of touch with reality.

I've interviewed numerous killers, some of whom practiced cannibalism and necrophilia. Their refrain was similar. They killed because it was thrilling and arousing. Their crimes gave them feelings of power and control over their victims and their victims' lives. They felt omnipotent, and that was a feeling they craved. They didn't do it because they were out of touch with reality or told to do it by voices in their head.

It is important to keep in mind that people who are mentally ill with a psychosis are less likely to act out violently than psychopaths are, and they are far less likely to be able to carry out a well-planned, cold-blooded,

Dangerous Truth

According to a survey done for the Screen Actors Guild, 60 percent of mentally ill characters were portrayed as criminals or as violent offenders, and 70 percent of stories that depict mental illness revolve around a theme of violence.[5] TV and movies are one of our biggest sources of information about violence and deviant behavior, and yet this source routinely provides an inaccurate portrayal of who is and who is not violent. Psychopathy is a personality disorder, one that should not be confused or linked with mental illness.

predatory act of mission-oriented violence. The vast majority of people who are mentally ill are not violent at all, and they are far more likely to become victims of violent crime than they are to be perpetrators of it.

Myth 4: Psychopaths don't know right from wrong.

They do know right from wrong. They know what the laws are, but they don't believe those laws apply to them. They know that killing, raping, stealing, and other actions are crimes and are against the law—and they choose to do those things anyway.

Myth 5: Brain tumors and brain trauma turn law-abiding citizens into psychopaths.

Psychopathy is the result of a person's genetics and environment; you don't snap into being a psychopath as the result of a brain tumor or other neurological injury.

Even Charles Whitman, who shot and killed fourteen people at the University of Texas at Austin, and who was, after an autopsy, determined to have been suffering from a brain tumor, didn't go up in the tower that day because of a tumor. Whether he had a brain tumor or not, his violence was well planned, predatory, cold-blooded, and purposeful, which are all indicators of psychopathy.

I was able to identify warning behaviors in Whitman's life going back to his days in the military, a full six years before the shooting. It was then that he wrote about preparing for a military siege. He wrote about the necessary supplies he would need and how to keep a door from being breached. (In the tower on August 1, 1966, he followed this plan to delay police officers from getting to him.) Five months before the tower shooting, he told his psychiatrist that he fantasized about killing people from the top of the University of Texas tower. The psychiatrist later admitted that he dismissed this revelation because Whitman seemed like "an all-American boy" and didn't look like a psychopath.

Myth 6: Most psychopaths were violently abused as children, their parents made them into what they've become, and most practiced cruelty to animals.

Some psychopaths may have been abused as children. For instance, I've interviewed Joseph Paul Franklin, who attempted to kill adult-magazine publisher Larry Flynt and was convicted of several murders. During that interview, Franklin claimed that his parents had yelled at him, beat him, and starved him. According to Franklin, his mother was a sadist and he once watched her physically abuse a stray dog that he'd brought home. He said that this abuse by his parents had turned him into a cold-blooded killer.[6]

Although people like Franklin may very well have been abused, many other people are abused as children and they do not turn into psychopaths or serial killers. Similarly, some psychopaths might have engaged in cruelty to animals, but not all of them have. And children who do engage in this behavior don't all become psychopaths. It is not a predictive behavior for psychopathy. It is certainly concerning behavior, and when parents see it, it should be addressed immediately with the assistance of trained mental-health professionals.

We know that heredity and environment together contribute to the development of psychopathy. The degree to which each contributes, however, is still uncertain, and very likely varies on an individual basis.

Myth 7: Psychopaths are capable of being in love.

Although in news reports I often read that a psychopath was "really in love with his wife," this is an emotion that they do not feel deeply or at all. Whenever I ask psychopathic serial killers why they did not kill their wives or children, they tell me that it's because they would immediately become a suspect in the murder of someone so close to them. Sometimes psychopathic serial killers will claim to love their wives or children. If I ask, "When was the first time you thought about killing your wife, girlfriend, or mother?" most will then tell me about all the ways they fantasized about doing their wives or girlfriends in.

Myth 8: Most psychopaths are violent.

When you hear the word "psychopath," the first thing that probably comes to mind is a serial killer like Ted Bundy. But most psychopaths are not serial killers. In fact, serial killing is rare and most psychopaths are not violent.

Psychopaths live on the edge by taking advantage of people. They manipulate people and lie to get what they want. But they don't necessarily end up in jail as a result of acting violently. They are not rule followers by nature, but many live right on the edge.

Myth 9: Psychopaths don't work in white-collar professions.

Many people think that psychopathy is a disorder that debilitates people to such a degree that they cannot go on to get an advanced degree or move up the corporate ladder. This just isn't true. Many of them excel in high-stress, high-risk professions. They are stockbrokers, ER physicians, bankers, lawyers, politicians, and even law enforcement officers. These professions are thrilling and provide psychopaths with the power that they seek. Paul Babiak's research into white-collar psychopaths even found that these individuals not only manage successfully in corporate America, but their glibness and charm, and risk-taking and sensation-seeking traits, are viewed as desirable assets despite poor performance appraisals. [7]

A psychopath can cause problems in the workplace. The white-collar psychopath will charm people initially. He or she will do this to win over fellow employees and bosses that they eventually manipulate to accomplish their objectives. These objectives could be anything from embezzlement to taking significant risks with company property (cars, money, investments) to sexual conquests.

Once white-collar psychopaths have people where they want them, they can become the company bully. They can stir up trouble. They can take credit for others' work, blame others for problems, prey on coworkers (through harassment or sexually inappropriate behavior), and create an atmosphere that pits employees against one another.

They can use and manipulate people to climb the corporate ladder or shine as the star of the company. People are in the organization for them to use. Their loyalty is to themselves, and they will betray the corporation if it serves their needs. They can cheat, embezzle, lie, take extraordinary risks, sabotage projects, and violate confidentiality issues while experiencing little if any remorse or feelings of guilt as they do so. They are not team players, but rather live by the philosophy that every man is out for himself. In a corporate culture, however, the need to be covert—"to fly under the radar screen"—is important for psychopaths to achieve their goals. Their calculated use and abuse of the company and its employees can be subtle and/or come out incrementally and selectively so as not to jeopardize their own employment.[8]

Myth 10: Psychopaths are smarter than the average person.

It's easy to mistake a psychopath for being brilliant, because of his or her inflated sense of self-worth (he or she will tell you of their brilliance) and the glib nature that enables them to engage with others on many different topics, albeit on a superficial level.

But psychopaths reflect the intelligence of the general population. There have been some exceptionally bright serial killers, such as Edmund Emil Kemper, whose IQ is thought to be around 160. Kemper, who I've interviewed several times, is rumored to have memorized the Minnesota Multiphasic Personality Inventory (MMPI). The test is used to evaluate the presence of mental illness. It has five hundred items on it, and Kemper knew precisely how to answer each of those items to support his insanity plea. He is one of the smartest killers I've ever interviewed.

On the other end of the spectrum, however, is Billy, whose last name I will not use out of consideration for his living family members. He was never tested for IQ, but he only had a fifth-grade education. When I interviewed him, he talked in one- and two-word answers such as "yup" and "nope." The most he ever said was when I asked him if he had heard of the word "psychopathy." I assumed he would say no, but he told me that he had.

"Really?" I asked. "How do you know about psychopathy?"

"I looked it up in the dictionary," he said. "Do you think I am one?"

"I think it's more important to know if you think you are one," I said. "What do you think?"

"Yes, and I think it's a good thing." He smiled and his eyes sparkled.

That was his most talkative moment. Billy is in prison for serial sexual murder.

Myth 11: People just snap.

As we've already discussed, after a crime is committed the criminal's friends frequently say, "I don't know what happened. He just snapped." They describe someone who was pushed to the brink by life stressors, and then morphed into a madman.

I call this "snap theory," and it comes up again and again and again when a human being behaves in a way that others find inhuman, bizarre, or violent.

Yet people usually don't snap. What happens is that their concerning behavior goes unnoticed. For instance, let's take a look at Andrew Kehoe, the man responsible for the worst school violence in U.S. history. Kehoe was a well-respected member of the Bath, Michigan, community and the treasurer of the board of the Bath Consolidated School. Did he snap when, in 1927, he blew up his property and later himself and a school, killing forty-five people and injuring fifty-eight? No, he didn't.

Kehoe was an injustice collector and was having financial difficulties. He blamed those difficulties on a number of people, including his wife (who had tuberculosis and was in and out of the hospital, racking up a lot of medical bills). He also blamed a property tax levy that was designed to raise money to upgrade the school.

Because Kehoe was trusted and well respected—a member of the board—he was allowed access to the school. For many months, he brought small amounts of dynamite to the school and stored it in various locations. Eventually he had stored hundreds of pounds of it there.

Meanwhile neighbors did notice strange behavior. He was bringing hay into a tool shed, for instance, and they could not figure out why anyone would need hay in a tool shed. None of them suspected, however, that he would later use it to set fire to the shed and other buildings on his property. They also heard him detonating dynamite on his property, but they accepted his explanation that he had just been testing it.

On the day of the incident, he blew up and set fire to his property, killing his wife. He even wired and blew up his remaining farm animals. He then drove to the school in his "machine," a truck he filled with explosives. It was likely the first car bomb ever to be seen in the United States. Using a timer, he detonated the truck shortly after he detonated the explosives at the school. He killed himself and at least forty-five children that day.

People were stunned when this happened, but there were many indicators ahead of time that Kehoe was prone to violence and planning to commit violent acts. He didn't "snap" at all. He planned every detail of his attack months ahead of time.

Similarly, Eric Harris and Dylan Klebold did not just snap. They planned the Columbine High School shooting for months. They meticulously and slowly gathered explosives and firearms. They planned the shooting down to the last detail. For weeks before the incident, they taped each other discussing how they would carry it out.

Dan White—who was convicted of shooting San Francisco mayor George Moscone and supervisor Harvey Milk—didn't just fall into a depression, start eating a lot of junk food, snap, and then murder two people while in a dazed state, as his attorney claimed in his so-called Twinkie defense.

I worked for the San Francisco District Attorney's Office during White's trial and my brother, Michael O'Toole, was the media officer and spokesperson for the San Francisco Police Department during the same time. Michael was there in City Hall when Supervisor Milk's body was found. I paid close attention to the case and sat in on the trial.

Yes, White may have been suffering from depression, but the depression was not the reason he snuck through a basement window and then shot Moscone and Milk. White had resigned from the board of supervisors and he wanted his job back. The mayor would not reinstate him, and White felt that Milk had influenced the mayor's decision.

White, a San Francisco native and a respected family man, was a former firefighter and police officer with an impressive career and pedigree. This made him a compelling defendant. Those who knew him said there were no warning signs of future violence. At the time, our knowledge of threat assessment, risk assessment, and warning behaviors for future violence was still in its infancy. This might be why his Twinkie defense helped to sway the jury to convict him of manslaughter rather than first-degree murder, even though he was predatory and mission-oriented when he committed the attack.

Your usual well-adjusted, law-abiding citizen doesn't "snap" and become a mass murderer or cold-blooded serial killer. There are usually warning signs that these people have the potential to become violent and are planning to carry out a violent act, but those signs often go unrecognized for a number of reasons:

1. We don't like to believe that the people we know—neighbors, teachers, school board members, spouses, and so on—can be plotting and planning violence.

2. People who are prone to violence can be quite good at hiding their plans from others.

3. Signs that someone might become violent are usually mixed with normal behavior. Some potentially violent people seem like normal, caring individuals at times. At other times they seem like angry, vengeful people. These characteristics are mixed together into a big soup, and sometimes it can be difficult to spot the indicators of violence until it's too late.

Kehoe, White, and others thought about their crimes ahead of time, and they exhibited a number of behaviors that indicated that they were contemplating violence. These warning signs, however, went unrecognized, or were misinterpreted or ignored until it was too late.

Myth 12: The maternal instinct protects children.

The mythical maternal instinct is somehow supposed to help mothers keep their children safe at all times. And all moms are supposed to have it.

It's quite possible that most mothers have such an instinct. But after seeing what I've seen during my time with the FBI, I can say that the maternal instinct is not a universal phenomenon.

For instance, when officials were negotiating with David Koresh, the leader of the Branch Davidian religious sect in Waco, Texas, some of them commented that the maternal instincts of the women in the cult would eventually "kick in." They anticipated that, as a result of these instincts, the women would send their young children off the compound and to safety. These instincts would cause the women to take whatever steps were necessary to keep their children safe.

But I wondered, "What maternal instincts?" Some of these women were already living in a situation where David Koresh separated mothers from children. Some of the mothers had already exposed their children to physical, emotional, and sexual danger. Now they were suddenly supposed to develop an instinct that would help to protect their children?

Belief in these so-called maternal instincts is what causes so many people to assume that strangers pose the biggest kidnapping threat to children. Part of this assumption, no doubt, is fed by the media, which has sensationalized the abductions of Adam Walsh, Polly Klaas, Jaycee Dugard, Elizabeth Smart, and many others. Another part of it, though, stems from a flawed belief that no parent—especially a mother—could hurt her own child.

Yet children are a lot more likely to be harmed by family members, caregivers, or others who are close to them than by strangers. Parents commit 34 percent of the sexual assaults on children; strangers carry out only 7 percent of them.

Parents hurt their children for many reasons that some of us find hard to understand. Sometimes it's intentional. Sometimes it is done out of rage. Sometimes it's an accident that the parents cover up. Sometimes it's out of convenience. For instance, for Diane Downs and Susan Smith, their children were in the way, preventing these women from getting what they wanted—romantic partners. They saw their children as objects that could be used, manipulated, and even discarded in order to accomplish their personal goals.

And if parents can hurt their *own* children, what leads you to believe a parent could not hurt *your* child?

The Dangerous Truth

Paraphilias are mental disorders that are defined as involving sexual urges, fantasies, and behaviors that fall into three categories:

1. Nonhuman objects
2. Children or other nonconsenting persons
3. Suffering and/or humiliation

Pedophilia—a specific paraphiliac behavior—involves sexual attraction to, and involvement with, children. Necrophilia involves sexual attraction to corpses. Sexual cannibals become aroused when they consume another human's flesh, and sexual sadists become aroused by their victim's response as the sadist inflicts physical and emotional pain.

Psychopathy and paraphiliac behaviors can manifest together in the same individual, creating a potentially very dangerous person. For instance, Canadian colonel Russell Williams engaged in voyeurism (a paraphiliac behavior) and residential burglaries during which he stole women's lingerie, which he later cataloged and photographed himself wearing. He engaged in these behaviors for years, eventually progressing to sexual assault and murder.

Myth 13: All strangers are dangerous.

A few years ago, I was asked to help Louisiana police investigate the disappearance of Melissa, a twelve-year-old girl. It was suspected that Melissa had run away. Yet she had disappeared from an area where we knew a serial killer had been hunting some of his victims, and I had been working intensely on this serial murder case.

The police wanted my opinion on whether Melissa was a runaway or might be the victim of this serial killer or of something else. I asked them to send me everything they had on the case. As I read the statement made by Carl, the girl's stepfather, I became suspicious. When I saw his arrest record, criminal history, and background, I knew the first step was to see if we could eliminate Carl as a person of interest.

So I asked the police to send me any video footage that had been taken of him. As it turned out, Carl had been interviewed by television reporters while handing out flyers about the missing girl. As I watched these videos, I saw that he was good-looking, articulate, and seemed normal. He expressed concern and worry over the disappearance of his stepdaughter. He seemed comfortable on camera. He appeared to be glib and charming and certainly didn't look dangerous.

Most grieving parents appear on camera out of obligation—in order to help find their children. But they usually seem sad, nervous, and stressed. They are scared and even in shock. This stepfather, however, seemed to enjoy being in the limelight.

I asked the police about his background. I learned that he'd recently been released from prison, where he had served time for a series of rapes of adult women.

I told them, "This is your suspect, right here." I flew down with two of my Behavioral Analysis Unit partners. As I drove to the crime scene, I was listening to the radio and heard a news report about another young woman's body being found in Louisiana. I would subsequently learn that this young woman was a victim of the serial killer I was already looking for.

I met up with the FBI agent on Melissa's case. We talked about Carl and his concerning behavior, and we identified personality issues that would be key to getting him to confess to us. Then we interviewed Carl. I knew that control was important to him, so I said, "You have a lot more control than you think you have." I reminded him that he could control his side of the story. He could say it in his own words and using his own narrative. I explained that he could choose to not take that opportunity, but if he did so others would tell his story for him, and they might make assumptions that could be right or wrong. Carl wanted to be in control, and he wanted to set the story straight. He ultimately took us to the girl's body. Carl was tried and convicted and sent to death row in a cell close to that of the man who was convicted for killing the woman whose body was being uncovered the night my plane had landed.

It might have seemed natural, in that case, to assume that Melissa was also a victim of a serial killer. After all, he was following women to their homes, going inside, and either killing them there or taking them to another location and then killing them.

In reality, however, I knew that Melissa was a lot more likely to be harmed by someone she knew than by someone she didn't.

The same is true of you.

When we think about taking steps to increase our personal safely, our most dangerous instinct is to stay away from the people we don't know and to place our trust in people we know more intimately—family, friends, coworkers, and neighbors.

For instance, if you were a young woman working late at the office, you might ask another employee to walk you to your car—just in case a dangerous stranger was lurking somewhere in the parking lot. The now famous crime writer Ann Rule did just that, years ago when she worked at a suicide hotline with a handsome young man whom she knew well and had befriended. He often walked her to her car at night and asked her to be careful. His name was Ted Bundy.

We are conditioned over and over again in life to fear strangers. We are not conditioned to fear people we know. And all too often, we use inductive reasoning to conclude that someone we have met casually and had a superficial conversation with is safe and poses no threat to us. Yet just as children are more likely to be harmed by their own parents than by strangers, you are much more likely to be harmed by someone you know than by someone you don't know. Consider that of 14,000 murders in the United States in 2008, only 1,742 were committed by strangers. Nearly four times more were committed by people who knew the victim.

And the more intimately you know someone, the more potentially dangerous the relationship is. Most of us generally do not invite strangers into our comfort zone—such as our homes or our cars. Most of us do not hand sensitive information—our Social Security numbers, credit card information, the password to our PayPal account—to people we don't know either.

No, we only trust such information with people we think we know quite well, which is why the people closest to us pose the biggest threat to us.

Myth 14: Dangerous people look scary.

I've interviewed many different neighbors, coworkers, friends, and family members during my career. No matter what a criminal has looked like or how a criminal has behaved in their presence, nearly all of them have told me that they had sized this person up and were shocked at his arrest, whether it was for murder, sexual assault, child abduction, espionage, or other crimes of violence. They said things like:

"I am so surprised. He's such a nice guy."

"We've worked together for years. How could I not have seen this coming?"

"He's been over to my house. Our kids are in the same class. He doesn't seem dangerous."

"He's my next-door neighbor. He says hello every morning when he walks his dog. He seemed so normal."

"I would have noticed something different or strange about him, because I am a good judge of character. I am shocked. He must have just snapped."

I'm guessing that, if I were called to investigate a crime that took place on your block, you'd probably tell me something similar. You would because no one taught you how to read people and assess them for dangerousness.

As a result, when you try to rely on instincts or intuition in order to get a read on someone, chances are you are not getting an accurate read at all.

Terms like "scary looking" and "creepy" are frequently used to describe people, but these terms are not synonymous with what makes someone dangerous. Many people think that dangerous people have a certain look about them. As a result, they think they have the ability to give someone a look up and down and tell whether he or she is dangerous. They bank on this ability whenever they open their front doors without knowing who is on the other side.

Let me tell you, I've spent my career studying the criminal mind and criminal behavior. I've interviewed some of the world's most prolific serial killers and other dangerous offenders. I've made it my business to know all there is to know about them.

I do not have the ability to look at someone and tell for certain if that person is dangerous. And neither do you. No one does.

Ann Rule, the author and former policewoman whom I mentioned earlier, writes in *The Stranger Beside Me* about her experiences working with and knowing the infamous serial killer Ted Bundy. She remained friendly with him for years, and she thought he was a handsome, empathetic, gentle, brilliant young man. There was nothing about him that made her think, "He's dangerous."

Even years later when she saw an artist's rendering of the man who was suspected of killing several young women in her area and noticed that the picture looked a lot like her friend Ted, she doubted herself. She didn't think the Ted she knew could ever be capable of such crimes.

She continued to doubt herself after his capture, and even after he was convicted of kidnapping.

Similarly, some of the women who met Derrick Todd Lee—now known as the Baton Rouge Serial Killer—thought he looked harmless. They described him to me as "incredibly good-looking" with a "beautiful complexion." They said he was clean-cut and soft-spoken—a gentleman for the short period of time it took him to assess the situation and decide to act out violently.

This inability to size up danger goes beyond killers. People lined up to give their money to Bernie Madoff. They voted Rod Blagojevich into office as governor. Plenty of tourists in the 1800s bought the Brooklyn Bridge from George Parker, even though the bridge was not his to sell. He sold it to unsuspecting tourists roughly twice a week for years. Frank Abagnale Jr. posed, before he was even thirty, as an airline pilot, a doctor, and a lawyer before his arrest by the FBI. He was considered one of this country's ultimate con men.

We like to think of the victims of such people as naive. We tell ourselves that we would notice something or that our intuition would tell us something that these victims didn't see. Yet not a single person who watched *The Dating Game* on the day, during the 1970s, when Rodney Alcala was on it thought, "He looks like a serial killer." Thousands of people watched the show that day. If it is so easy to spot a serial killer based on appearance or first impression, don't you think someone who watched that episode would have called the police?

As I mentioned earlier, Charles Whitman was so all-American and clean-cut looking that his psychiatrist did not think that he would carry out his threat to shoot people from the tower, even as Whitman was telling him about his homicidal fantasies.

Robert Hanssen is recognized as one of the most dangerous spies in U.S. history. The fact that he was able to engage in espionage activity while employed as an FBI agent was stunning, not only to the FBI, but to the entire counterintelligence field. What behavior was overlooked or not recognized? How was he able to pull it off for such a long time? If dangerous people actually look dangerous, would he have gotten away with it for as long as he did?

Dangerous people generally don't look any different from regular, everyday people. They don't have a certain look in their eyes. They don't smile a certain way, and they don't wear a uniform or a certain haircut. If they did, we would run away or avoid them.

Sure, some dangerous individuals might look like the shifty-eyed, straggly haired stranger that television dramas have conditioned us to expect, but many of them don't.

CHAPTER 4 RAP SHEET

- Dangerous people can be so good at impression management that your gut feelings will tell you that they are safe and "good guys" when they are anything but.
- Psychopaths lack empathy and remorse. They do not feel guilt about the lives they've ruined.
- People capable of hurting others can look very normal and come across as charming and nonthreatening.
- You and your loved ones are more likely to be harmed by someone you know than by a stranger.
- Dangerous people do not necessarily stand out in a crowd. They don't look different from other people.
- Dangerous people usually don't snap. They exhibit red flags that warn that they might become threatening or violent.

Chapter 5

Why We Miss the Details
That Matter

Many years ago the FBI sent me to help find a teenage girl. Julie had walked away from her grandmother's home. She was one of a series of girls who had gone missing in California over a period of time.

When I arrived at the command center, the pressure was on to broadcast the disappearance on every media outlet and to call in every type of support available—helicopters, rescue teams, bloodhounds, evidence response teams, and lots of human power.

Doing so, though, would likely cause some degree of public panic and could even impact the local economy. We were walking a fine line. Underinvestigating the girl's disappearance might allow the kidnapper enough time to escape detection and possibly kill her and dispose of the body. But ratcheting up the investigation and classifying the case as a kidnapping when there was no factual basis for that assumption had its own problems. It could trigger a media frenzy, involve lots of human power, time, and money, and could even involve the apprehension of people as suspects in a crime that never occurred.

What was the right course of action?

As I listened to the detectives at the briefing, I read through diaries and journals that local authorities had gathered from Julie's home. I attempted to develop a victimology (a study of the victim, her personality, habits, interests, thoughts, fantasies, experiences, reactions, perceptions of life, and her fears).

She was a prolific writer. I had a lot to read and only a short time to do it. Time was of the essence. Law enforcement wanted to develop a strategy and wanted my assessment of what I thought had happened as soon as possible. I had only a few hours to hear what they were saying, visit Julie's home, and find out as much as I could about her and surmise what had happened.

I went to the condo where Julie had been staying with her grandmother for the summer. She'd recently arrived there from the Midwest.

From her grandmother, I learned that Julie seemed lonely. I thought she was more than lonely: She was sad. She had no friends in California, was on the quiet side, and didn't have a boyfriend but really wanted one. She had also been spending less and less time with her grandmother, but her grandmother didn't know why. Julie's grandmother had been fairly lenient and had not kept track of her every movement.

From what I'd already read in the journals, and from talking with her grandmother and visiting her home, I could see that Julie was not your typical high-risk victim. She was not an out-of-control child. Rather, she was introverted. She appeared to be a responsible, caring, and loving girl with a heavy dose of teenage insecurity. I also knew that she would not purposefully do something to hurt her grandmother or her family.

The singular theme throughout her journals was her loneliness and her desire for a boyfriend. This loneliness was so pervasive that I felt sad for her as I read about it. She wrote extensively about wanting to find a boyfriend, using phrases like "I want to have someone in my life" and "I wish I had a boyfriend" over and over again.

It was as though she'd made it a mission to find a boyfriend once she got to California.

I went through her bedroom and her closet. There I found a dress that her grandmother had purchased for her. It looked like a wedding dress. I asked her grandmother about it. She told me that she was not thrilled with the dress and didn't know why her granddaughter needed or wanted one like it.

I had my own suspicions about that.

Soon I was back at the command center. "So what is your assessment?" the head of the task force asked.

My opinion was one that would likely be met with skepticism and perhaps even some anger. If I was right about my assessment, we would eventually find the girl and she would be safe. If I was wrong, I risked losing credibility as a profiler and feeling horrible if something happened to her because we had not been aggressive enough from the beginning.

"My opinion is that she came out to California to find a boyfriend, that she met someone, and that she's with that person. She has not been kidnapped, and now she is probably frightened to come home," I said. "This is a situation that snowballed before she could stop it."

I'd come to this conclusion by adding up what we in law enforcement call "the totality of the circumstances." The circumstances were these: This was a low-risk victim in a low-crime area. She had a lot of freedom to go wherever she pleased and had little supervision. She was shy, lonely, insecure, and in search of a boyfriend. She had a wedding dress in her closet. Based on those details, it was my opinion that she had run off either to meet a boyfriend or to find one, and that she might come home on her own if she thought that neither she nor the boyfriend would get in trouble.

I suggested that we tone down the media coverage of the disappearance as much as possible. We asked the media to broadcast that Julie should come home with her new friend, and that she would be loved and welcomed.

Her parents arrived from the Midwest. They were scared and upset. I'm sure they were thinking the worst. Two days later I was sitting with the girl's father. I was going over Elisabeth Kübler-Ross's five stages of grief. He was kind and he held on to my every word as he sat shaking at the kitchen table. I could tell he was depending on me to take care of him, his family, and his daughter. I felt like there was nothing I wouldn't do to help him.

"In the next couple of days, you will find yourself angry with me," I said. "That's normal, if anything can be considered normal during a missing-child investigation. Most parents of missing children feel angry at this point in the investigation, but this is when I am going to need your help the most."

As I said those words, the front door opened and in walked Julie.

Her father fell to his knees and wept. He grabbed her, hugged her, and sobbed uncontrollably.

Julie had been staying with a boy who was about four years older than she was. She hadn't come home one night, and then she'd stayed subsequent nights with him at his family's home. She did know that her grandmother would worry about her, but she didn't realize things had gotten so out of control. She'd never thought that her grandmother would suspect that she had been kidnapped, that her photo would end up on the news, or that her parents would fly in.

A short while later, I left the kitchen, got in a car, and drove away. I never saw Julie or her father again. I wonder what their lives are like now. I hope they are well.

It would have been easy to get caught up in the wrong details that day. I could have fixated on the fact that other girls had gone missing and come to the conclusion that Julie was probably also abducted by a stranger. Had I done so, and had we conducted a full media blitz about Julie and her alleged kidnapper, Julie may have left the area or the state, thinking that the problem was insurmountable. The time, effort, and expense of trying to find her would have been enormous.

Underestimating Risks, Overestimating Benefits

When making critical decisions, most of us weigh the pros and cons. For instance, when deciding whether to take a new job, you might list the points in its favor, such as a bigger salary, a better job title, and job responsibilities that are a better fit for your interests. The negative considerations might include the need to move to a new location, the learning curve, leaving behind your support network, and so forth. There are some people who just don't like change, so any change is a real con for them.

I've found, however, that most people overestimate the potential benefits of various decisions and greatly underestimate the risks. Many of us have suffered from the "shiny ball" syndrome at one time or another in our lives. The new job, the new car, the new house seems to shine, and we want that shiny new ball, so we suspend the good judgment that would be based on an in-depth risk assessment.

In a marriage, for instance, a new bride might notice how her husband dotes on her, but she might ignore his controlling, dominating behavior or his jealousy and suspiciousness. She might even see them as a plus. Perhaps she feels special: She must really be something to have a guy be so jealous over her. Years later, however, his controlling personality really bothers her. She tells people that he's changed: He's not the same man she married.

In reality, he hasn't changed, but she has. She's finally taken in the whole picture. She realized that what at first seemed controlling is in fact dominating. What she initially saw as her husband's jealousy is actually suspicious and threatening behavior. Her husband's personality has not changed. She has taken off her rose-colored glasses and finally seen his behavior for what it really is.

Similarly, when an employee starts a new job she might notice the friendly coworkers and the flirtatious charm of one of her new colleagues, who she even considers sweet. It's not until the sweet, charming, flirtatious guy begins sending inappropriate e-mails and leaving inappropriate gifts on her desk that she realizes she has a problem. Yet his behavior was present all along. She just didn't put it all together at first.

The Riskiest Blind Spot

We don't just underestimate the risks of various decisions; we sometimes don't see the risks at all. And the risks we fail to see are often the very ones that are likeliest to hurt us the most.

For instance, many parents in the suburbs take their children to indoor amusement centers. These places offer lots of fun for the kids: climbing walls, bowling alleys, laser tag, bumper cars, sliding boards, and more. Many also include entertainment for the parents, such as a bar or gambling games.

The benefits of going to such a place? If you are a parent, you can probably rattle them off for me. Your kids get to run around and have fun. They burn off excess energy and get some exercise, and you get to relax.

The obvious cons, however, include the price tag. Such places are also loud and overstimulating, which means the kids might be crabbier later on.

But there are two risks that many parents probably just don't think of.

Risk 1: Physical harm to your child

How safe is the equipment, and how well-trained is the staff? Most people assume that such places are safe simply because they are open for business. They assume that some state agency regulates such places and therefore kids can't get hurt. But these places are not necessarily safe. In Indianapolis, for instance, a five-year-old boy was critically injured on a mini-teacup ride at an Xscape entertainment center that state officials later realized never had a permit to operate. The injuries were caused by a ride that was not properly maintained, and because of that, it jerked so abruptly that the child fractured his skull in two places.

Risk 2: Child molestation and/or abduction

As I've mentioned, kidnappings by strangers are rare, but think about how easy it would be for another adult to walk out with one of your children while you are relaxing at the bar. Incidents of child molestation are much more common and are frequently underreported. Pedophiles and other predators are drawn to places where they know children will be.

———

Consult the chart on the next page to see a number of other similar decisions and the risky blind spots associated with them.

The Decision	Benefits	Risks	The Blind Spot
You allow a person to rent an apartment or room from you.	Income, the place is not sitting vacant, and it will be maintained.	The tenant loses his job, falls behind on the rent, and then you have to go through an eviction process.	You know little about the tenant's background, behavior, whom he will bring to the house, and if he poses a danger to you or your family if you have to evict him.
A colleague offers to drive you to and from the airport.	You don't have to pay for a cab or a shuttle.	Your colleague might expect a similar favor later on. Your colleague might show up late and you'll miss your flight.	The colleague uses a medication like Xanax that affects his alertness and as a result gets you both into an accident.
You're at a bar. A handsome guy chats you up. You have great chemistry. You decide to go home with him.	He might be the one.	He could have an STD.	He might have a serious anger-management problem that is exacerbated when he drinks. It's rare, but he also might be a rapist and this is how he cons his victims.
Your son comes home and says he heard one of the kids in his class say he was going to bring a gun to school. Your son tells you that this boy is angry at the assistant principal because she suspended him for making verbal threats to a teacher when he was only joking around. Your son asks you not to say anything because he worries the friend will retaliate if he finds out that he tattled. You are considering keeping the secret.	Your child might not be bullied as a result of him sharing this information with you. He won't be blamed for going to his parents about the threat.	This other student brings a gun to school and shows it to some of the other kids.	School counselors and mental-health experts are unaware of this student's new threat (called "leakage") to bring a gun to school. He might escalate to acting out violently, and others at the school could be hurt, including your son.

Why We Are Blind to Risk

In the last chapter I mentioned a number of myths that tend to get in the way of us noticing dangerous people. In addition to those myths, six factors tend to cloud our observations of others and of situations.

Our first impressions: We tend to form a first impression of someone else within minutes, and this impression is often shaped by superficial details: what the person looks like, how they are dressed, their political or religious affiliations, a facial expression, body language, and tone of voice. If our first impression is a positive one, we will likely look for details that support this positive view and filter out details that do not.

Similarly, if the first impression is negative, we look for details that support the negative view and filter out details that support a positive one.

Sometimes we size up other people just to compare them to ourselves. Are they smarter? Are they prettier? Rather than assess them, we compare them.

This is a particularly dangerous blind spot because dangerous people—especially psychopaths—can be masters at impression management. They know precisely how to make a good first impression and win your unwavering trust. They can be charming and glib and seem like the life of the party. At the very least, they seem harmless.

Recommendations from others: Perhaps even before meeting someone, we already have an impression because friends, family, and coworkers have referred to this person as a "good person" or "nice guy." Then, as with first impressions, we filter out the negative and focus on the positive. We assume that they've been prescreened and there's no more work necessary.

Superficial details of normalcy: We trust people who seem normal and distrust people who seem abnormal. As a result, we trust those who fit in—they have a well-groomed front yard, 2.5 kids, an easy smile, and a job. We trust people who do what everyone else does, who look like everyone else, and whose houses and yards look like everyone else's.

For these reasons, initially, many people were duped by Susan Smith, who tearfully went on television asking for the safe rescue and return of her children. She certainly didn't *look* like the type of person who would drown two little boys. No one could imagine that any mother would be capable of doing such a thing.

In reality, however, if a criminal or dangerous person is intent on you *not* knowing what is really going on behind his or her front door, he or she is going to make a concerted effort to look normal. His front lawn will be well manicured. He will dress nicely. He will go to work every day, and he will wave and smile as he drives by. He will even marry and have children because that's what normal people do. Yet you don't know what he is doing to that seemingly perfect family behind closed doors. He could be abusive mentally and physically. He could be engaging in high-risk behaviors that put his family and even his neighbors at risk.

Personal biases: Various biases may cause you to unfairly and incorrectly sort entire groups of people into "dangerous" and "safe" categories. For instance, many people have a bias that causes them to categorize all monks with shaved heads and brown robes as safe. The same goes for most religious clergy and also for many people who attend religious services regularly. For instance, think about how often you've heard the line, "He's a good guy. He's really active in the church." Yet this is a false bias. Little about someone's religious affiliation offers any indication as to whether that person is dangerous or safe. More important, dangerous individuals know about this bias and will mention that they are religious or fans of gospel music just to disarm you.

You may have other biases that cause you to unfairly sort others into dangerous categories. You might do this with people of a certain race, ethnicity, gender, socioeconomic status, or sexual orientation. Think about your natural reaction when you see a Latino youth with tattoos, a do-rag, and loose-fitting jeans that allow his boxers to show. He might be the nicest, most innocent kid around, but your instant reaction may be fear.

Our own personalities: Your personality affects how you view other people. If you are opinionated and rigid, you might sort people into black-and-white categories and have a hard time seeing the gray area in between. If you are selfless and naturally optimistic, you might frequently let down your guard (or never put it up in the first place) because you tend to see the good in people, even the ones who pose a threat to you.

Past experiences: Negative past experiences with certain types of people can cause you to erroneously sort people into good and bad categories. For instance, children of alcoholics might see anyone who takes a drink as having a drinking problem.

How Blind Spots Persist

In late summer 2010, a fifteen-year-old girl, her thirteen-year-old friend, and his eleven-year-old brother pooled some babysitting money, took a cab to the airport, bought three airline tickets, waltzed through security, and boarded a plane. They flew from Jacksonville, Florida, to Nashville, Tennessee—all without their parents' knowledge. Their destination was Dollywood.

When they realized the Nashville airport was two hundred miles from the theme park, they called home and asked for help.

When this story broke, people kept asking the same question: "How do three children walk through an airport and get on a plane without anyone noticing?"

I'm guessing that at least a few people—ranging from the employees who sold the children the tickets to TSA officials to other passengers to flight attendants—did notice. And these folks probably did, initially, wonder where the kids' parents or guardians were but immediately concluded that the adults must be nearby—probably in the restroom or grabbing a cup of coffee.

But they asked few if any questions because they rationalized and normalized the risk away. The airlines were quoted as saying that employees asked no questions because of a company policy that allows children age twelve and older to travel alone without a parent. They said the eleven-year-old was okay because he was with older companions.

TSA officials have commented that they asked no questions because children under age eighteen do not need identification to go through airport security.

I'm guessing that various passengers thought, "Well, the flight attendants are not saying anything, so it must be okay," and the flight attendants probably thought, "They got through security and they have tickets, so it must be okay."

Some other people probably suspected that these kids were not supposed to be on the plane, but they opted to believe that their parents must be somewhere.

Five Ways People Misinterpret Details

The airline incident illustrates how a blind spot can persist. Many times people see behaviors that are odd or even suspicious, and even though they might be skeptical about what is going on, they frequently assign these details into the most logical or ordinary scenario. If these suspicious details are misinterpreted, either purposefully or inadvertently, it is usually for one of the following reasons.

Normalizing: When you normalize, you find a normal explanation for what at first seemed to be a risky behavior or situation. Whenever you put too much emphasis on *superficial indicators of normalcy* and too little emphasis on other telling details, you normalize the situation. For instance, maybe your daughter's boyfriend has complained about how he has been treated at work. You don't know him very well, but there were a few times when you thought he got angry with a neighbor over an unimportant situation in a way that felt a little scary. You might have heard from your daughter that he is spending a lot of money and time going to gun shows, that he just bought a membership in another gun club, and that he never seems to have the money or time to take her out to dinner. Yet you normalize these hints by reminding yourself that he looks like a regular guy; your daughter seems to care about him; and although you are not around him a lot, he does seem to be respectful most of the time. You tell yourself that he's just a guy who is caught up in a bad work situation and his interest in firearms is his way of relaxing. It's his only release. He's normal, therefore his hobby is normal. This normalizing may prevent you from seeing the very real threat that your daughter's boyfriend might be an injustice collector who plans to use some of those guns against his coworkers and bosses or even your daughter.

Similarly, if you've ever worked in a secure building that required you to swipe an access card to get in, you've probably normalized potentially dangerous situations numerous times. Did you ever hold the door for the person behind you, even though you didn't know that person? If so, you probably told yourself that the person must be an employee. See? He's got a cup of coffee in his hand. Who else would he be but an employee? In reality, thieves commonly gain access on the coattails of employees in just this way, and then roam the building.

Similarly, let's say you notice a strange car parked in front of your home and see a man sitting inside that car. You keep glancing out the window. Ten minutes pass. Twenty minutes pass. Finally he leaves. The man's behavior is unusual and concerning, but, instead of calling the police, you normalize the behavior by telling yourself, "Maybe he's just waiting for someone," or "Maybe he's eating his lunch." You don't tell yourself, "Maybe he's casing the neighborhood," do you? Yet that is a very real possibility.

Rationalizing: When you rationalize a situation, you doubt your ability to properly interpret risk, and you mentally talk yourself out of doing something about the very real risk in front of you. For instance, going back to the strange car parked outside your home, you might talk yourself out of calling the police because "The police officer is going to think that I am overreacting," or "I'm going to get that guy in trouble and he isn't doing anything wrong."

Parents sometimes rationalize allowing their children to do dangerous things—such as walking to school by themselves—by telling themselves, "If I don't let him do this, he will never grow up," or "I shouldn't be such a helicopter parent." At other times they rationalize risky behavior by telling themselves that their kids are "good." For example, I can't tell you how many mothers have told me that their daughters were "good parents," even if their daughter was heavily involved in the use of illegal drugs and engaged in high-risk behaviors like prostitution and completely neglectful of her children.

People also tend to rationalize risky behavior because they are too scared to get involved. For instance, you might see a parent lose it in a store and scream at her kids and possibly even swat them on their bottoms. You might find the parent's behavior concerning, but you rationalize it by telling yourself, "She probably just had a really bad day. I'm sure she doesn't act like this all the time. I remember when my children were little, and I know what it feels like to be exasperated." In reality, the frightening issue is what this woman does at home when no one else is watching.

Explaining it away: People often explain away a telling detail by focusing on other details that seem to tell a different story. For instance, in a child-abduction case I worked on years ago, the parents turned the missing child's bedroom into a home office, and they did it within days of the child disappearing. This was concerning behavior. Yet many of the investigators were already convinced that the parents were not involved, so they explained away this behavior with comments like "The house is really small, and they need this space to serve as a command center where flyers can be created." This child has never been found.

Ignoring: Ignoring is a type of magical thinking, pretending that a situation, circumstance, or person is not what it appears to be. People often resort to ignoring when all of the evidence is saying otherwise, but they want—for various reasons—to hold on to their positive view of a person or situation. The mother of a rapist or murderer, for instance, might ignore all the evidence presented against him at trial. The owners of a vicious but beloved dog might ignore all the people who complain of feeling threatened by the dog. A parent might ignore the warning signs of a brooding son who is an injustice collector and has recently been suspended from school. They might even ignore his recent purchase of bomb-making materials.

Icon intimidation: We tend to ignore risky details if someone is iconic; that is, in a position of great power, status, or fame. For instance, many people trusted Bernie Madoff with their money, in part, because he used to be a nonexecutive chair of the NASDAQ stock exchange. How could someone with such an impressive title be a crook?

Whenever I worked a case and was told, "We've got to be careful here," I knew icon intimidation was going to be a factor. Investigators only used that phrase if a suspect had hired a high-profile attorney and they were intimidated by that attorney, if the suspect came from a prominent family, or if the suspect had a powerful job with a powerful title.

We automatically put more trust in CEOs and other successful business leaders, and we tend to discount signs of their wrongdoing for a longer period of time than we would with people of lesser status. We do the same with people who hold positions of trust, such as religious figures, law enforcement officers, and doctors. For instance, would you trust someone who worked for the FBI? I would, and I did. I worked down the hall from Earl Edwin Pitts, the FBI agent who was later charged with spying for the Soviet Union and Russia. We all assumed that the lengthy background investigation, interviews, and application process involved in getting a job with the FBI ensured that the folks we worked with were trustworthy. It didn't occur to anyone—not even me—that Pitts was a spy. His position also allowed him to gain access to the country's secrets and all of us to overlook the initial warning signs.

The status of someone's family can play a role in icon intimidation too. The arrest of Kevin Coe—known as the South Hill Rapist—left Spokane, Washington, residents reeling because he came from such a "fine" family. His father, managing editor of the *Spokane Chronicle*, and mother, Ruth, were considered upstanding citizens. His family was very well-known and well-respected. They were considered leaders of the community.

Now that you know how details tend to get misinterpreted, let's take a fun look at a few hypothetical situations and see how they can be interpreted correctly or incorrectly.

Secret Profiler Tricks

In the popular crime shows, profilers famously walk into a room, look around, and then, based on one small detail—usually a family photo— spout off a litany of conclusions that they've reached about the person who lives in that house. For instance, based on a tiny detail, a TV profiler might conclude that the father has been molesting his daughter for years or that the mother has a drug addiction.

In real life, it just doesn't work that way. FBI behavioral analysts (known colloquially as profilers) don't take one small detail and hang an entire profile, or even a definite conclusion, on it.

For instance, let's take a look at how a TV profiler and real-life profiler (me) would interpret the following details differently.

Detail 1: An Armani suit

TV profiler: The wearer is a company CEO who likes to flaunt his self-importance by wearing expensive clothes and buying expensive things. He has a narcissistic personality disorder. He may even be a malignant narcissistic who feels so grandiose and entitled that he abuses his wife without any concern for her welfare or feelings and has multiple extramarital affairs because he is so handsome and successful.

Mary Ellen says: Expensive clothes don't tell us whether someone is honest or dishonest. Does the rest of him fit with the picture? Does he have a cheap watch and unshined shoes? Or is he wearing an expensive watch and expensive shoes that go with the expensive suit? If the whole look is good, then maybe appearances are important to him.

How does he talk? Is it all about him? Does he constantly seek attention by talking loudly and dominating the conversation? If so, then perhaps he is a narcissist. If not—let's say he asks questions about others around him, behaves graciously or humbly, and is more reserved and quiet—probably not. The Armani suit by itself offers little insight into his personality. His behavior, however, shows a lot more.

Detail 2: A neat and tidy living room with no photos on the walls

TV profiler: The woman of the house is a "clean freak" who is controlling and rigid. She doesn't have photos because they collect too much dust. She has an obsessive-compulsive disorder. If you look in her dresser, you'll find that she color codes her underwear.

Mary Ellen says: What does the rest of the house look like? Is it possible that the living room is the only neat and tidy room in the house? Maybe it's neat and tidy because the owners never use it.

Or maybe the woman of the house is like me and keeps her living room neat and tidy because that's the room where she entertains guests and she wants to have a pleasant and nice place for them to relax and feel comfortable. I can assure you that if were you to walk into my garage, you would not find it to be neat and tidy.

I, too, do not have photos on my living room walls. Yet I own plenty of photos. They are not on the wall because I've never gotten around to hanging them.

Detail 3: An office adorned with framed plaques, degrees, and awards

TV profiler: This guy should ditch his wife and marry himself instead. The guy is in love with himself.

Mary Ellen says: Yes, it could mean that the man is a raging narcissist, but the plaques also could mean that he is proud of his work and loves what he does. It's possible that he's created a special work space that he enjoys coming to every day.

It's also possible that he lives in a small home with no office space. In a very selfless move, he's given all of the wall space at home to the family so they can display their photos and artwork. The only place he can hang his treasured mementos is in his office.

Detail 4: Someone with her arms crossed over her chest

TV profiler: This woman is clearly defensive and has something to hide.

Mary Ellen says: Yes, that's possible, but it's also possible that the gal is cold, isn't wearing an outfit with pockets (and therefore has nowhere else to rest her hands), is trying to cover up a ketchup stain on her shirt, or just stands that way routinely because she's comfortable that way.

Detail 5: A guy who looks away as he says something

TV profiler: This guy is lying, and I don't need a polygraph to prove it.

Mary Ellen says: We assume that people who look down, away, or who seem shifty-eyed are either lying or hiding something. This might be the case. But it could also be true that the person is just shy and his or her interpersonal skills are lacking. People often assume that someone who is guilty will not be able to make eye contact, but this isn't true. Psychopaths are exceptionally good at making eye contact, even when they are telling one lie after another.

Detail 6: Her bookshelf is loaded with books about psychopathy, serial killers, and sex offenders

TV profiler: She's married to someone she's suspicious of. She thinks her husband might be a violent offender, and she's reading these books so she can better understand what makes him tick.

Mary Ellen says: Maybe she's writing a book called *Dangerous Instincts* and these are books she's reading for background.

As we were working on this book, my coauthor had the following titles on her desk:

- *The Biology of Violence*
- *Snakes in Suits*
- *Without Conscience*
- *The Psychopath*
- *The Psychopath: Emotion and the Brain*
- *The Stranger Beside Me*

She was using the books for research. Yet it would be easy for someone to see those books and assume something else. She also has about thirty diet books on her bookshelf. Someone might see all those titles and assume that she has an eating disorder or a weight problem. In reality, she's collaborated on about fifteen diet books. The ones on her bookshelf are either books she's written or books she's consulted for research purposes.

Look at the Totality of the Circumstances

When you sum up a person or a situation based on just one detail, it's like trying to get a sense of what a book is about by reading just one page.

Later I'll show you specifically how to assess risk and make decisions based on the totality of the circumstances. Rather than taking isolated pieces of information—such as someone's body language or a snippet of their conversation—you will learn how to read people and situations and to make smarter decisions as a result. Once you start assessing the behavior of those around you, rather than isolated pieces of information, you will have a better understanding of who people really are and whether they pose a threat to you.

CHAPTER 5 RAP SHEET

- When weighing pros and cons, we tend to underestimate the cons and overlook the biggest risks of all.
- We assume that we can tell at a glance whether someone is dangerous, but even the best FBI behavioral analysts cannot do this. Dangerous people can look about as normal or abnormal as everyone else.
- If a first impression is a good one, we will tend to filter out negative information we notice later on in favor of details that support our first impression.
- Positive recommendations from others can bias our judgment and keep us from noticing danger.
- We tend to become disarmed by superficial indicators of normalcy, even though there is nothing to stop someone who seems normal from also being dangerous.
- We tend to normalize, rationalize, explain away, and ignore risky details.
- If you take one detail and focus on it without taking other details into account, you will likely come to an incorrect conclusion or form a poor decision.

Chapter 6

How to Improve Your Judgment

I was in Baton Rouge trying to help local authorities track down a serial killer.

Eyewitnesses had thought they'd seen a white man with some of the victims either just before they disappeared or around the areas where they had been killed. Still, I knew that the serial killer could be of any race since the races of the victims varied. To learn more about this killer, I had been encouraging local authorities to study assaults that had happened long before, looking for possible survivors from the days when this serial killer was still perfecting his technique.

Eventually authorities traced the incidents back a full year and uncovered three reports from various women who might have been approached or assaulted by the killer, but all of whom had survived. All three women described him as an African American male.

This description, however, did not fit with the eyewitness accounts.

Now investigators faced many perplexing questions. Had the eyewitnesses been mistaken? Was their information flawed? Or were we looking at two separate offenders?

I was sent to see what was similar and what was different about the respective patterns of behavior and to reach a conclusion. As I readied to leave to interview the three women, Pat Englade, the head of the Baton Rouge serial murder task force, pulled me aside. I had built a rapport with him, and I had come to admire him greatly. He'd taken an unfair beating by the media and from the public for not catching this serial killer more quickly. This was an extremely high-profile case, one that had already drawn lots of criticism from armchair profilers. Some of them—retired FBI agents and homicide detectives—were very proactive, even to the point of coming in and trying to take over the investigation.

Still, Englade did not attempt to micromanage our progress. He gave all the investigators the freedom to do their jobs. He trusted us and gave us positive feedback and credit for our work.

"Mary Ellen," he said. "Don't come out of these interviews and tell me that this rapist is a person of interest, because I can't do bullshit with that. That's not helpful. If you don't know if this is our guy, then you don't know. If it's not connected, it's not connected. If it's not him, fine. But tell me straight." I promised I would.

I interviewed all three women extensively. I asked them how this man had approached them, what he had said, and about other details that they might have noticed. I went to each of the locations where the offender first contacted the women. I walked through each scene with the women and made note of every detail. I focused much of my attention on the last victim, who had spent the most time with the offender. Through her eyes and ears, I studied his behavior and learned about his personality.

Then I spoke with Englade.

"Mary Ellen," he said, "I will do what you tell me to do here. I need you to tell me whether this man is the same person we are looking for in connection with the murders in Baton Rouge. Don't give me any BS. Are they connected or not?"

I felt tremendous pressure to get it right. The forward progress of the investigation hinged on my opinion.

If I was wrong, I not only risked slowing down the investigation, I also risked maligning my entire profession. I knew that whatever I told the chief would be broadcast to the media. I might eventually have to testify in court about how I came to my conclusions.

I would have to live with this decision for the rest of my life.

I took a deep breath. Was I the right person to make this decision? Was I ready to make it? Yes and yes.

I knew my craft. I'd been profiling crime scenes and assessing personalities for years. My assessments had helped law enforcement catch rapists, murderers, and child abductors.

I knew what I was doing.

I also had interviewed the three victims extensively. I had considered every piece of new evidence. The offender had approached Diane, one of the victims, at her front door in a nonthreatening manner. She described him as charming, pleasant, polite, and very good-looking. He'd told her that he liked the Christian music that she was playing inside her home. He'd claimed to be lost, and he'd asked for directions to find a job site and to use her phone. I knew phones had gone missing from the homes of other victims. His asking to use her phone was a telling detail.

Then, when Diane handed him the phone, he'd asked if her husband was home. When Diane answered no, he quickly shifted from a polite and charming man and into a brutal killer. He pushed his way through the door, got inside the home, and attacked her. Had her son not come home and scared him away, the attacker might have strangled her to death.

The two other women had described a similar man: good-looking, beautiful skin, hair that was well coiffed, charming, and polite. He'd approached one of them at home too. He'd also asked to use the phone because he "needed directions." As the second survivor retrieved her phone, he walked inside and began looking around at her family photos and asking questions about the people in her life. That's when she'd ordered him out of the home. Fortunately for her, he'd left.

The third woman had caught his eye when she'd been walking to her car in a parking lot. He'd followed her from the lot and then across the street to a restaurant. He parked and asked her to walk over to his car. She thought he was very handsome, had beautiful skin, and hair that was well coiffed. Intrigued, she approached him. That's when she noticed his stunning behavior: He was masturbating in his car. She said, "You are too good-looking to have to do that."

These women were all independently describing the same cluster of behaviors, and those behaviors—high risk and sensation seeking as well as impulsive—were consistent with the other murders we'd been investigating. These women also described a charming man. That explained why the murder victims did not have defensive injuries. This was a man who used his good looks and charm to con women into thinking he was not a threat to them. That charming, nice-guy style, however, dissipated once he was in their comfort zone and could take control, which happened in only a matter of minutes.

"The guy who did these things is the Baton Rouge Serial Killer," I said. I briefed Englade on what I thought he should tell the media and the public so that someone, somewhere, would think, "That describes a guy I know."

Englade held a press conference. He held up an artist's rendering, based on the description Diane had given of her attacker, as he delivered the information I'd suggested. He said that we were looking for a man who was glib, charming, and good-looking—a man who could approach women in a way that was endearing and disarming. Englade said that this man would be a risk taker, and that he'd likely entered other people's homes before when he hadn't committed a murder. People who knew him might have discovered him snooping around their bedrooms, for instance. He also said the man was of African American descent.

Before the conference was over, someone called the task force hotline and said, "The person you are looking for is Derrick Todd Lee." Derrick Todd Lee was later convicted and sentenced to death.

If I had told Englade that the murders were not connected, the Baton Rouge serial murder task force would not have continued to unravel these sexual assaults. A more accurate composite sketch would not have been drawn. A buccal swab (obtained by swabbing the inside of the cheek) had been obtained from Lee several months before, but a judge later determined that it had been obtained in violation of his constitutional rights. At the trial, the judge ruled that the DNA was not admissible evidence in court. Then the judge later readmitted the DNA findings based on the "inevitable discovery exception to the exclusionary rule." This exception allows evidence (DNA) to be admitted back into a legal proceeding even though it was seized in violation of the Constitution based on the presumption that the evidence would have eventually been discovered and lawfully obtained using other investigative techniques. It was the judge's ruling that police would have eventually arrested and gotten a warrant to obtain Lee's DNA because of the behavioral work of the FBI and the task force that resulted in the identification of Lee following the press conference.

If someone had not come forward after Englade's press conference and fingered him as the suspect, Lee would have gone on to kill more women before getting caught, and he may not have been convicted at trial after his arrest if the DNA was permanently excluded as evidence.

Why Your Decision-Making Style Matters

I could have waffled on the day I made that decision. I was tremendously stressed and had a knot in my stomach, but I had to make an informed, analytical decision. How was I able to make such a definitive decision when I was under so much pressure? How was I able to be so confident about my conclusion?

I was able to do so, in part, because I had developed an effective decision-making style for this type of high-stress situation and had extensive experience in making similar decisions. Those factors allowed me and the FBI's BAU to complete an analysis that helped to lead to the conclusion that eventually allowed the task force to catch the killer.

Your level of experience in making high-risk or stressful decisions, as well as your personal biases and your emotional state at the time you make them, will all affect your ability to make a SMART decision. In other words, more effective decision making starts with you. In particular, it depends on your ability to understand your:

- emotions, especially knowing when not to make a decision because of them or in spite of them
- experience and information, especially knowing when you don't know quite enough to make a decision
- resources, especially knowing when and whom to seek out for help

In this chapter you will find self-assessments and reflective questions that will help you to test how well you make decisions and to see what might be clouding your judgment. These exercises will help you to do the following:

Make SMART decisions. People think decision making is a talent you are born with, but that's not necessarily the case. Yes, some people are naturally better at choosing correctly. Still, decision making is a skill that you can learn and improve with practice. When you learn how to make SMART decisions, you will feel more in control of your life. When risky situations come up, they won't feel overwhelming because you will have a system to follow that will help you to make the decision on your own or consult the opinions of others.

When you use the SMART model to make decisions, you do not feel as if you are flipping a coin, picking an option, and then hoping for the best. You will know that you've made a decision that will keep you and your loved ones as safe as possible.

Track your progress at making safer decisions. In a few pages, I will ask you to assess your current decision-making effectiveness. This will allow you to reassess your decision-making effectiveness later on so you can see if you are getting better.

Know your decision-making weaknesses and strengths. Most of us are pretty good at making decisions in some areas of our life and not so good at making them in others. For instance, I'm strong when it comes to deciding whether someone's behavior is problematic or threatening. I'm much weaker when it comes to deciding whether a new computer meets my needs. Purchasing the wrong computer for my needs can result in a significant financial loss as well as long-term problems and frustration. I know this is a weak area for me and that I lack the knowledge and experience others have. As a result, I take my time in deciding whether to purchase a computer, and I will likely consult with other people for insight and information.

Procrastinate less and reason more. Procrastination is a problematic decision-making style that some of us resort to when we feel overwhelmed. Rather than taking ownership of a situation and choosing a course of action, procrastinators continually put it off and remain passive. The SMART model will help you to move beyond procrastination. You will know the difference between indecision—the inability to make a decision because you don't know what to do or how to do it—and a slow, reasoned, careful decision. You will know when the time is right to make a decision and when it's appropriate to wait before making a decision.

How Effective Are Your Decisions?

Let's evaluate the effectiveness of your current decision-making skills. This exercise is not designed to humble you. Rather, I'd like you to complete this exercise so you can learn more about yourself, and so, after some practice, you can take it again to see just how much progress you've made. I encourage you to participate as you read. Go get a notebook or open a file on your computer. Jot down notes and date your entry. Then you can take the test again later and use your first set of notes to see how much progress you've made.

I'd like you to think about three different types of decisions.

Category 1: Rare decisions

What they are: Rare decisions are the ones you make only a few times in your life.

Why they can be dangerous: Rare decisions can affect you for years to come. For instance, the decision to marry the right person could lead to years of happiness. The decision to marry the wrong person could lead to years of misery, painful divorce, and possibly financial devastation. Because you don't make these decisions often, you will feel out of your comfort zone. You may lack important skills or the knowledge needed to make such decisions. You will probably need to consult friends, experts, consultants, or other resources before making a rare decision. Many rare decisions generate a lot of emotion, both positive and negative, which can cloud your judgment.

Types of rare decisions:

- Whether to get married or divorced or to break off a relationship
- Whether to initiate an intervention for a family member or friend
- Whether to buy or sell a house
- Where to attend college
- Whether to get pregnant, adopt, or have more children
- Whether to relocate
- Whether to change jobs or careers
- How to respond to someone who seriously maligns you professionally
- To fire someone (if you rarely do this)
- Whether to purchase or give away a pet
- Whether to seek medical treatment for a friend or loved one

Category 2: Occasional decisions

What they are: You make occasional decisions every so often—perhaps once a year or so.

Why they can be dangerous: While you do have some experience making these kinds of decisions, it's not a skill that you've developed and honed. You might feel more familiar with these kinds of decisions, but if you don't have a good decision-making system in place, you are not likely to be any better at making these than you are at making rare decisions. Because you feel more familiar, though, you might be more cavalier when making an occasional decision.

Types of occasional decisions:

- What car to buy
- Whether to tell family friends something intimate
- Whether to hire (or fire) an employee or household help
- Whether to make a financial investment
- Whether and how to confront a supervisor or a colleague

- Whether to go out with someone you just met online
- Whether and how to ask for a raise
- Where, when, and with whom to travel
- Whether to buy your teenager or preteen a laptop, cell phone, or other expensive piece of equipment
- Whether to report someone or something to law enforcement
- Whether to allow your child to associate with new friends you know little about

Category 3: Frequent decisions

What they are: You make frequent decisions as often as several times a day.

Why they can be dangerous: There is a desensitization that sets in when you make a decision over and over again. You make these decisions so often that you may not even be aware that you are making a decision at all. Also, frequent decisions often lull people into a false sense of safety, especially when they don't, at first, result in negative consequences.

This desensitization can result in everything from reckless or hasty decisions to decisions based on flawed or partially flawed data. As soon as a decision becomes routine, you will need to ensure you give that decision specialized attention to avoid making mistakes due to this desensitization.

Types of frequent decisions:

- Whether to hand over your car keys to your teen or tell your teen that it's okay to catch a ride with a friend
- Allowing your children to walk to school alone
- Allowing your children unmonitored use of a laptop, cell phone, or credit card
- Whether to get into a car with someone who has just had two drinks
- To open your front door when someone knocks without looking through the peephole first

- Agreeing to carpool with someone who has a poor driving record
- Continuing to associate with a friend or associate who displays all of the dangerous behavioral characteristics mentioned in chapter 9
- Not to lock your doors
- To walk alone at night

Think about your life. Come up with examples of a rare, occasional, and very frequent decision you've made. Jot them down in your notebook. Then ponder the following questions and write some notes next to each decision accordingly:

1. How did your decision turn out? What was good about it? And what was bad about it? Did it cost you money, time, stress, worry, a damaged relationship, health problems, or peace of mind? Don't assume a decision was "good" because everything turned out okay. For instance, you might have pulled off texting while driving without getting into an accident. That doesn't mean the decision was a good one.

2. Who helped you make the decision? With whom, if anyone, did you consult?

3. How would you decide differently? If you could go back in time and do it over, what would you change about your decision and why?

4. If the decision did not result in a good outcome, what happened? What led to this outcome?

5. Was this outcome fixable? If so, what did you do to try to fix the situation? And how did that work for you?

6. What factors influenced how you made the decision? Were you emotional, under pressure, or lacking in important information? Did you fail to do something that led you to make a poor decision?

7. Would you make the same decision today? If not, what are the factors that would make you decide differently? What would you now do instead? What was it that caused you to make that decision in the first place? Who would you consult and why?

8. What did you learn about yourself because of this decision? Do you default to flipping-a-coin-style decisions when you are tired or under stress? Do you tend to get lulled into a false sense of safety when making very frequent decisions? Do you get frustrated and say, "Lets just go for it"? Do you use magical thinking, telling yourself, "It will be fine. It will be okay"? Do you default to groupthink, telling yourself, "Everybody else does it"? Or do you use the Scarlett O'Hara of the epic *Gone with the Wind* philosophy of "I will worry about it tomorrow"?

Look over your notes. What have you learned about yourself and about how you make decisions? Don't be too hard on yourself. Even if the majority of your decisions did not turn out well, that only means you have room to learn, practice, and improve. Use this exercise to learn about yourself and your past mistakes. Evaluating what influenced past decisions will help you to avoid allowing those factors to influence your decisions in the future.

On the flip side, try not to get overly confident if most or all of your decisions turned out well. Chances are you still have some room to learn and grow too.

I encourage you to take this assessment every six months to see how your decision-making skills are improving. Give it to your family members, too, especially your children.

How Do People Make Flawed Decisions?

Most people take part in risky behavior from time to time. For instance, many people text while driving, even though they know about the dangers of doing so. Others might get into a car with someone who has had a few drinks, even though they know that alcohol impairs driving ability. I see plenty of people jogging in remote areas in the dark and while wearing headphones. I also know many people who routinely leave their doors and windows unlocked.

Yet these folks are not bad people. They are not sinister, and they don't have a death wish either. Their risky behavior is, however, the result of a flawed decision-making style.

Any regretful decisions you identified in the previous exercise were probably based on a flawed system of decision making as well. Look over your notes and think about what led you to make those decisions. What factors came into play? For instance, did you make the regretful decision because you did any of the following?

Caved under pressure. Have you ever made a purchase because a salesperson talked you into it, only to regret that purchase later? Have you ever decided to do or not do something solely because you didn't want to upset someone? Think about decisions you regret. You caved under pressure if you've made the decision because:

- you worried you would inconvenience someone else
- you didn't want to upset someone else
- you felt pressured to do it
- you wanted to be polite
- you were influenced by your own strong feelings, negative or positive

Were lulled into a false sense of safety. We get lulled into a false sense of safety in a few ways.

1. When everyone else is doing the same thing. If you live in a neighborhood where no one locks their doors, you might think it must be safe to leave your doors unlocked, even if it's not. If all of your friends are piling into a car with a driver who has had a few drinks, you might get in, too, even if under any other circumstances you never would feel safe driving with someone who has had a few drinks. One of the reasons motorists in the Washington, D.C., area feel safe when they are "slugging" (carpooling with strangers they meet in park and ride lots) is because lots of other people are doing the same thing.

2. You've done it before. The more often you practice a dangerous behavior and get away with it, the safer that behavior will feel to you, even though it's not safer at all. The probability of something unfortunate befalling a slugger is the same every single time that slugger accepts a ride from someone he or she doesn't know.

3. Your biases lead you to deem someone harmless when you really don't have enough information to make that judgment. This happens most often when the person in question seemingly shares something in common with you. Perhaps you are members of the same church, alumni of the same school, or volunteers for the same charity. It also tends to happen when someone belongs to an organization or group that you have deemed good, trustworthy, or virtuous. For instance, many people automatically trust anyone who is dressed as a Buddhist monk or Catholic nun. They also trust people who are in positions of authority, such as police officers, members of the military, security officers, or bouncers. Sometimes people blindly trust those who are elderly because they think of them as physically less threatening or less imposing or because of the stereotype of wisdom and weakness coming with age.

Talked yourself into it with rationalizing statements. Rationalizing statements give you a reason to do what you want to do, despite the risks. You might talk yourself into taking a dangerous risk with rationalizing statements like the following:

- It will make my life easier.
- It will save time.
- It will save money.
- It will be much more inconvenient if I don't do it.
- I'm doing it because I love my family.
- You have to trust your child sometime.
- I don't want to get involved. It's someone else's problem.

Didn't have all of the information. The problem with lack of information is this: If you don't know you are missing a key fact, how can you know if you should include it or exclude it from your decision-making process? For instance, if you are buying a house and don't know there will be future problems with the basement when there is an unprecedented amount of rain, how can you factor that possibility into your decision? This is why it's so important to ask yourself, "What is it that I don't know?" It's also a reason to consult others who may know more about this type of decision than you do. They can fill you in on all of the information that you should gather before committing to the decision.

Think about how often you've made a similar decision. If you have made them rarely, then it's a good idea to consult with an expert who can help walk you through the steps and help ensure that you have all the information you need.

Discounted some of the information. This is when you choose to focus on the positive side of a decision and fail to adequately consider potential negative consequences. For instance, many parents allow teens to travel overseas with friends or with school-sponsored trips. They focus on all the positives: what their children will learn, the great opportunity, the affordable price, and so on. They push the negatives out of their minds. For instance, that their home country's law enforcement may not be able to help if they get into trouble in another country. And what happens if they get sick? Does the country they're visiting have a good health-care system in place? How would they get home in an emergency? Does the family have enough money to medevac them or to pay for shelter or food if they get stranded for days, or longer, and can't get out? What if their friends get arrested for an alleged crime? Who would the family contact if they inexplicably stopped communicating? Will there be enough or any parental supervision? What if there is a natural disaster and there is no communication with that part of the world for hours, days, or even weeks?

Didn't have all of the information because you were too timid to ask for it. This might happen if, for instance, you fail to ask the salesperson about a car's accident record. It could happen if you are about to sleep with a new sexual partner and you can't bring yourself to ask for medical reports showing that he or she does not have an STD. It could happen if you take a new job and realize that it will eventually require multiple moves that your new spouse refuses to make.

Were emotional when you made the decision. Fear, anger, sadness, and other strong emotions can cloud your judgment and cause you to overlook potential future consequences. Strong needs can do the same, like a need for revenge, security, money, prestige, acceptance, etc. For instance, have you ever sent an angry e-mail to someone only to later regret having pressed the send button? Have you ever said something during the heat of an argument that changed your family dynamics forever? What would you do to be able to take those words back?

Even positive emotions can cloud your judgment. For instance, many people have rushed into flawed decisions because they've been in love with someone or have loved an idea or a material item.

You may not be able to keep your emotions in check 100 percent of the time, but you can do the following:

- Think about your emotional state before committing to a decision. Ask yourself, "Am I too stressed, sleep deprived, in love, sad, angry, or out of sorts to make this decision right now?"
- Slow down whenever you notice yourself thinking or saying things that begin with "I just want" or "I just need." For example: "I just need some peace in my life . . ." "I just need to get that . . ." "I just want to get this over with." "I just want to show her/him . . ." "I just want to teach her/him . . ." "This is all I've ever wanted."
- Put off making a decision until you are feeling less emotional and less conflicted.
- Make a point of saying, "I'll think about that and get back to you" whenever anyone presses you to make a decision.
- If possible, give yourself some time and distance before making a decision. The greater the consequences, the more time you should take.
- Talk over potential decisions with a level-headed friend and ask questions like "Do you think I'm too emotional to make

this decision right now?" "If you were me, what would you do?" "What am I missing here?" "What factors am I not taking into consideration?"

Didn't consider the long-term consequences. Flawed decisions are often made with the short term in mind. Try to remember to weigh the long-term consequences too. Ask yourself the following:

- Will I still be able to live with this decision tomorrow or next week?
- Will I still be able to live with this decision six months from now?
- Will I still be able to live with this decision a year from now or even for the rest of my life?

Didn't consider what would happen if you got caught. We've all watched as any number of politicians' and other prominent figures' hopes and dreams were dashed by decisions they'd made in the past because they assumed they would never get caught. Gary Hart, Bill Clinton, Tiger Woods, John Edwards, and the infamous sexting congressman Anthony Weiner all come to mind.

Many people cheat on their spouses because they assume they will never get caught. Many people cheat on their taxes for the same reason. If "not getting caught" or "no one finding out" is an important factor when making a decision, it's probably a good idea to reassesses whether that decision is a SMART one. Will you still be able to live with that decision if you do get caught or if people do find out? Have you thought about how you will deal with this decision if everything does go bad?

Allowed personal biases to overshadow rational judgment. As I was writing this book, the suicide of Rutgers University student Tyler Clementi was in the news. He jumped off the George Washington Bridge after his roommate allegedly secretly videotaped him having sex with a male student and then broadcast it on the Internet. News of the incident resulted in a public outcry. Various people began wearing purple in support of bullied gay and lesbian youths. Then a school board member in northern Arkansas did something stunning. He reportedly posted on Facebook that the only way he would ever wear purple would be if "they all committed suicide."

Word of his posting spread through the Internet. Soon people were calling for his resignation, and he eventually stepped down from the school board and apologized for his "unfortunate" remark.

I'm guessing that this school board member did not think very far into the future as he posted that remark. He probably did not think of the long-term repercussions or foresee that the posting would eventually result in his resignation from the school board. His bias against gays clouded his judgment. His remarks made him look as if he had no empathy for others.

You don't have to be racist, sexist, homophobic, classist, ageist, or anti-Semitic to dehumanize someone. You might dehumanize a person during a moment of anger. You might do it because they are faceless—someone you are interacting with on the Internet or a driver in another car on the freeway.

The Dangerous Truth

Negative biases cause you to put a group of people in the "bad" category and dehumanize them. Positive biases cause you to put them in the "good" category, and once you do that you are a lot less likely to perform a critical risk assessment on them. You might have a positive bias toward members of your class or your religion or those who share your political views. Yet just because you have something in common with someone doesn't mean that person is not dangerous or could not pose a threat to you.

How to Know If You Are Ready to Decide

To ensure that your choice is truly SMART, ask yourself the following questions before rushing into any decision:

1. What is the key decision I am trying to make? (For example, am I deciding to buy a house?)

2. What are the possible long-term and short-term consequences, good and bad? Once I make this decision, how am I likely to feel?

3. What is my past experience in handling this problem or situation?

4. How often do I make decisions about situations like this? Do I make them rarely, occasionally, or frequently? Have I taken steps to overcome my lack of experience in making this type of decision? Have I taken steps to overcome the problems I have encountered when I made this type of decision in the past?

5. What is influencing this decision? Am I feeling pressure to make it? What factors are causing me to feel pressure? Am I in the right state of mind to make this decision? What are my emotions?

6. What is my decision-making style and how does it help or hurt me in handling this problem?

7. Do I have all the information I need to make the decision? Is this information reliable? Am I relying only on the Internet to make this decision? Do I have all the information I need to make a strong decision? If not, or I'm not sure, have I consulted with a person or resource who does know what information I will need to make a good decision?

8. What are the long-term effects of this decision on me, my family, my friends and colleagues, and my place of employment? Have I thought about the consequences, not only in the short term, but also in six months or a year or more down the road?

CHAPTER 6 RAP SHEET

- When you use the SMART model to make decisions, you reduce your risk of negative consequences and gain a sense of control over your life.
- Your ability to make SMART decisions can be honed with practice.
- Rare decisions can be risky because they put you out of your comfort zone and force you to lean on others for help.
- Very frequent decisions can be risky because than can lull you into a false sense of safety.
- Regretful decisions are usually influenced by pressure, a false sense of safety, rationalizing statements, lack of information, strong negative or positive emotions, failure to consider the long-term consequences, failure to consider what would happen if you got caught, or personal biases.

Chapter 7

How to Assess and Mitigate Risk

While we were putting together this book, my coauthor traveled to Italy with a close friend. One evening the two were walking from a restaurant back to their hotel. It was around 11:00 p.m., but they didn't have far to go. It was only a ten-minute walk at the most. The streets they would traverse were well populated, well lit, and lined with shops that were still open.

You'll soon learn how to evaluate the risk of any given situation as low, medium, or high. Since you have not learned how to do that just yet, I'll tell you that my coauthor's risk was medium. It wasn't high, because she was not in a life-or-death situation. But it also wasn't low, because she was in a foreign country where she didn't know the language and she was walking the streets after dark. She also was missing key pieces of information. For instance, she didn't know what sort of crime problems there were where she and her friend were walking.

One's risk is quite dynamic, and it can change quickly. My coauthor's risk was quickly moving up, and her exposure to physical injury was increasing. The farther she walked from the restaurant the higher her risk became as she got deeper and deeper into unfamiliar territory. She and her friend probably stood out as foreigners, making them easy targets for thieves and pickpockets who prey on people from out of town. Because of that, we'd have to upgrade this situation from medium to high, and it could have ultimately become a life-or-death one.

My coauthor and her friend attempted to take a shortcut, one that led them to a busy road that was not well lit. Now their risk was very high. Before reading on, can you think of why?

They were about to walk down the road in the direction of the hotel when my coauthor said, "You know, there are cars whizzing past. There's a blind curve up ahead. It's 11:00 p.m., which means the probability of some of these drivers being drunk is high, and I'm dressed from head to toe in black, which means the drivers can't see me."

She and her friend decided to turn around, backtrack, and take the long way back to the hotel. This decision required that they walk back up a very steep hill. It added another ten minutes to their walk. They were anxious and jittery when they got back to the hotel, but they were also both alive.

What had initially seemed like a benign situation had quickly become a risky one. In hindsight, my coauthor says she would have tried to get more information about the crime problems in the area. She would have asked locals about the best and safest routes to walk at night. She would have found out—before embarking on the walk—who to call and where to go for help if needed. All of this would have taken only a few minutes, but it would have been a few minutes that could have saved her from a lot of potential trouble.

Why the Situation Matters

The nature of the specific situation in which you find yourself affects two aspects of your decision making.

1. How much time and effort you will want to put into a given decision. For instance, in a low-risk situation, the possible consequences of a bad decision are minimal, so it might be okay to rely on quick judgments. But in a high-risk situation the outcome of a bad decision might be physical injury or even death. In such a situation, you will want to assess the risk factors, look ahead, consider the most likely consequences, and then craft your options.

For these reasons, you probably can make a swifter decision when ordering a pizza than when hiring a cleaning person. The consequences of ordering a pizza are minimal. Even if the delivery person is a dangerous character, the exchange is made at the front door and not inside your house. Also, the delivery person must interact with dozens of customers every day. If there's a problem, it will be reported back to the pizza company sooner rather than later. The pizza place creates a built-in danger filter. If this delivery person had created problems for customers, it's likely he would have been filtered out, because customers would have complained.

On the other hand, a cleaning person will be coming into your home, where you are much more vulnerable. Most cleaning people work for themselves. So even if there have been hundreds of complaints, you'd never know it. The potential consequences of hiring the wrong house cleaner could be theft of your belongings, damage to your property, or even identity theft.

Conversely, the cleaning person, Realtor, or service person who willingly walks into a variety of homes and interacts with numerous strangers every day is at an even greater risk. The person she works for could refuse

---

The Dangerous Truth

Not long ago, a bank was robbed near where my coauthor lives in Emmaus, Pennsylvania. The police chased the robbers, first by car and then on foot. The robbers shot at the police. Other police responded from nearby areas, and the state police and FBI got involved too.

What do you think many of the residents and storekeepers of this small town did when they heard scores of police sirens roaring down Main Street?

They went outside to see what was going on.

By doing so, they greatly increased their risk of getting hurt. Of course, none of them knew that the robbers were on foot, and were armed, dangerous, and willing to take hostages and shoot civilians. That's why the safest thing to do when you hear sirens is the response that is least instinctual: Stay inside and lock your door.

to pay her or write her bad checks. Much worse, she could face down an unfamiliar or dangerous pet. A home owner could falsely accuse her of stealing, assault her, or even attempt to murder her. There could be aspects of the home that might cause her physical injury, such as deteriorating steps, toxic mold, cigarette smoke, or pet feces.

The higher the risk, the more careful your assessment needs to be.

2. Whether you take steps to mitigate the risk. Again, in a low-risk situation you might not take steps to mitigate the risk at all. But in a high-risk situation, you will want to take every precaution possible, and in medium-risk situations, you want to take precautions that will prevent the risk from becoming higher.

You'll learn how to mitigate the risk of any given situation later in this chapter. For now, let's talk about how to determine the level of risk in the first place.

How to Assess Risk

You can use the following scale to determine the level of risk.

High risk: The likelihood of your decision resulting in mental, physical, emotional, or financial harm is high. The consequences are serious to extreme. A flawed decision in a high-risk situation could result in job loss, prolonged legal problems, a marred reputation, harm or loss of a loved one, debt, physical injury, and even death.

Medium risk: These situations have potential to escalate (and become high risk) or subside (and become low risk). For instance, having a teen driver in the home leads to dozens of medium-risk decisions every day. If your teen is a good driver and follows all the rules of the road and does as she or he is told, the risk could drop to low. If your teen texts and drives or is operating an old car that is likely to break down as he is driving home from school or work at night, the risk could swing high.

Note that sometimes you will rate a decision as medium risk because you don't have enough information to deem it high or low, and these unknown factors can easily swing a medium-risk situation into the high-risk category. For instance, my co-author didn't know about the crime problems in the town where she was walking in Italy. If she was in a low-crime area, the risk would have been low. If it was a high-crime area, the risk would have been high. She didn't know the nature of the local crime problems, so the risk was medium.

Low risk: Low-risk decisions result in minimal conse-quences to your health, livelihood, and loved ones. These deci-sions include, for instance, what to cook for dinner and whether to buy the shoes that you see on sale. Don't sweat these deci-sions. Even if you flip a coin and make a flawed decision based on the result, it's not a big deal. Choosing poorly in a low-risk situation won't result in years of regret.

Your level of risk in a given situation is dynamic. It can shift back and forth, from low to medium to high and back down again, based on where you are, what you are doing, and the variables in your environment. Sometimes these shifts are subtle and sometimes they are seismic.

You'll face different types of risky situations. Many people think only of their risk of physical harm when it comes to staying safe and avoiding problems, but there are many types of risky situations, all of which are dynamic and changing. Factors that can quickly turn a low- or medium-risk situation into a high-risk one include the following:

Physical risk: Personal harm due to severe weather events (floods, mudslides, hurricanes, snowstorms, tornadoes, and so on) and harm that results from unstable or unsafe surroundings (earthquakes, dilapidated or poor construction, fires, avalanches, and so on), as well as car accidents, sudden falls, and crime.

Health risk: Food poisoning, flu outbreaks, a new diagno-sis (cancer, heart disease, diabetes).

Social or emotional risk: Loss of a loved one, a loved one develops sudden and serious health issues, a loved one moves farther away.

Professional risk: Backbiting coworkers, unfair supervisors, poor company performance that eventually results in layoffs.

Financial risk: Stock market or real estate crashes, identity theft, job loss, robbery.

When trying to decide if a situation is low, medium, or high risk, consider how many different areas of your life the situation affects (professional, personal, financial, health, and social). Think about what might cause the risk to move up and down, and keep in mind these important factors:

1. What are the possible ramifications of this decision six months or a year from now for you and others around you? If the ramifications are high and a lot of people are impacted, you will want to spend more time making the decision.

2. What are the worst possible outcomes of this decision? Are those outcomes serious to extreme? Then the risk is high. Is it minimal? Then the risk is probably low. Does it depend on a number of factors? Then the risk is probably medium and you need more information.

3. How do your physical surroundings factor into the risk involved in this decision? Are your surroundings safe (I'm in my home with the doors locked in a low-crime neighborhood) or not so safe (I'm looking for my car in a deserted parking lot in a big city with lots of crime)? What is going on in your surroundings that could prevent you or someone else from being and staying safe? If the surroundings are safe, the risk might be low. If the surroundings are unsafe, the risk might be high. If you don't know the safety of your surroundings, the risk is medium and more information is needed.

4. Are you about to move into or out of a safety zone? For instance, if you are walking from your place of employment (a safe zone) into a poorly lit, unattended parking garage (unsafe zone), your situation has moved from low to possibly high.

5. Are you about to allow someone you don't know well or at all into a comfort zone? Your home and your car are your comfort zones. Whenever you invite someone into these places, your risk level goes up. Conversely, are you going into a comfort zone of someone you don't know?

Test Your Risk Assessment Smarts

Use the following chart to get a sense of the risk zone into which some decisions fall. Think over the various situations and the reasons you think I ranked them as low, medium, or high.

Situation	Risk	Why
A friend you know very well invites you out for the evening and offers to drive.	Low (Physical risk)	You know the friend well. That means you know she doesn't drink and drive, that she's a safe driver, that she maintains her car, and that she is responsible and won't leave you stranded if she meets someone while you are both out. (Note: If you don't know these details about your friend, your risk level goes up.)
Your cousin asks if she and her two young children can move in with you because she's going through a divorce and financial hardships and needs to pull herself together.	Medium (Financial and physical risk)	You don't know enough about the reasons for her divorce and specifically about her soon-to-be ex-husband. Do you know whether he has threatened her? Is he likely to come to your home and try to hurt her? You also don't know about her disciplinary practices with her children, and you might not know about her personal habits. Does she drink or do recreational drugs? Is she a closet smoker who tends to fall asleep with a cigarette in her hand? You also may not be aware of possible behavior problems that her children might have, and you may not know if she makes a habit of living with others. What if she is parasitic and moves into your home anticipating that you will support her and her children?
You are traveling abroad with a friend. She wants to avoid hotels in the interest of saving money and to look online to see if there are any local families willing to put you both up.	Medium (Financial and physical risk)	There is a lot about this situation that you do not know. You don't know which sites this friend is looking at online. You don't know about their reputation. You don't know if they screen host families. You don't know about the kinds of families who advertise on the sites this friend is considering. You don't know their background, the living conditions of their homes, or their personalities. You also don't know about their previous experiences when hosting international travelers or the experiences of other travelers who have stayed with them.

Situation	Risk	Why
Your fifteen-year-old daughter wants her own computer in her bedroom.	High (Physical risk to both you and your family)	If the computer is in her room, you will have no way to oversee her computer habits. Online predators target young children and teens with unsupervised computer access, and your teen is not old enough to be able to effectively screen who is a threat to her online and who is not. In some families, the son or daughter exercises exclusive rights to their room, their computer, and other possessions. When the parents allow this behavior, or even inadvertently encourage it, they need to understand that they may be encouraging behavior that could evolve into a serious threat to their child's well-being. Parents also need to understand that they inadvertently put their children at risk whenever they allow them to make major decisions about their lives and well-being. Children and teens do not have the maturity or emotional ability to spot Internet predators.

How to Minimize Risk

In the movie *The Blind Side*, Sandra Bullock plays Leigh Anne Tuohy, an upper-class mom who takes in Michael Oher (played by Quinton Aaron), a homeless and traumatized boy who later becomes an all-American football player and first-round NFL draft pick.

In the movie, Oher becomes upset and runs away from the Tuohys' home, which is located in an exclusive area of Memphis, Tennessee. Tuohy decides to look for him and, in the process, drives to a dangerous part of Memphis.

In the movie, Tuohy knows she is driving into an area with a high crime rate. She knows that, as white women in an expensive SUV, she would be noticeable and stick out.

But she doesn't feel she has any other choice. She loves Oher and cannot wait at home while he possibly gets into trouble.

She does, however, take some precautions. She goes to this part of town during the day. She doesn't stay long. She travels in a reliable car that she knows will not break down. She has a cell phone with her. But she gets out of her car to confront members of a gang regarding Oher's whereabouts, and that one action catapults her risk level from medium to high.

She could have taken additional precautions. For instance, she could have called the police and told them where she was headed. She could have gone there with someone else.

Tuohy made a choice that many parents would probably make. No amount of danger will get in the way of the desire many parents have to protect their children. This is why parents are known to run into burning houses. They would rather die than stand back and do nothing while their children perish or are hurt.

This is understandable, of course. Just because a situation poses a great deal of risk doesn't mean you won't willingly find yourself in the middle of it. But you can, as Tuohy did, take steps to minimize your risk. Let's walk through some hypothetical situations and minimize the risk together.

Situation 1

Your college-age daughter calls on her cell phone to tell you she has a flat tire and had to pull over. She is two states away from you.

The possible negative consequences: It's dark, which means other motorists might not be able to see her if she attempts to change the flat. It also means she is easy prey for any predators who happen to be passing by.

The risk level: High.

How to minimize her risk: Stay on the phone with her and have her describe her location, giving you as many landmarks as possible.

Keep her on the phone with you. Use another phone to call 911 and let the police know about her situation. If a cruiser is nearby, an officer can park behind her car to provide a safe buffer while she changes the tire. You might worry that you are being a nuisance by calling the police about her flat tire, but trust me. It's a lot more convenient for one police cruiser to aid your daughter while she fixes a flat than to dispatch the entire police and fire department because a passing motorist hit her car and then proceeded to cause a ten-car pileup.

- Tell her to stay in the car with the widows up and doors locked, even if someone stops and offers to help.
- If she needs a tow, stay on the phone with her the entire time. Ask to be put on speakerphone when she's in the cab of the tow truck. You can also call a taxi or shuttle service to arrange for her to be picked up.
- Advise your daughter not to accept a ride with a stranger even if he looks normal and appears to be willing to provide assistance.

Situation 2

Jenny is a college student. She's recently met another group of students, and they invite her to join them at a local pub.

The possible negative consequences: Jenny doesn't know much about any of these students. She doesn't know if they are the type of people who will look out for her if she gets into trouble with another bar patron. If there are men in the group, she doesn't know if they have anger-management problems that get worse when they drink. She doesn't know if there have been problems at the pub. For example, there may have been recent incidents of men slipping women flunitrazepam, the date-rape drug. She also doesn't know much about the employees at the pub. Do any of them have a criminal record and, if so, what for? Will any of them prey on her if she compromises her judgment and ability to think quickly by drinking too much?

The risk level: High.

How to minimize the risk: Many people attempt to minimize the risk of a situation like this by assigning someone to be a designated driver, but the risks posed by this situation call for much more than that. Jenny will be with unfamiliar people in an unfamiliar setting. She needs her wits about her because she might need to make a quick decision. Drugs and alcohol will compromise her ability to think strategically. She doesn't want to slow her thinking and her reaction time with alcohol. She could search online to see if there have been any reports filed for criminal or suspicious activities at the bar, such as women being harassed or assaulted. Prior to leaving, Jenny should absolutely tell someone where she is going and who she will be with.

Situation 3

Another student is bullying your eleventh grader, who tells you that the student bragged about having access to a gun and said he was going to take it to school and "hurt a few people who deserve it."

The possible negative consequences: There are many unknowns here. You don't know if this student was bluffing. You don't know if he really has access to weapons. And, unlike me and other FBI behavioral analysts, you don't have expert knowledge of the behavior and personalities of people who are likely to commit school violence. Most kids who threaten to shoot do not carry it out. That's a good thing. Still, there is no way—without having a trained expert do a threat assessment—for you to know if this person is serious.

As a result, you do not have the ability to decide—without outside help—if this student is making statements only to scare fellow students or if he is a serious menace. If he is serious, then many students could potentially be harmed or lose their lives if he decides to bring a gun to school.

The risk level: Medium.

How to minimize the risk: Tell a school official what this bully told your son. You want school officials to do a threat assessment or bring in outside help to do one.

When a threat like this comes in, there is usually a protocol already in place to address it. These days most schools do not use just one strategy to respond to a threat, whether it is serious or benign. Over the past decade, most schools have created threat-assessment programs with behavioral assessment and intervention teams. These teams are trained to assess the threat and consider different levels of intervention based on the seriousness of the threat.

This threat should not go unreported out of fear—fear of reprisals, fear of antagonizing the bully, and so on. Your failure to act would enable the bully to continue his behavior unchecked.

Situation 4

Your next-door neighbors create a lot of problems in your neighborhood. The wife, in particular, seems to target neighbors with passive-aggressive behaviors like playing music loud late at night and cluttering her yard with "crap" that has become an eyesore. This woman has been known to call the police on neighbors who are not doing anything out of the ordinary and to scream and yell across the street for no reason. You have seen her and her friends drinking in the yard. Her behavior seems to get worse at these times. She's recently filed a police report about a theft in her home, and now she is accusing your child of the theft.

The possible negative consequences: You know that this woman is volatile, but you don't know where her line is. Will she be able to manage her behavior, or will she escalate to worse and more threatening and harmful behaviors? If you do not handle this situation correctly, the threat could increase even more. She could focus her aggression on you and your family.

The risk level: High.

How to minimize the risk: The natural inclination of many people is to fight fire with fire and retaliate, but that is the opposite of the way to minimize risk in this situation. What you want to do is defuse the situation and keep it from getting worse. Make an effort to stay away from her, her family, and her property. You want to avoid continuing this battle on personal terms. You want to refer the matter to an entity (such as a home-owners' association or the local police) and let her fight it with them. They will have procedures in place to handle these problems. They have both the power and the legal and financial resources to enforce appropriate rules and regulations. They are the best entities to address her behavior, particularly if it begins to escalate. Deferring the problem to one of these entities also puts a buffer between you and her, which is critical.

Situation 5

There is a serial burglar operating in your area, and he's hit all the houses around you. You worry that yours might be next, but you have a guard dog and you work out of your home during the day. Maybe that's enough?

The possible negative consequences: You fear that sooner or later this burglar is going think about breaking into your home. What you don't know is (1) whether the police might catch him before he does, (2) whether your dog is enough of a deterrent to persuade the burglar to stay away, and (3) what the burglar will do if he does manage to break into your home. Will he only take some of your property? Will he also destroy and vandalize your home? Will he hurt your beloved dog? Is it possible the he might break in while you are home and harm you or your family? Is he watching your home right now, and if so, how is he doing it? How has he managed to be successful so far? Why hasn't anyone seen him in your neighborhood?

The risk level: High.

How to minimize the risk: There are many things you can do to make your home harder to break into, and I'll get to those in a little bit. First, however, let's talk about catching this burglar before he or she takes an interest in your home.

This person has been able to gain access to many homes over time. He or she has gotten away with this time and time again. Think about why that might be. Could it be that this person is very normal looking— perhaps someone who does not look like the type of person who would burglarize a house? Could it be that this person has not been caught because he or she blends in? You and your neighbors may very well have seen this person in the neighborhood but didn't think anything of it. Maybe your eyes skipped right past this person because he or she was so good at blending in and creating a facade of normalcy.

To catch this burglar, you and your neighbors will want to be aware of people who might be casing homes. Burglars do not stand in front of a home wearing a mask and holding a laundry bag. They do things that allow them to blend in. This person might walk a dog, jog, or ride a bicycle through the neighborhood. He or she might sit in a car while it is off or idling and appear to be on the phone or texting. Perhaps he or she goes door to door under the pretense of selling something, dropping off flyers, or asking for directions. Chances are you are not looking for someone who appears suspicious. You are looking for someone who does *not* look suspicious. If he looked suspicious or out of place, he probably would have been caught already.

Keep notes on what and who you notice in your neighborhood and compare those notes with your neighbors.

In addition to keeping watch over the neighborhood, do everything possible to make it seem as if you are always home: Keep lights on, keep the shades drawn, and keep a radio or the TV on when you are not home. Make sure your yard is well lit so it's harder for someone to break in without being seen. Make your house harder to break into: Keep the doors and windows locked. Consider getting an alarm system. Talk to your local police about the break-ins and ask them what you should look out for. Make sure you have the local police on your phone's speed dial, and make sure your phones are easy to access.

Brief family members about answering the door or giving out information about your home. Change your routine. Come and go at different times. Change your parking habits so it's not obvious that you are not home when there's no car in front of the home. Show that it is not easy to assume that you are, or are not, at home by making the signs of your presence less predictable. Finally, consider starting a neighborhood watch. Ask police to come in for a public briefing on best practices.

What to Do When the Risk Is Too High

When I was in graduate school, I moved into a small apartment in another town and lived by myself. One night, during my first week there, someone knocked at my door. It was the landlord. I let him in. He proceeded to tell me that he found me attractive and suggested that we have a romantic relationship.

I felt uncomfortable, and I thought he was forward and rude, but it didn't occur to me, at that time in my life, to think any more of it.

Then I called my mother. I told her what had happened and ended the story with "Can you believe he did that?" I was living alone for the first time in my life. I had sized up the situation as low risk, but my mother sized it as high. I was viewing it through the lens of a twenty-year-old who did not have a lot of experience at assessing risk.

My mother told me to start packing. She then called an uncle who lived nearby and asked him to drive over and help me move out. She saw the situation for what it was: extremely high risk. Here I was, a young, vulnerable woman living alone. I had a landlord who was both interested in me and rude and impulsive enough to tell me so. He was in a position of power, and he had a key to my apartment.

My mother didn't leave any room for mitigating that risk. She got me out of there. Within days, I was living in a new apartment.

There will be times when you will want to do the same. You will want to abruptly pull yourself or someone else out of a risky situation, or you will want to avoid getting into a bad situation in the first place. Here are some reasons why you would want to get out of a situation:

1. There isn't enough time to mitigate the risk. There is potential for danger or even imminent danger to yourself and/ or others.
2. Even if you take steps to mitigate it, the risk is still very high.
3. No matter how creatively you think, you can't come up with a way to mitigate the risk.

Some examples of times when you would want to pull out or ignore rather than attempt to mitigate the risk include:

- domestic physical or emotional abuse
- a group dynamic in which the group leader is suggesting that everyone do something dangerous (bullying someone else, drinking and driving, texting and driving, engaging in character assassination of a colleague, etc.)
- someone poses a threat to himself and others

In the next chapter, you will learn how to gather information so you can use that information to mitigate risk and make better decisions.

CHAPTER 7 RAP SHEET

- Take more time when making decisions that are high and medium risk.
- High-risk situations can have extreme consequences. Medium-risk situations can swing high or low, depending on the circumstances. Low-risk situations threaten only minimal consequences.
- Try to mitigate as much risk as you can in high- and medium-risk situations.
- Some situations cannot be mitigated. In these cases, the best strategy may be to extricate yourself or others from the situation.

Chapter 8

How to Uncover Information

Many years ago I was interviewing Tina, the spouse of an alleged serial killer. As I read Tina her Miranda rights, she started to cry. She fell out of her chair, onto the floor, and sobbed.

It's common for people to break down during an interview, especially when they are facing possible prison time. It's possible that Tina was both terrified at the possibility of being charged as an accomplice to her husband's crimes and remorseful for potentially ignoring telling signs that he might be terrorizing and murdering women.

I felt for her, and I was concerned, too. She was a rather large woman, and she was heaving so intensely that I worried that she might suffer a health problem as a result.

Still, I had to read her the rights. The interview could not move forward without me doing so, and we wanted to get her side of the story. I'm a compassionate interviewer, but I know better than to stop an interview over a few tears.

I calmly got out of my chair and I knelt next to her. Then I continued to read her rights: "You have the right to remain silent. Anything you say can and will be used against you in a court of law . . ."

As I neared the end, she abruptly stopped crying, sat up, composed herself, and lost all of her symptoms of sadness. She looked at me and said, "It always worked with James."

I was floored, and so were all the detectives, FBI agents, and profilers watching the interview through a two-way mirror. I'd watched people pretend to fall asleep to evade an interview. I'd listened to them as they'd threatened me and other agents with bodily harm. I'd seen a lot of people attempt to evade my questions in many creative ways.

And I'd even seen people turn on the tears, but I'd never seen someone behave in such a manipulative way as Tina had. Her display of emotion was the most convincing display of emotion I'd ever seen. She was a phenomenal actress. She'd been malingering: faking her sadness, fear, and distress for personal gain. She'd put on the show in order to get me to stop the interview and stop reading her the rights, to push me away and refocus the interview so I'd feel sorry for her. She thought her tears would end the interview before it started. They didn't.

How to Conduct an Interview

In this chapter, you will learn how to interview people (including your coworkers, neighbors, family members, and friends) in order to persuade them to tell you what you need to know. You will find out how to put people at ease so they are more likely to reveal important details. You will discover how to tell if someone is lying or being evasive. And you will find out how to observe someone's behavior so you can gain access to critical information about what is going on with them.

An interview is a situation in which you are attempting to obtain information. The word "interview" may sound quite formal, but I think it helps to think in those terms. If you think of this sort of conversation as an interview, it will keep you focused on information, both giving it and receiving it. If you call it something else, it will be easier to lose focus.

An interview is *not* the following:

1. A *confrontation* involving lots of emotion and battle lines being drawn.
2. An *accusation* that involves you telling someone what he or she did or did not do and not allowing this person room to explain his or her position.

3. An *intervention* that involves you telling someone else what his or her problem is and how you are going to fix it.
4. A *lecture* or *sermon* during which you do all of the talking. (Unless you are a preacher, don't preach.)

Confrontations, accusations, interventions, and lectures are all examples of communication styles in which you come at someone from a position of superiority and dominance. There is a time and a place for lecturing, confronting, and so on, but you want to be aware of when and why you are using these confrontational styles, along with the likely consequences.

During an interview, you do not want to act as if you are the person in power. Rather, you want to do everything possible to put your interviewee at ease, to listen, and to ask questions that will get you the information you seek. Ripping someone's head off might allow you to feel better if you are very angry, but it will not get you to your goal. As soon as you walk in and start taking your interviewee down a peg, you will cause that interviewee to shut down, reject what you are saying, resent you, become angry with you, and avoid further communication with you.

The more judgmental, opinionated, accusatory, or angry you are during an interview, the less the person you are interviewing is likely to reveal.

The Dangerous Truth

On TV and in movies, suspect interviews include lots of shouting and even some bodily harm. Foreheads are banged against tabletops. Backs are thrown up against walls. Threats are made, and the suspect is called any number of names. All of this eventually breaks the suspect, reducing him or her to tears and a full confession.

This overly aggressive method of interviewing is not how modern law enforcement, including the FBI, conducts interviews. The best way to get someone to shut up and shut down is to get in his or her face and start yelling.

Do This Before the Interview

To conduct an effective interview, you'll want to prepare for it and put some thought into your strategy before you ever ask a question. I would suggest the following:

Set some goals. What do you want to accomplish during the interview? What are your goals for this interview? What is your objective? What do you hope to find out? Keep in mind that most people do not open up and tell all in just one interview. It might take several interviews for you to pull the full story out of your sullen teen or stonewalling spouse. Make sure your goals are realistic and not intentionally cruel or harmful.

Calm down. The angrier or more aggressive you are, the less effective your interview will be. If you are thinking any of the following phrases, you are probably emotional and now may not be the best time to conduct an interview:

- I've just had it!
- If I don't do this now, I'll never do it.
- I just can't take this anymore.
- That does it!
- I have had it with him.

If needed, take a break and calm down before asking a single question. Again, if you are feeling emotional it's probably not the best time to try to get the information you seek.

Think about how your interviewee will react to the interview. What kind of a person are you dealing with? What will this person likely do if he or she does not want to give you the information you seek? Is he or she likely to cry, shut down, change the subject, walk out of the room, or something else? Think about past conversations and interactions you've had with this person, especially those that might be similar to the one you wish to have now. How did he or she react then? Take what you know about this person's personality and behavior into account and craft your questions and interview style around what you know.

If you worry you'll lose your cool, write a script to follow. Without a doubt, one of the most memorable cases I ever worked on involved the kidnapping, for ransom, of a wealthy and very high-profile computer executive. Such a crime of violence rocked the foundation of his family. For six days, this man was kept by his kidnappers who taunted the family with regular phone calls to dictate the terms of the ransom. The kidnappers had given strict instructions that the FBI was not to be contacted, so I determined that Kathy, the daughter, would be the best person to communicate with them.

Kathy was only in her early twenties and had absolutely no experience with criminal behavior, "bad guys," or the FBI. Kathy was frightened for her dad's safety and worried about what this whole situation was doing to her mom, who already had health problems. She was also very angry that this was happening to her father—to their family. I didn't want Kathy to be blindsided by anything they said to her, or for her to lose control, so I wrote her a script—questions for her to ask the kidnappers. I also wrote out a variety of responses she could provide them, depending on their comments or questions. Before each call, she and I practiced, and I told her how she was going to feel during the calls. I told her they would say things to her that would scare her about what they would do to her father if she didn't follow their demands. I told her they would say things like "kill your father" and "you will never see him again" and that they would try to push her buttons to get a reaction from her. I counseled her on keeping her cool and how to not get angry, demanding, or too emotional.

Every time the phone rang, Kathy and I both jumped, and I know her heart must have been pounding, because mine was too. She would pick up the receiver while I listened in on the other line. I stood right next to Kathy and held on to her as she braved her way through the kidnapper's cruel comments and questions. I would point to the script throughout the call, so she would know what to say. When Kathy started to get angry or emotional, I would tighten my grip on her and point to my long list of directions: "Don't get angry. Don't yell. Don't call them names." Following these phone calls, Kathy would sometimes shake or break down in tears. But she did an incredible job. We eventually found her father and brought him home safely, and the kidnappers were arrested and convicted.

I hope you will never find yourself having to conduct such a high-risk interview. But, if you know there is a lot at stake, and that emotions will run high, prepare a script. Write down what you want to communicate and how you will want to respond to the questions you might expect. Anticipate how your buttons will be pushed. Refer to your script when you find yourself getting upset or off point. Also, practice ahead of time.

Decide where you will conduct the interview. I didn't do much undercover work while in the FBI. Working as an undercover agent requires a special talent that I just didn't think I had. But one time I went undercover to keep an eye on a white-collar suspect who was believed to be offering bribes to other bankers in return for favoritism. The suspect wanted to do business with the bank where I supposedly was working, and he asked for a meeting at a restaurant during lunchtime. I was wired to record our conversation. Obviously this was a pretty important conversation and I wanted it to go well. However, it was loud, hot, and crowded in the restaurant. Other people's conversations were drowning out ours, and I didn't think the recorder was picking up the conversation. I tried to sit closer to the suspect while maintaining some decorum. The waiters, who had no idea what was going on, would come over to the table at the most critical times to fill water glasses or ask if we needed anything. It broke our rhythm. Every once in a while, I would look over to the table where the other agents were sitting, just to make sure they could still see me, but there were too many people around to have a clear view of them. It really was not the best place to have a sensitive conversation.

Another time, when I was not undercover, I went to interview a murder suspect. I wanted it to be somewhere he was comfortable so he would be more likely to open up and talk. I knew an interview room at the precinct was not such a location. He would just clam up if I took him there. On the other hand, we knew he often visited a graveyard late at night, so I suggested the cemetery as a meeting spot. I normally don't interview people while sitting on a grave, but I knew it was the best way to get him to talk, and it worked.

Think about the type of environment that will be the most conducive to your reaching your goal. If your conversation could result in you or the other person crying or having some other emotional response, pick a place that affords both of you privacy and respect. Also think about distractions that could stall the interview—a ringing phone, a blaring television, a bleeping text message, a crying baby, and other people—and try to minimize them if possible.

Decide when to conduct the interview. If possible, find out what is going on in your interviewee's life that might complicate the interview. Check his or her emotional vitals. Stress, depression, grief, anger, and other strong emotions will make it tougher for your interviewee to pay attention, open up, and talk.

For instance, let's say your teen just found out that he was not selected for the varsity football team. He's sullen and has spent much of the afternoon in his room with the door closed. You want to talk to him about his girlfriend who has been practically living in your home, the negative influence she's having on your family's life, and how you want her out. But today is not the best day to talk about his girlfriend. Save it for a better day, when he's not so troubled.

Occasionally you might have no other choice than to interview people during inconvenient times. You might need to do it in an emergency, when time is of the essence and you need to gather information as soon as possible. In such situations, incorporate the problematic timing into your initial delivery so the interviewee will buy into the urgency. For instance, you might say, "I wish I could pick a better time to talk with you about this. I can tell what happened today will make it tough for you to talk with me. I want to make sure you know that I am sensitive to what is going on with you, but this other situation we need to discuss is really urgent."

Decide how you will conduct the interview. Whenever possible, interview someone face-to-face. Face-to-face interviewing allows you to observe behavior. If you cannot interview someone in person, then the phone is your next best option. E-mail and texting are the least desirable because these mediums are so impersonal. They raise the risk of your interviewee misinterpreting your questions, motives, and feelings and of you misinterpreting the interviewee's answers, feelings, and motives.

Some people prefer to handle tough conversations by phone or by text, but I would encourage you to counter any tendency you might have to do such a thing. When you attempt to have a tough conversation in these manners, you are unintentionally broadcasting a message that says, "You are not important enough to me to do this in person." It can leave the other person feeling insignificant, hurt, marginalized, resentful, and unimportant.

Do an assessment of your own style. Use the information you learned about yourself in chapter 6. Also think about how interviews and important conversations have gone for you in the past. Do you tend to become angry? Are you more of a talker than a listener? (See "Are You a Good Listener?" on page 159.)

Do you tend to lecture or become accusatory? For instance, do you tend to say things like "I just tell it like it is," or "I'm just brutally honest," or "I don't have time to figure out what to say—I just say it," or "I don't have time for all that warm-and-fuzzy crap." These are all statements used to justify insensitive and bullying behavior. You might not think of yourself as a bully, but whenever you try to exert power over someone else and shove your opinion down his or her throat, you are bullying, and it most likely feels like bullying to the other person. Once you move into a bullying state, you become dominant and controlling and a lot less likely to get the person you are interviewing to open up.

Think about what adjustments you might want to make to your interviewing style. How might you adapt your natural style to the person you are interviewing? How have interactions between you and this person gone in the past? If things have not gone well, how might you adapt your interview style so things can go better this time around? In my thirty-two years in law enforcement, this is one of the most important concepts I learned. If you are the interviewer, you are in a leadership role and it is up to you to make the necessary changes, modifications, and adjustments to help guide the person you are interviewing to give you the information you are seeking.

The First Five Minutes of the Interview

The first five minutes of the interview can be the most important. During this time you will want to do the following:

Set up your physical surroundings. Limit distractions. Turn off the TV. Put your phone on vibrate or, better, turn it off entirely. Create an atmosphere that will make you and your interviewee comfortable.

For instance, whenever someone comes to my home—whether it's a neighbor, a friend, or hired help—I offer them a refreshment. I say, "I'm going to make some coffee, would you like some?" If they stay longer, I might offer them something to eat too. It's a way of extending an olive branch.

Now let's say you offer the olive branch, and the person you wish to interview says, "No, let's get on with it." Well, then it's best to get on with the interview. The interviewee is already annoyed and doesn't want to be there. No amount of coffee is going to change that. Someone like this is going to be impatient. Forgo the comfort and get right to the point. You might say, "Okay, it sounds as if you want to get right into this conversation and so do I."

Make introductions. If you already know the interviewee, then this might be as simple as saying hello. If you do not know this person, you'll want to introduce yourself and explain who you are. Keep your introduction to just a few sentences. Try not to go on and on and on, listing your credentials or use stalling phrases like "I hate to bring this up," or "I'm not sure how to say this," or "I'm not comfortable with this."

Here are examples of effective and not-so-effective ways to introduce yourself.

Say this: "Hi, I'm Jane—I'm Tyler's mom. Your son and my son go to the same school and they ride together on the bus. We live across the street."

Don't say this: "Hi, I'm Jane, your neighbor. I've lived here for twenty years and my house is on the historic registry. I work as a lawyer and am one of the most respected attorneys in the state. My son, Tyler, is on the honor roll and the captain of the football team . . ."

Build rapport. When you build rapport, you are creating a connection that puts your interviewee at ease, making him or her more likely to open up. There are two situations in which this doesn't work. First, rapport building does not work with psychopaths because they do not have the same feelings of empathy as you do. They do not bond on an emotional level with other people. Instead, they feel superior to you and any connection with you is meaningless.

Second, it's important to note that you don't want to spend much, if any, time building rapport if you are in an adversarial situation and your interviewee has already asked you to "get this over with already." This person has his or her mind made up and is impatient for you to finish talking. In this case, do not ramble. Just give the person quick bullet points and come to your conclusion quickly.

But in all other situations rapport building can help get the answers you need. Here are a few ways to build rapport:

1. Explain how much you care about the person or the outcome. For instance, if you are interviewing a family member, you might say, "Because I really care about you," or "Because you are so important to me," or "Because I don't want anything bad to happen to you." Just make sure your comments are sincere. When someone I hardly know starts off a conversation by saying, "I really care about you, Mary Ellen," I think, "If you lied to me about that, what else are you going to lie about?" Insincerity leaks out your pores.

2. Say that you need help. Adults like to give opinions and to fix things. (This isn't necessarily the case with children, who usually just want to be listened to.) When you give adults the opportunity to state their opinions, they will often open up. When you take that opportunity away from them, they will often shut down. To get a person talking, give him an opportunity to help you. Ask questions like these:

- What do you see as the problem here?
- Could you help me with this?
- I would really love your advice about this. Do you mind helping me?
- How would you resolve this if you were me?
- How do we fix this?
- How do you view this situation? What do you think is going on here?

- What do you think I should do?
- How do you think I feel about this?
- What is your perception of this?

You can also make statements like "I don't know how best to handle this. I could really use your help or advice," or "I could really use your assistance. I am not sure how to handle this situation."

This tactic works especially well with people who are reticent to offer advice, ideas, or suggestions. For instance, not long ago, three workers came to repair my roof. One of them was a young woman who seemed very reserved and shy. I also think she may have felt a little intimidated after she learned that I had been an FBI agent. She and the others were at my home for most of the day, and she didn't say more than a few words the entire time. I offered them lunch, which they accepted. As they were eating, I said, "You probably have noticed these color swatches on my wall. I've been planning to paint this room, but I can't seem to make a decision about the color. I am not very good at this."

I turned to the young woman and asked, "Which one do you like?" Well, her face just lit right up. She picked a color. I asked her, "Why do you like that one?" That's when she opened up like a flower. "This is a warm color and you are a warm person. This color speaks to your personality." She went on and on and on. I was just stunned. As it turned out, she was studying interior decorating. Had I not made the effort to draw her out, I would never have gotten the benefit of her expert opinion and insights about decorating.

3. Chat about a common interest. I'm an animal lover, so whenever I interview someone who has dogs or cats, I might say something like "Oh, I see you have cats. I have three feral cats that I feed." If your children are the same age, you could build rapport by talking about your children. Or perhaps you share a similar hobby or political views.

4. Reveal personal information—with caution. By briefly telling your interviewee that you are not perfect and you know it, you help them to relax and they will be more likely to see you as less threatening and less intimidating.

Of course you don't want to tell someone something off-putting. It's probably not a good idea to mention the time you spent in a mental hos-

The Dangerous Truth

Probably the most common way people bring up a potentially tense conversation is by saying, "We need to talk." As a general rule, however, this phrase comes across as quite threatening to people. It forecasts problems, pending doom, and ultimatums. Your loved ones probably have a history of hearing those words and of the resulting conversation not going well. As a result, those words might trigger someone to prepare for battle rather than relax and talk easily.

Even in a serious situation, you don't want to start off this way. For instance, let's say you suspect your boyfriend or spouse of cheating. Try not to go into this type of interview fueled by very strong negative emotions and thoughts such as these:

- I will kill him if he is cheating on me.
- I am so angry.
- That SOB! How dare he?
- He has ruined my life.
- I want to ruin him.

Have goals in mind before approaching your partner. If your goal is to uncover the truth, the advice in this chapter will help. If your goal is to accuse or unload or verbally abuse, this book can't help you. Just keep in mind that words are not retractable. The damage is done forever.

Also remember that emotionally laden interviews can escalate and lead to serious problems. You can evolve into an emotional and verbal abuser. If this happens, you are going to look bad. If your partner is thinking strategically, you will give him more and more reasons to stop the relationship. In the worst-case scenario, the conversation will turn physically abusive and the police could get involved.

pital or a past drug problem. But you might say, "I'm a little nervous right now," or "I'm thinking I might be a bit rough around the edges with this interviewing process, so please bear with me."

5. Introduce the goals of the conversations. Briefly state what you hope to achieve. For instance, you might say, "I hope by the time we are done talking we can reach an agreement on how best to handle this." This is an important piece of the conversation because it forces you to focus on your objective and it helps to prevent you from launching into an accusatory rant. It also tells your interviewee what to expect from the interview. Surprising someone with information may be necessary and, in some cases, part of a well-thought-out strategy, but it can also be very off-putting if used as a weapon to catch someone off guard or box him or her into a corner.

When you introduce the goals of the conversation, try to be as nonconfrontational as possible. For instance, let's say you want to talk to your husband about why he doesn't want to install an alarm system in your home. The factor motivating you is the recent spate of burglaries in your neighborhood, which has pushed this topic to a level of greater significance. Here are examples of how, and how not, to approach the subject.

Say this: "I know you've worked all day and are probably pretty tired. I bet the last thing you want is to sit down with me. You've been really patient, and I appreciate it. I'd like to talk with you about your concerns about getting an alarm installed. I'd like to understand your views on the matter."

Don't say this: "We need to talk about this alarm and why you don't want it."

How to Ask More Effective Questions

For the rest of the interview, you want to ask questions and listen and observe the interviewee as he or she answers, or doesn't answer, them. If you are interviewing someone who is reserved or uncomfortable opening up, intersperse different kinds of questions. Some questions should be focused on how he or she feels ("How did you feel when your boss told you that you were not getting that raise?"), and others should focus on what your interviewee actually did or observed ("What did you tell your boss?"). If you alternate "feelings" questions with "behavior" questions, you will not only get more facts but you will also hear more about emotions, motives, and perceptions.

Listen to what your interviewee is saying as you notice how he or she is saying it. Is this person slumped over and hanging her head on her chest while she talks quietly? Or is she animated and enthusiastic? Is he becoming more and more angry and responding in a combative and defensive manor? All of this is interpersonal intelligence. It gives you information about what your interviewee is thinking and feeling, and how she is reacting to you.

Periodically paraphrase what you've heard the person say. This validates your interviewee, assures her that you've been listening, and will encourage her to open up even more.

Here are some additional pointers that will help you to improve your interview and disarm your interviewee so he feels more comfortable and less defensive:

Offer a few compliments. Even if you are interviewing someone you find contemptuous, you can find a way to give a compliment here and there. You might say, "You are doing a really good job of explaining this," or "Thank you so much for taking the time to talk to me. I know you are very busy and your time is very important."

Ask open-ended questions. These are more likely to get someone talking and to soften up the conversation. Instead of questions that generate one-word answers, ask questions that allow the person to talk and explain. Usually these questions start with "what," "how," or "why."

Slow down your line of questioning. Avoid making your questions come off like machine-gun fire. You don't want to sound like the stereotypical cop from the 1960s crime drama *Dragnet*: "Where were you? Who were you with? Why were you there? What were you doing? Just the facts ma'am. Just the facts."

Such a line of questioning generally makes even the best of people nervous and uncomfortable. It causes many people to shut down, become evasive or angry, or start denying everything.

Use silence to your advantage. Many people become uncomfortable when there is a period of silence in a conversation, and this discomfort causes them to talk in an effort to fill the silence. Give your interviewee ample time to think about and answer every question, and allow a period of silence at the end, giving him or her ample opportunity to say more.

Resist the temptation to fill the silence yourself. If you patiently wait it out and allow a pause, your interviewee just might say a little more.

Acknowledge someone whenever he or she provides you with an honest and sincere answer. Give periodic positive feedback during the entire time the person is talking. You might say, "I appreciate you telling me that," or "I know that was difficult for you. Thank you for opening up."

Don't allow emotion to get them off the hook. Like the woman I mentioned earlier, who cried during the interview, some people will use emotion to stall the conversation. Even if the emotion is authentic, stepping in and catering to the emotion will derail your interview. It's okay to gently put a hand on someone's back or make another conciliatory gesture (as I did when I kneeled next to the woman I was interviewing), but do so with caution. Also keep in mind that crying during an interview can be cathartic and positive, which is why it has always been my practice to allow people to cry. I just pause and let the person cry, without handing them a tissue or gently touching their arm. A touch, a gesture at that point, could cause them to prematurely stop crying.

When a person becomes angry during an interview, I let them have their angry outburst too. I will sit quietly and let them yell, even rant. Once they calm down, I continue. If their anger moves toward aggression, however, it becomes a safety issue, and it will become necessary to terminate the interview and reschedule it for another time.

Reflect back what they say. Summarize what you think your interviewee has said, to make sure that you've got it correct. As you do, acknowledge his or her feelings, especially if those feelings are obvious. For instance, you might say, "It seems like this is a very tough topic for you to talk about. I appreciate you taking the time to talk with me about it."

What Not to Do

As we were working on this book, my coauthor was worried about her daughter, who'd said a little boy in her first-grade class was bending her fingers back until she said uncle. Obviously this concerned her. But it was also a sensitive situation. If she handled it poorly, she risked alienating herself and her daughter from the first-grade teacher. She also risked having the behavior escalate.

She wasn't sure of the right course of action. She needed advice and information. So she called the school principal. She explained the issue and said, "I don't know what to do. I could really use your advice. I'm not sure how to handle this. This is the first time I've ever encountered this problem, but I'm guessing you've dealt with problems like this hundreds of times. Could you tell me what you think I should do?"

The principal did one better. She offered to talk to my coauthor's child and to the little boy in question, get to the bottom of the story, and then do something about it if needed.

As it turned out, my coauthor's daughter was not entirely innocent! The little boy had come up with the idea of bending her fingers back until she said uncle, but she had done it back to him too. The principal gently talked to them both and explained that this was not acceptable behavior.

The situation was resolved.

This might have gone much differently, though. My coauthor could have called the principal and chewed her out for allowing such bullying to go on under her watch. She could have insisted that the little boy be punished or even expelled from school. She could have told everyone in the school what she thought of them and what she thought they should do about this situation. She could have been demanding, threatening, and insulting, which would have gotten her negative results.

She would have derailed the interview, and she would not have gotten what she wanted. There are other ways to derail interviews. Here are some examples.

Don't hijack the conversation. You hijack a conversation whenever you interrupt the person talking and bring the topic back to yourself. For instance, whenever I go to social gatherings, people generally ask me what I do for a living. Usually after I say that I am a retired FBI profiler, the person hijacks the conversation like this:

> Oh, really? That is so cool. Well, you know, I just love watching *Criminal Minds*. That is my favorite TV show of all time. I always wanted to be a profiler. I am really good at reading people. You know, people say that I've got this special gift that allows me to get inside somebody's head. I'm really not sure how to go about doing that because maybe I am too old to be an FBI agent, but I think I could be really good at it . . .

And then for ten minutes or so the person continues to talk about him- or herself. Because I'm never asked another follow-up question, I shut down and just let them go on and on. I provide them with no other information. This person who was so interested in FBI profiling goes home that evening with no more information about me or my work.

If you make the interview all about you, you will turn off the other person and shut that person down. Conversation hijacking embarrasses interviewees. It can make them feel that whatever they were talking about is not important to you. It can make them less likely to bring it up again. They might resent you for being rude, self-focused, and self-absorbed. Every time you do this during an interview, it will be tougher and tougher for you to keep your interviewee talking and on point. You'll also have a tougher time getting this person to communicate with you in the future.

Frequently I will ask people about specifics of a conversation they have had with a friend or a family member. They often tell me that they don't know what their friend or family member said about topic A or B. I ask them why they don't know. They tell me that they didn't ask in-depth questions because they weren't really interested in what the other person had to say. I am always floored by this. An "I don't care attitude" is hard to hide. The person you are talking to will see that attitude on your face and in your behavior, and it will negatively impact your communication with them.

Unless it's vitally important, don't cut off the person with statements like "Oh, hold on one second while I grab this phone call," or "Oh, that reminds me of something," or "Hey, did you see that beautiful house we just passed?" Save those thoughts for later. If you interrupt the interview with such passing thoughts, you are broadcasting one thing and one thing only: "I just asked you a question, but I really don't care about your answer. I am not listening. This conversation is not important to me."

That is not the message you want to send during an interview, particularly a really important interview. If you send that message, the person you are interviewing is probably going to shut down.

Are you a serial interrupter?

You might be a serial interrupter if you:

- check for calls or texts or e-mails during a conversation with another person
- change the topic midstream and pull it back to something you remember in the past
- hoard the conversation
- go off on tangents that only relate to you and your areas of interest or preference
- say things like "Let me stop you here" or "Let me just say this"
- look away and act as if you are not engaged

Don't jump in and fix someone's problems. Many adults are fixers, and many adults are also insulted when someone tries to fix their problems. When fixers hear about a problem, they immediately want to give advice. Are you a fixer? If you are, you will want to hold back your desire to fix during your interview. If someone really just wants to be heard and you jump in to fix things, your interviewee can end up feeling insulted, as if you are treating him or her like a child. This person might feel as if you think he or she is insignificant, incapable, or unintelligent. Most adults know how to fix their own problems. When they come to you with an issue or a problem, ask yourself, "Does this person want to be fixed or does he or she just want someone to listen?"

Don't talk for more than 15 percent of the time. If you are talking this much, then you are not getting the information you seek because you are not listening.

Don't note your displeasure at what the other person is saying. Don't sigh loudly. Don't roll your eyes. Don't make sounds like "pfft."

Don't threaten, manipulate, or bully. For many of us, it's our natural reaction to raise our voices, become argumentative, or become inappropriately forceful or confrontational. Yet these tactics rarely—if ever—get us what we want, especially during an interview. If you don't believe me, think about the one person in your life who you just can't stand because of the way he or she has treated you in the past. Now imagine telling this person the most intimate detail of your life. Would you do it? Hell no. Now think about the people in your life with whom you feel most comfortable sharing your most intimate details. Chances are these people do not talk down to you, bully you, shout at you, or threaten you. If you make someone not like you during an interview, chances are they will not tell you what you want and further conversations with them will become more and more difficult.

Don't tell the other person how he or she should feel. Just as certain things are likely to put a dog in the "red zone" and lead to an attack, certain topics will generate strong emotions or reactions from humans. For instance, laying someone off from a job, breaking up with someone, or informing someone that they or a loved one has a serious health issue are "red zone" topics.

When you are discussing such a topic, your natural reaction might be to tell the other person to not get emotional. Don't do that. For instance, try to not use phrases like "Now, don't get emotional," "Don't get upset," "Don't take it personally," "I don't want you to feel bad," or "Just calm down." These are all attempts to push emotion back down someone's throat, and they don't work. If anything, they will make your interviewee even more emotional. If someone becomes angry, yells, cries, or rants without any move toward physical aggression, you can let that person emote until he or she calms down. If there is a move toward physical aggression, whether against you or self-directed, you need to immediately terminate the interview, attempt to de-escalate the situation, and move to another location if you continue to feel threatened.

Don't blame. Phrases like "You never . . ." or "You always hurt me" or "It's your fault" or "You are a . . ." will likely push your interviewee toward the red zone and derail your interview.

Don't daydream or multitask. Paying close attention to what your interviewee is or is not saying—and how he or she is saying it—will require every ounce of your attention. If you try to multitask by checking e-mail or straightening up the house, you will miss important, telling details and you won't end up with all the information you need.

More important, you'll annoy the person you are interviewing. Think about how you feel when you are talking to someone and her cell phone rings. She looks at the caller ID, and she says, "I've got to take this one." When she finishes the call, she'll say, "I am sorry about that" and you'll say, "That's okay." But is it really okay?

Chances are it's not. Chances are you're annoyed. You're annoyed because this person just subtly told you, "You are less important to me than this call." Answering a cell, sending a text, or checking e-mail while you are having a conversation sabotages that conversation. Don't multitask. Don't check your e-mail, glance at your phone, sort the mail, or flip through a magazine. Being a good listener and multitasking are not compatible.

Don't get emotional. It's important to stay in touch with your emotional state. Getting emotional really limits the outcome of your interview. As soon as you become emotional, you change the direction of your interview and the goals become more about winning, beating up on the other person, and getting your point across than about conducting an interview. If you feel any of this happening, take it as a warning sign.

The more uncomfortable or upset you become, the less effectively you will be able to observe and listen and the more likely it is that the conversation will evolve away from being an interview and become a confrontation. And, at the other end of the spectrum, remember that if you are bored, it's a sign that the person you are interviewing is bored too.

Don't accuse or confront the other person. As I mentioned earlier, you will be asking people to reveal personal information about themselves or something they did. They will not do this if they feel threatened, judged, insulted, or put down by you. These approaches cause people to shut down.

Never call the person you are interviewing derogatory or insulting names. Don't assassinate that person's character by making statements like these:

- You are such a jerk. You don't care about me!
- You're such an ungrateful child!
- What kind of a friend are you to do that behind my back?
- You play favorites with people all the time. You should never be in your position!
- I hate you so much, I am going to call your employer and tell them how you have been abusing me!
- You are just like [your mother, father, or person you both dislike]

I am sure when you read these phrases you can feel the sting in them. What would you feel if you were on the receiving end of them? Would you feel the environment was safe for you to talk and open up? I don't think so. For the same reason, avoid "always" and "never" accusations as well, such as "you always do this" and "you never listen to my side of the story." Phrases like this paint people with a broad brush of previous failures. Their reactions will be varied, but they will most likely be negative. The person will become immediately defensive and try to argue that your perception of them is wrong. Their anger—and yours—will escalate and possibly move into the red zone. If this happens, both of your risk levels go up as well.

To keep the lines of communication open, keep the focus off you and on them. Use statements that do not blame the other person. If you want to tell someone how his or her behavior has impacted you, reference the behavior, not the person. Here are some examples:

- I felt hurt when this happened.
- I did what I did because at the time I thought it was the best choice.

- I am so hurt by all of this. I need to walk away and think before I say something too cruel and hurtful.
- I know that expecting great things from you is exactly how I should feel. I know you want to work to your potential as well. Let's talk about some of the issues you think are getting in your way of doing that.

Don't filibuster. Albert Einstein has been quoted as defining insanity as "doing the same thing over and over again and expecting different results." Yet many people do just that during an interview. They ask a question. They don't get the response they want. So they ask the same question again and again and again. Or they repeatedly say, "Just answer the question. Just answer the question. Just answer the question." Sometimes people will just keep talking louder and louder, without stopping, and they will refuse to be interrupted or halted.

This style of communication goes nowhere and is certain to shut down meaningful discussion.

Are You a Verbal Abuser?

If you use words as weapons to hurt, stun, shock, insult, overwhelm, and overpower, you might be a verbal abuser. Keep in mind that the damage your words inflict may be permanent and irreversible. You can't rescind words communicated in interviews, conversations, e-mails, texts, or letters. You can apologize and say you are sorry, but the original words are there forever. Words can ruin a relationship forever. And they have. So when you hear, "Choose your words wisely," there is a reason for this caution. If you have a tendency to say things that are harsh, critical, and judgmental, don't delude yourself by saying that it is up to the other person to interpret the words correctly or to take what she or he had coming. If you want positive results, change your delivery style from negative to positive.

Are You a Good Listener?

You just learned about many ways to derail an interview, including poor listening skills. How effective of a listener are you? To find out, think about how you would answer the following questions. Also, for a reality check, ask a couple of close and honest friends and/or family members to rate you as well.

1. Typically, how emotional do I get when I am attempting to interview someone? Rate this on a scale of 1–3, where:
   - 1 = very emotional (angry, sad, frustrated)
   - 2 = nonemotional and detached
   - 3 = I remain interested and tempered

2. Typically, how often do I interrupt?
   - 1 = several times during a conversation
   - 2 = just once or twice during a conversation
   - 3 = almost never

3. Do I say things like "What? You've got to be kidding me," or "That reminds of me of the time I . . . ," or "You think that's bad, let me tell you about . . ."
   - 1 = frequently
   - 2 = sometimes
   - 3 = rarely

4. Do I roll my eyes, put my head down, shake my head back and forth, throw myself back in my chair, turn away, get up and walk away, show signs of anger or threatening behavior, or otherwise display that I am not paying attention or do not like what the other person is saying?
   - 1 = frequently
   - 2 = sometimes
   - 3 = rarely

5. Do I fidget until people stop talking and then immediately respond without considering what they've said?

1 = frequently
2 = sometimes
3 = rarely

6. Do I let my mind wander to all the other things on my "to do" list and keep thinking that I just don't have the time for this?
1 = frequently
2 = sometimes
3 = rarely

7. Do I wait until the nanosecond when the speaker goes to take a breath to pounce on him or her with my opinion?
1 = frequently
2 = sometimes
3 = rarely

8. Do I hijack the conversation? For instance by saying something like "Look we've been over this a million times. Your ideas are just not going to work. This is what we are going to do"?
1 = frequently
2 = sometimes
3 = rarely

9. I reflect the person's thoughts and feelings back to the person I am listening to.
1 = frequently
2 = sometimes
3 = rarely

10. I ask open-ended questions to encourage the other person to talk.
1 = frequently
2 = sometimes
3 = rarely

Although this is not a scientific test, it can give you a gauge of where you stand. The higher your score, the better your listening skills. If you scored 8 or less, your listening skills are below average. Make sure to read the next section carefully for ways to practice and improve your listening skills.

How to Be a Better Listener

Years ago I was traveling to a city with some colleagues. One of them was a young, inexperienced agent. On the way to this city, this young agent talked about himself for nearly the entire trip. He didn't ask me or another agent a single question. It was all about him and his exploits, opinions, suggestions, and observations.

On the way home, he did the same thing. As we neared our destination, I said, "If you listen more and talk less, you will learn so much more about people." He readily agreed that listening was important and that he would work on it.

I watched the clock.

Roughly five minutes later, he began talking about himself yet again. He even began boasting that he could talk forever without running out of things to say.

The other agent and I just gave each other a look, and then we tuned him out. I wondered, "How in the world is this guy ever going to conduct an interview with a suspect if he does this much talking?"

This young agent thought that he was blessed with the gift of gab—a natural comedian. As it turned out, his so-called gift was really his downfall. He suffered from "the arrogance of ignorance." He was ignorant of his own arrogance and how it affected his job performance.

During an interview, you want to be listening and observing most of the time. You communicate so much when you sit quietly and just listen and watch. This is the behavior that will create an atmosphere of empathy and sensitivity. This will encourage your friend, child, peer, or spouse to trust you and open up.

Chances are this amount of listening might be difficult for you at first. For years and years, you may have been practicing and strengthening poor communication habits. You can't just reverse them overnight. It will take some practice. It took years and years to develop these poor habits. It will take some time and effort before you learn a new communication style. Interpersonal skills such as listening are perishable and require practice to stay sharp.

To improve your communication habits, practice interviewing a few people in your life—friends, family members, acquaintances. Ask them open-ended questions designed to elicit information. These practice interviews are just for fun—and for you to improve your skills. As you practice interviewing, see if you can craft questions and conversations that allow you to do the following:

1. Create a nonjudgmental environment in which people will become comfortable physically, mentally, and emotionally and open up as a result.

2. Help them to identify and talk about their feelings (happiness, sadness, elation, excitement, anger, frustration, guilt, remorse).

3. Help them evaluate their own behavior and its consequences.

The Dangerous Truth

Many people attempt to fake the appearance of listening by saying "uh-huh" a lot and nodding their heads. It's important to know that if you look like a bobblehead and say "uh-huh" at the wrong moment, it will broadcast to the other person that you are not listening at all. This type of behavior is distracting at best and an interview derailer at worst. I can't tell you how many times I have had conversations with people during which I've watched their heads bobble up and down. I was never sure what they were agreeing with or what they were hearing. When you are listening to someone, your nonverbal behavior must appear genuine and consistent with your words and your feelings. It also cannot be distracting. Others will know if you are being disingenuous, just like a bobblehead doll—mechanical and without empathy.

4. Help them see the implications of their behavior and/or decisions in the future.

5. Help them redesign their strategy and reassess their decisions or conclusions.

6. Communicate your willingness to be supportive.

How to Listen Between the Lines

As you listen, you want to pick up on more than just the content of what is being said. This is why listening requires all of your attention and practice. You want to listen for the following:

1. What they say. What is the person telling you? Do they accidentally let anything slip?

2. What the person doesn't talk about. What *isn't* the person telling you? Is there a pink elephant in the conversation? If yes, it is okay to say that you feel he or she is avoiding the main issue. Your interviewee will let you know if you are off base.

3. How they say it. What emotions does the person seem to be experiencing? Base this on both verbal and nonverbal behavior.

For instance, many years ago I interviewed a serial killer who had already confessed to more than a dozen murders. At the time of the interviews, he was on death row, and I was trying to get more information from him, before his execution, about other murders he may have committed.

I was accompanied by another homicide detective, named Pat, who was a phenomenal interviewer. She was also pretty and petite. Dave, the convicted serial killer, liked Pat a lot and, as a result, had opened up to her.

Dave was talkative but also cagey, dominant, and macho. He attempted to gain control of the interview by making threats. For instance, he casually mentioned how easy it would be for him to reach across the table and strangle us—that he could do it so quickly that the guards would not be able to get to the room and intervene before it was too late.

Still, he talked about the murders he wanted us to know about and was vague on those he didn't want to discuss. He would shift from memories that were crystal clear to memories that were vague, sketchy, and incomplete. He played games with us to let us know that he was in charge.

We had no specific case information about child murders, but I knew it was a possibility that he could have killed a child, even though he had insisted, up to that point, that all of his victims had been adult females. I knew that serial sexual killers evolve into their psychopathy and sexual deviancy. As they develop and learn their preferences for victims, killing, and ways to evade detection, they tend to go through a period of trial and error when they will kill various people around them, even close to them. It is in this period of time that they will make many mistakes and will experiment on victims of different ages, genders, races, and cultures. Because of this, it made sense for me to ask Dave a general question about whether he had ever killed a child.

When I did, he became dark, defensive, and angry. He was adamant about never victimizing children. He used phrases like "How dare you accuse me" and "What do you think I am? A pervert?"

I strongly suspected that he had a psychopathic personality, and I knew that psychopaths have no moral compass or code of ethnics. They don't draw lines in the sand about whom they will or will not victimize based on society's rules of right and wrong. So when he aggressively denied ever abusing children, it told me a lot.

His sudden change in demeanor—from glib and charming to defensive and angry—convinced me that he probably had victimized a child at some point in his past. The proof wasn't in what the man said. It was in what he didn't say and in the change in his behavior.

You might think that this convicted killer had nothing to lose. He was on death row after all. Why not admit to every single murder, including the murder of a child? At that time, he was thought to have only killed women. If he admitted to killing a young child, he would likely have had problems with some of the other inmates in the prison. He wouldn't want to be known as a child killer, since they tend to fall at the bottom of the pecking order in prisons.

Shortly thereafter Pat and I interviewed Dave's estranged wife. She told us a very interesting and chilling story. She said a boy had gone missing in their neighborhood years before. She described Dave as showing a great deal of interest and excitement in the media coverage of the case. He followed the investigation closely, and he'd often ask her to look at the articles in the paper with him. Then, one day, he took her for a drive so he could point out the last route this boy had taken on his bicycle before he was kidnapped and murdered. The case was still unsolved at that time.

It wasn't what Dave had told us that led us to look for this kind of information. It was what he refused to tell us.

This is one of many examples I could give you that shows just how important it is to listen for what isn't being said. Here's just one more.

A friend of mine, Cindy, was at a gas station filling up her car when a man approached her. He was on foot and asked her about the location of a shopping center that was about fifteen miles south of the filling station.

"Are you walking?" she asked.

"Yes," he said. "My car broke down at that shopping center and I need to get back there."

"You are going to be walking all day," she said.

She was in a hurry to get to my house, and the shopping center was in the wrong direction. He seemed helpless and innocent. She said, "I wanted to help him. I feel badly about not helping him. He was a young man, close to my son's age."

"Stop feeling so guilty," I said. "He might not be as helpless and innocent as you think."

Why do you think I came to that conclusion? What was it about what he didn't say that would have led me to conclude that his intentions were not pure? Think about it, and then read on.

He didn't say how he got to where he was. If his car had broken down fifteen miles away, how did he get to the gas station to begin with? Why did he travel more than fifteen miles away from his car, on foot, if getting his car repaired was his primary intention? And if he'd walked from the shopping center, wouldn't he know the way back to the shopping center?

It was what he didn't say that was most important.

It's also what he didn't do. There were many workmen in the area who had vehicles and would have likely been headed in the direction where his car was supposedly located. Cindy noted that he had approached her but none of the men.

As it turns out, there's a police station across the street from this particular gas station where my friend happened to be pumping gas that day. It was eight in the morning. What this person probably didn't want her to know was that he'd been arrested the night before and had spent the night in jail. Cindy could have increased her risk level if she offered to give him a ride to his car.

When listening to your interviewee, it's incredibly important to listen between the lines.

In particular, listen for leakage—information the interviewee may accidentally or purposely allow to slip out. These details are usually collateral to the questions you are asking. For instance, let's say you are interviewing a job candidate about how he views himself working on a team, and you get this answer:

> I think working with teams . . . Well, here's the thing. With the
> kind of work I've done in the past I've had tight deadlines and
> meetings with clients and bosses several times a day. It just
> didn't lend itself to working with others. It would have really
> slowed down the project.

If you take this person at his word, it sounds as if he's given you a good answer. In reality, however, he hasn't. What he's done is completely evade the question, and he's indirectly told you that, no, he's not a team player at all. He tells you about deadlines, about being responsive to clients, about working hard, and about being independent. You didn't ask about any of those things. The one thing you asked about is the one thing he didn't mention.

Let's look at another situation. Let's say you are considering carpooling with another parent to take your kids and hers to and from soccer practice. You don't want your child being driven around by an unsafe driver, however, so you want to make sure she doesn't have unsafe habits like texting and driving. You have asked her questions like "What do you do when you have a carful of screaming kids and you get an important call? Do you ever have problems with that?" She's given you this answer:

> Oh, you know, I just tune the kids out. When I'm driving the kids around, I just turn up the radio and I let them sit back there and have their fun. I'm one of those parents who is so used to being around kids that I can just tune them out. I don't answer my cell phone unless it's an emergency. As far as texting—not really . . . I used to text, but, no, I don't do that anymore, and, no, I don't really have any problems when I'm driving a bunch of loud kids in my car.

What did she accidentally allow to leak out? Think about it and try to spot all the leakage in her statement. Then read on.

This is what I'm seeing leak out: She just tunes the kids out. Sometimes she texts. And she talks on her cell phone while driving.

This means she's not focused on what the kids are doing and saying. She's not attentive. She tunes out. You didn't ask her if she tunes out, but now you know. She accidentally told you.

She accidentally told you something else too. She does use her cell phone while she drives. She might not use it very much, but she does use it. Her use of the phrase "not really" is also problematic. You'll find out why later in this chapter. But for now, just know that her "not really" probably means that she does text while driving. What constitutes an emergency call for this woman? Is it a call from the hospital? From her client? Her boss? Her husband? Even if it is true that she will only talk on her cell phone if it is a true emergency, it is even more frightening. Driving a group of children while you are distracted by a crisis you are trying to handle via phone is going to put all of you at an even greater risk for something bad happening.

The important point, though, is this: Just from the leakage, you have all of the information you need to make a decision to *not* carpool with this mother. You don't need to follow up with a hard line of questioning to find out just how often and under what circumstances she takes calls and texts while she drives. Instead you can just say, "No thanks," and either drive your child all the time yourself or make plans to carpool with a different parent.

How to Observe Behavior

When you interview someone, you are not just listening. You are also watching. In particular, you should take notice of the following behaviors.

Tuning out: Is your interviewee doing something else? Does your interviewee seem interested in you, or is he or she losing interest quickly? Maybe he or she is watching television, checking his or her

---

The Dangerous Truth

Many people attempt to read body language as if it were a black-and-white science. For instance, if someone has his or her arms crossed, they say it's a sign of defensiveness. Yet some people with big barrel chests stand with their arms crossed simply because it's comfortable. Other people do it because they are cold. To know if such body language really is a sign of defensiveness, you must observe the behavior over a period of time and listen to the words the person is saying. Does this person usually stand this way? Or does he suddenly start standing this way in response to a particular line of questioning? A sudden change in body language is much more telling than the body language itself. In order to know if someone's behavior is out of the ordinary or inconsistent, you have to have a baseline by which to gauge his or her behavior. In other words, you want to know what their normal behavior is. You can't call behavior unusual, deceptive, or out of the ordinary if you don't know what is ordinary.

---

smartphone, or obsessively grooming (stroking his beard, putting on her lipstick, picking lint off his slacks, brushing her hair). Or maybe he just appears bored with you. One of the things I learned while doing graduate training in counseling is that if the interviewer feels bored during the interview, the interviewee is probably feeling the same way.

If your interviewee is bored, you will need to find ways to shake up the interview. For instance, I was once less than an hour into an interview with a murderer on death row in Louisiana when the defense attorney walked me outside and told me that the inmate was bored. She was right. Sam was bored, and I had to change things if the interview was going to be successful. I knew I was not likely to get the information I sought if I continued to conduct the interview in the same way, so I changed the approach. Rather than continue to interview him myself, we switched interviewers. We would go from one interviewer to another to another. We changed the questions too. The constant change added variety to the interview, and it kept Sam engaged and interested. He talked with us for nearly eight hours.

Avoidance: Is your interviewee trying to stall the conversation? Maybe he or she answers the phone or invents a reason why he or she has to call someone right now. Other avoidance behaviors include the following:

- Repeated or long bathroom breaks
- Falling asleep or appearing to doze off
- Walking away
- Retreating to a different room
- Sudden displays of emotion (as with the woman I mentioned at the beginning of this chapter who broke down and sobbed)
- Derailing the interview by changing the topic and getting off track
- Blaming you or someone else for the problem
- Clamming up
- Reading a book or newspaper or watching TV or a movie and not responding
- Staring straight ahead or downward and being unresponsive

Hijacking: Does this person take over the interview and steer it into a completely different direction? If this happens, he is trying to take the conversation off track, deflect the heat, or take control of the interview. He is telling you that this conversation is now on his turf and that he is in charge.

Inappropriate emotional response: Does your interviewee show the appropriate emotion for the interview topic? For instance, if you are talking about a sick relative, does the interviewee seem somber or does he or she seem nonplussed? Does the person have a smirk on his face? Does he shake his head at you as if you are wrong and he is dismissing you and what you are saying? Does the person become angry in a way that's disproportionate to what you are saying? Does the person start crying before the interview has really begun? This could mean he is hiding something and doesn't want to talk about it.

Signs of strong, negative emotions: Does your interviewee get angry or red in the face? Do you see veins in his head start to pulsate? Are her fists clenched and pounding the table? Has he raised his voice? Is she swearing and pointing her finger in your face? These are all signs of imminent danger. You have to de-escalate the conversation, and you must do it quickly, especially if other variables like drugs and/or alcohol are involved. Drugs and alcohol could exacerbate the situation and even push the person into his red zone.

Addressing Deceitfulness

Deceitful people require you to use special interviewing skills. In order to get around their deceit, you must be able to spot the dishonesty and also understand why they are being deceitful. Here are some ways a person can deceive you.

Lying or distorting the truth: Your interviewee might give you some truthful information but also a few pieces of false information designed to throw you off track. Or maybe your interviewee is a compulsive liar and everything he or she says is a lie, even the inconsequential details.

Withholding the truth: Your interviewee might give you some information but then refuse to talk about certain topics or begin to filter the information he or she provides.

Evading: Your interviewee might continually change the topic or otherwise try to take the conversation in a different direction.

People engage in deceitful behaviors for a number of reasons. Possible reasons might be that he or she:

- is afraid of the consequences of being open and honest
- is afraid of your reaction
- doesn't want to be judged by you
- doesn't trust you
- doesn't like you
- doesn't want to get other people in trouble
- doesn't want you in his or her business

If your interviewee feels strongly that you are going to judge her harshly, and feels this way because you've judged harshly in the past, it

---

The Dangerous Truth

You may have read that you can tell someone is lying if he avoids eye contact or looks away when answering a question, if he touches or scratches his face while answering a question, or if his facial expressions are out of sync with his words (for instance frowning when he says, "I'm so happy to see you!").

Although all of this *may* be true, using body language alone to evaluate whether someone is lying is like navigating a ship by only looking at the stars. Very few people have the experience and knowledge to do it correctly. Reading body language and facial expressions is an art form that is a lot more complicated than most people realize. For instance, you can't always assume that a lack of eye contact means someone is lying. It could be that you are dealing with a person who lacks social skills and doesn't make eye contact whether she is telling the truth *or* telling a lie.

---

will be very difficult for you to get her to open up. You'll want to remove as many barriers as you can. You don't get people to tell the truth by bullying them (by shouting, "Just tell the truth! Just tell the truth! Just tell the truth!"). You do it by making them feel safe enough to reveal the information you seek. If you can address your interviewee's reason for not giving you the information, you've removed the barrier that is preventing her from opening up.

To tell if someone is being deceitful, think about whether any of the following factors are present.

There's no denial. When you ask someone a yes-or-no question and they don't give you a yes-or-no answer, you may have reason to believe that they are hiding something. For instance, if you ask your spouse, "Are you cheating on me?" and you get any of the following answers, you probably are not getting the whole story.

1. **"Not really."** When an answer is qualified by "not really," the respondent is not denying your accusation, and there's usually more to the story. To get the whole story, ask a follow-up question such as, "What do you mean when you say you are 'not really' cheating on me?"

2. **A question.** Instead of a yes or no, you instead get, "Why do you think I would do something like that?" or "Why would you ask me a question like that?"

3. **Protests.** Instead of a yes or no, you hear, "How could I do that? You know I love you," or "How could I do that? I'm too busy to have an affair."

4. **Defensiveness.** Instead of answering your question, he or she is overly sensitive about accusations, innuendo, criticism, and questions about his or her behavior.

5. **Counterattacks.** The person attacks you, your words, your behavior, and anything else about you. This can be a form of hijacking the conversation.

6. **Change of topic.** Instead of answering the question, he or she asks you a question about something else or starts talking about something else.

7. Hair splitting. The most famous example of this is when President Clinton said, "I did not have intercourse with that woman." When a person splits hairs, he or she does not directly answer your question with a yes or no. Instead he or she changes the question slightly to match their answer. For instance, you might ask, "Are you cheating on me?" and he or she might answer, "I am not having an affair."

There's too much denial. In investigations, we would become suspicious if we asked a person about a murder and he answered with a question: "How do you even know she's dead? You can't prove she's dead."

In nonpolice matters, this type of deception might come up if you are confronting your spouse about porn you found on his computer and he says, "There's no porn on that computer." Or maybe you have brought up some charges made to the credit card bill and your spouse says, "There aren't any strange charges on that bill."

The story doesn't add up. If you continually ask open-ended questions and keep your interviewee talking, you can look for places where the story just doesn't make sense. For instance, let's say you are talking to a man you are considering dating. He tells you a sad story about how his wife died of cancer just three years before. A little later on he mentions that he just broke up with his girlfriend of two and a half years. And then he tells you about several other women he has dated recently. Do you see anything wrong with the story? I do. If his wife died three years ago and he had a girlfriend for two and a half, when did he have time to date all of those other women? Did he do it in the past six months? Or was he cheating on his wife and his girlfriend? He is unable to stay on top of his own story.

It's important to note that you might not be able to pull the entire story out of someone. For instance, a pathological liar will lie about every single detail, even about what he or she ate for breakfast. These people have used lies and deception their whole lives and can be masters at it. It's easy for them and almost automatic. You don't need to dig down to the ultimate truth with such a person, and you probably will never be able to. All you need to know is that this person lies about everything and that you should walk away from the relationship. This is a person who will only bring heartache, pain, and many problems to your life.

Similarly, you might not be able to find out all the details of a partner's affair, but you might find out enough to know that his or her story doesn't add up or is improbable. You might not be able to get your teen to tell you about all his reckless driving behaviors, but you might be able to get him to tell you about some or just one of them—enough for you to know that it's time to revoke his car privileges.

How to Interview a Child or Teen

Sometimes as you attempt to interview or have a conversation with a child—especially your own and especially about a sensitive topic—he or she will throw up a brick wall that you just can't jump over. Frequently this brick wall comes in the form of "always" and "never" statements like these:

- You are always accusing me of things I didn't do.
- You never trust me.
- You always treat me like I'm three years old.
- You never let me do anything.
- You never listen to my side of the story.

It's important to be prepared for such comebacks because they can be emotional triggers for you. If you are prepared for them, it's less likely that they will trigger you to switch to bullying or some other nonproductive tactic.

As you address such statements, consider using these pointers:

- Try to not respond to them with an "always" or "never" statement of your own. Try to throw absolute words such as "always," "never," "should," "need to," and "must" out of your vocabulary. They indicate that life is black or white, with no gray area. Real life is not black and white.

• Consider whether there's any truth to the statement. If so, acknowledge it. For instance, if your child says, "You never give me a chance to talk," you might say, "That may be true and I am working on that. I'm sorry that has been my reaction in the past. Let's start fresh. I want to hear what you have to say."

• If there is no basis to the allegations made by your child, resist arguing and having the conversation default to an "I say–you say" standoff. Move beyond these types of barriers or communication blockers. Instead say something like "When are the times you felt comfortable about talking with me or another adult?" or "Let's take a break and take a walk or watch a movie" or "Let's go to our rooms and reconvene in an hour."

Now that you know how to get the information you want out of someone else, it's time to learn what to do with that information. Learn how to size people up and assess them for dangerousness in the next chapter.

CHAPTER 8 RAP SHEET

• Be willing to suspend old habits and communication styles and to develop new and more effective ones to help your interpersonal communications, sharpen your listening skills, and enhance your ability to make better and more sound decisions.

• Interviews require care, consideration, and compassion for others and the ability to show people that you care about them, their circumstances, their feelings, and their future.

• Listen when you'd rather give advice, interrupt, or offer a quick opinion. Look and listen for emotions and learn to recognize them accurately.

Chapter 9

How to Size Someone Up

Years ago I worked on a case involving a nanny. She had told the police that she feared for her life. She said she had been the victim of satanic ritual abuse while growing up and that a relative and former member of this satanic cult had plans to assault and kill her.

We attempted to corroborate her story of prior ritual abuse but were unable to do so. Likewise we could not locate any family members who were planning to travel to where she lived and attempt to hurt her. Nonetheless, this young, soft-spoken, educated woman insisted that her allegations were true. I asked her about the cuts and scratches I noticed on her arms. She told me a stranger had inflicted them.

Although the nanny's story might sound bizarre and unusual, this was not the first time I'd heard such allegations. I'd interviewed other men and women who said they had been victims of ritual childhood abuse. We could never corroborate these stories. We could not find physical evidence, and we couldn't uncover human remains either. We couldn't find graves. We couldn't find evidence of murder, torture, human sacrifices, or cannibalism. When we told these victims that we could find no evidence to support their claims, their responses were hauntingly always the same. They explained that their abusers were masters at covering their tracks and destroying evidence. They had destroyed or consumed all the evidence, and no one in the group would talk.

It was always a perfect conspiracy.

Let me tell you that in all of my years in law enforcement I have never seen a perfect conspiracy. When more than two people know about a crime, the chances of someone talking about it go up exponentially.

Based on all of this, I seriously doubted the nanny's story. Still, I was astounded by her commitment to it and her willingness to accuse family members of such a serious crime despite the absence of any physical evidence.

I asked the nanny to come into my office for one final interview to make sure I had all the details. Clearly there was something wrong in her life, and I wanted to find out what it was.

She walked into my office slowly and cautiously, as though she were in a great deal of pain. I noticed blood on her legs but none on her socks. I asked her what had happened, and she implied that she had just been attacked. She asked to use the restroom. I went with her. In the restroom, she began crying and saying she was in pain. I asked her if she had purposefully done something to hurt herself. After a lot of reassurance from me, she eventually admitted that she had inserted a razor blade inside herself. We called the paramedics and she was rushed to the hospital.

You probably agree with me that this young woman posed a danger to herself and others. She was involved in self-destructive cutting behavior, and her current injuries were serious. Her willingness to implicate a relative in a crime that had never occurred indicated that she was willing to file false charges against people despite the possible criminal implications and consequences.

And she worked as a nanny. When she was released from the hospital, her employers—who now knew about her false allegations and cutting behavior—welcomed her back into their home to care for their young children. They didn't even ask her to undergo a mental-health assessment or intervention.

You might think that this family is an anomaly—that they were either more naive or trusting than most. I don't believe they were anomalies, though. I believe many people would have made the same flawed decision.

Let me tell you about a similar case. Paula (not her real name) met

Dave, a man serving a long prison sentence for serial sexual assault. Although this might seem unusual, women frequently meet men who are serving time. Sometimes they meet them when they are visiting another prisoner, perhaps a relative. Other times they follow the case and get to know the prisoner by writing letters back and forth.

Once Dave was paroled, he and Paula continued their romantic relationship and ultimately married. Dave moved into Paula's home with her young daughters. Not much later there were allegations of sexual molestation involving one of the girls. Then, a short time later, one of the girls went missing. Dave eventually confessed to the murder.

Whenever I tell this story, people look incredulous. They can't understand how Paula could have thought that a man convicted of serial sexual assault was a safe person to date, let alone marry, and to live in the same home with her daughters. But Paula and the parents I mentioned earlier were bright, educated people who cared dearly about their families and children. They were not stupid. They were not naive. And they were not cavalier.

They just didn't know how to tell if someone posed a threat to them or their families. I've seen people make the same kinds of mistakes so many times. They misread others, ignore dangerous behaviors, normalize those behaviors, and delude themselves into believing that dangerous people will automatically stop being dangerous without any kind of intervention.

In this chapter you'll learn how to overcome these common mistakes. You'll find out how to gather and interpret information so you can more effectively spot and understand three types of problematic behavior:

- *Concerning* behavior
- *Threatening* behavior
- *Dangerous* behavior

CTD behaviors, as we'll call them, are all problematic and important to spot and understand, but some are more serious than others. Think of problematic behavior as falling along a continuum. Concerning behavior falls toward the less serious end of the continuum. Dangerous behavior falls toward the most serious end. Threatening behavior falls in the middle. Behavior is dynamic. It is fluid and can change rapidly, so concerning or threatening behaviors can quickly become dangerous.

Like other skills, recognizing and correctly interpreting CTD behaviors will take practice. But once you learn this skill, and practice it, you will be less likely to be duped into believing that someone has "changed" or "snapped." You will no longer misread people and be fooled by them. You will not be surprised or blindsided down the road. You will see trouble early and be able to respond to it before it gets out of control.

This process will free you from black-and-white rules that you may have leaned on in the past, rules like "Don't talk to strangers" and "Don't trust people you don't know." You'll also be able to go beyond meaningless descriptions like "He's a nice guy," "She's harmless," "He's acting out of character," and "That was in the past and people change." Rather, you'll really and truly get a sense for whether someone could manifest CTD behaviors and pose a threat to you, your possessions, your loved ones, your career, or your financial livelihood.

What Makes People Dangerous

Many people ask me how to get "inside someone's head." In reality, you can't. You will never be able to read a person's thoughts, or know their inner world completely, or know with certainty the motives for their behavior. You will never be a mind reader, and neither will I.

You can, however, gain a sense of someone's personality by studying and understanding his or her behavior. Behavior is an expression of a person's personality traits and characteristics. One personality trait does not produce one specific behavior. It's a lot more complicated than that. Personality traits cluster together to form patterns of behavior that can become hardwired for life.[9]

In the pages that follow, you will learn about many possible CTD behaviors and the personalities behind them. The key is to recognize clusters of behaviors and interpret those patterns correctly. Don't take one isolated behavior out of context and use it to form an opinion about what someone must be like. But also don't ignore it, rationalize it, explain it away, or delude yourself into thinking that a person who is dangerous or violent toward someone else "will never turn on me." Try to identify the whole behavior picture, and assess it correctly.

The following is not an exhaustive list of CTD behaviors. Rather, this is a list of behaviors that I have seen over and over in my years of investigating and profiling violent crimes and in studying the people who engage in these behaviors. I will briefly explain many CTD behaviors here. Then, in the section that follows, I'll go into the five CTD behaviors that I think are most important for you to understand, recognize, and interpret in greater depth.

Impulsivity: Behaving with little if any regard for long-term or short-term consequences to self and others.

Inappropriate or out-of-control anger: Repeated eruptions of anger in a variety of situations where anger is not appropriate or warranted. People with inappropriate anger are either unable or unwilling to control their anger. They have a controlled and systemic undercurrent of anger

Narcissism: Acting self-centered, arrogant, and grandiose, with little or no insight or concern for others. People who behave narcissistically have a sense of entitlement and superiority over others, and an expectation of special treatment and consideration. They believe they are special, unique, and superior to others.

Lack of empathy: Inability and unwillingness to understand the feelings, concerns, and opinions of others. People without empathy lack compassion for others.

Injustice collecting: Injustice collectors do just that: They collect injustices—real or imagined—over their lifetimes. They respond to them in ways that are extraordinarily disproportionate to the perceived injustice.

Objectification of others: Dehumanizing others and not seeing them as humans. People with this behavior may view others as nonpersons or possessions and treat them accordingly.

Blaming others for failures and problems: Seeing oneself as a victim and refusing to accept responsibility for one's life problems. It's always someone else's fault.

Paranoia: Suspicious of the motives and intentions of others.

Rule breaking: The life philosophy that the rules of society do not apply to you.

Use of violence: A history of committing dangerous or violent behavior, including assault, abuse, intimidation, road rage, and more.

Thoughts and fantasies of violence: Suicidal, homicidal, and nihilistic thinking. The manifestation of these behaviors requires immediate intervention by mental-health professionals or law enforcement.

Drug and/or alcohol problems: The use and/or abuse of drugs and/or alcohol that exacerbates other CTD behaviors.

Poor coping skills: Inability to deal with stressors, disappointments, problems, and/or everyday life problems

Equal-opportunity hatred: Dislike for and/or hatred of other people or groups because of real or imagined wrongs or other beliefs and opinions.

Thrill seeking: A pathological or extreme need for thrill, excitement, and/or attention from others, despite the harm or worry it causes.

Problem Behaviors in Depth

To help you better spot and understand some of the most problematic CTD behaviors, I've explained five of them in more detail in the pages that follow.

Problem 1: Impulsive behaviors

When you act impulsively, you tend to consider only momentarily—if at all—the possible consequences of your actions, and then disregard the consequences of your actions. Impulsivity can range from occasional and minor impulsive acts to regular and serious impulsive acts.

We're all impulsive from time to time. Most of us have impulsively run a red light in order to get somewhere more quickly. Or we have occasionally made an impulsive purchase because something was on sale.

People who are routinely impulsive, however, do it often and in every area of their lives. They might quit their jobs because of a momentary hassle they just had with their supervisors. They might repeatedly call in sick at the last minute so they can take a vacation. They might drink too much at parties and then decide to drive home. They might buy a home on a whim, because they "loved" it, but fail to take the time to find out they cannot afford it. They will marry someone whom they don't really know.

Impulsivity becomes a CTD behavior when it is a pattern evident in many aspects of a person's life—at home, at work, while driving a car, from relationship to relationship, and so on—and the behavior compromises their safety and welfare and that of others around them. When it is compounded by the use of drugs and/or alcohol, it can really create problems and increase the likelihood of financial ruin, social problems, and even violence.

Problem 2: Angry behaviors

Some people have a long fuse, whereas others have a very short one. People with a short fuse can become enraged or even explosive over things that the rest of us think of as quite minor. Like impulsivity, anger is something we are all familiar with. We all lose our temper every once in a while. Anger becomes dangerous when it is disproportionate to the events that trigger it; becomes out of control and excessive; results in physical harm or threats of physical harm to others; cannot be easily, quickly, or voluntarily brought under control; and occurs on a regular basis.

For instance, a few years ago it was reported that a disgruntled husband shot and killed his wife and four others because of how his wife cooked his eggs. Clearly there was more to this violence than poorly cooked eggs. It is not unusual, however, for such a minor precipitator to be the trigger that sets into motion a disproportionate response in people with anger-management problems. Someone who wasn't so quick to anger might have sighed loudly about his undercooked eggs rather than pull out a shotgun.

People who are quick to anger often get into trouble when driving. They become easily irate at other drivers and retaliate by cutting them off, tailgating, or throwing objects at their vehicles. You can tell a lot about someone's personality by the way he or she drives a car, and people who are constantly peeling out, driving recklessly, tailgating, and traveling well above the speed limit very likely have problems with anger in other areas of their life.

People who are quick to anger tend to have interpersonal problems with others, too, and these interpersonal problems can erupt over seemingly minor things. For instance, they are the people who will ream out a waitress for bringing them a steak that's well done instead of medium rare. They are the people who will shout at hospital staff when they show up after visiting hours and are not allowed entrance to the hospital. The bagger at the grocery store, for instance, might mix their meat in with their vegetables and the customer will end up telling off the store manager over it.

Drugs or alcohol will exacerbate anger, but someone with a CTD anger problem will become angry without the influence of either.

In addition to the explosively angry individual, there are others who maintain an undercurrent of anger all the time. The anger is right below the surface. Their anger seems controlled, cognitive, and less likely to erupt. These individuals can be quickly frustrated, verbally abusive, and quick to judge or malign others. They maintain strong negative opinions of others without apparent reason or justification and even with evidence to the contrary. They are quick to damage interpersonal relationships.

Problem 3: Narcissism

The word "narcissist" is in vogue right now and is often tossed around to describe people who are somewhat self-absorbed. Those are not the types of people I'm referring to here. I am describing someone who views him- or herself as the center of the universe. Narcissists tend to be elitist and arrogant and see themselves as special and above everyone else. They have a sense of entitlement, a grandiose sense of their own importance, and an unrealistic expectation of favorable treatment. Narcissists are always searching for attention and admiration.

People who are narcissistic will do the following:

- Make choices that meet their needs, ignoring the needs of others.
- Talk endlessly about themselves but want to know little if anything about you.
- Hijack conversations. You will say a line or two about yourself and a narcissistic individual will interrupt and say something like "Let me tell you about me and my opinions." (After all, their opinions are the only ones that matter and therefore more important than anyone else's.)
- Make inappropriate remarks because they don't realize and don't care about how they affect or impact others. They will talk about how great they are, for instance.
- Take credit for an entire project, even if other employees helped get it done. Everything they do is one of a kind, special, unique, and superior to anyone else's work. In reality their work is a mess.
- Not accept blame or failure in a work or personal situation.

In a marital relationship, everything will be about making the narcissistic individual shine. For instance, a narcissistic individual will expect his wife to dress a certain way because how she looks affects how others perceive him. Narcissistic individuals will seek accolades and recognition in everything they do. They will exaggerate, lie, brag, and do whatever they think is appropriate to get what they want, because it is all about them.

Problem 4: Lack of empathy

Some people are exceptionally good at sensing the feelings of others and of anticipating their needs. They are sensitive and compassionate toward others and display this empathy in their words and actions. Other people are more callous, and it's much harder for them to understand the feelings of others. They can't easily walk a mile in someone else's shoes. Sometimes they can't do it at all.

Someone with an inability to empathize will be a poor listener (because he or she doesn't care about you or your problems and feelings). If you have a problem and really need someone to talk to, they may give you a few minutes. Then they will turn you off quickly, respond to you harshly or coldly, or change the topic as quickly as possible. If you try to have an ongoing relationship with someone who lacks empathy, you will feel cheated in the relationship. You will become the listener and never the one who is listened to. You will feel used and taken advantage of.

Problem 5: Injustice collecting

I coined this term back in the late nineties when I was the FBI's lead researcher in school and campus violence. At that time I saw a pattern of behavior in students who seemed to maintain an ongoing pattern of collecting and never forgetting real or imagined injustices. Despite the amount of time that passed, these individuals never forgot. They frequently blew injustices way out of proportion and would never forgive the person they felt had wronged them. They use words like "wronged," "persecuted," and "destroyed" to describe the injustices others have inflicted on them.

Injustice collectors occur in all age groups and in all professions. These individuals do not forgive easily and cannot move on. They take offense easily and hold on to grudges for years. They can even feel slighted by events that never occurred the way they claimed they occurred. They see personal and professional injustices wherever they go.

Injustice collectors might feel slighted if an employee accidentally parks in their space, and they will never forget the day it happened, the time it happened, and the response of the human resources department when they filed a complaint about the incident.

If injustice collectors are passed over for a promotion because someone else was far more qualified, they will see it very differently and perceive it as a major personal and professional insult to them that has ruined their life.

They will still remember and feel slighted about the anniversary a spouse forgot ten years ago.

They are still mad at their mother for things that happened during childhood, even if their mother died years before.

Themes of vengeance are common in the thinking of an injustice collector. An injustice collector will have a long list of grievances about a long list of people. They may even maintain a "hit list." They will tell you about their mean siblings, disloyal friends, backbiting coworkers, good-for-nothing spouses, and terrible mothers.

Injustice collectors begin to move toward CTD behaviors if their response is significantly disproportional to the perceived or real injustice. For example, most people who feel they are being singled out at the workplace for a poor performance rating, or are terminated because of their performance, will go home and cry or have a drink with a friend. An injustice collector who has shifted toward CTD behavior might decide to go back to work with a gun and attempt to harm his former bosses and coworkers. Obviously this reaction is completely disproportionate to the action of the company.

As CTD behaviors cluster together and form a pattern, they can become more and more problematic. Here are some tips for using the information I just provided so you can accurately assess the people in your life.

Screen the people who matter most. You won't have to screen for CTD behaviors in every single person you meet. Don't worry about the waitress who serves you at the diner, or about the pizza delivery person. But you definitely want to screen for concerning, threatening, and dangerous behaviors in your close and intimate relationships. And you'll want to assess someone before granting them access to your intimate life details—such as your Social Security number, the key to your house, and so on.

Look for clusters, not for just one trait. It's when these traits and behaviors cluster together to form a pattern that an individual can move along the behavioral continuum toward becoming dangerous. Someone who is only impulsive, for instance, isn't nearly as threatening as someone who is impulsive, angry, narcissistic, and an injustice collector with homicidal and suicidal thoughts. Many CTD traits can be clustered with narcissism, and when this happens it can create the perfect storm. Narcissism means "it's all about me," which means the narcissist's needs and well-being and future are going to be paramount to yours. It exacerbates other CTD traits.

Don't judge someone based on just one action. Accurately assessing someone's behavior requires establishing a baseline. You want to know how that person typically behaves most of the time. Ideally you want to observe someone in a variety of circumstances, over a period of time, and with a variety of people.

Put it all into context. You also want to be aware of the context in which these behaviors occur so you can assess not only degree of the threat but its long-term and short-term implications.

Where Are Your Danger Zones?

Now that you understand some of the traits, characteristics, and behaviors that can cause people to become dangerous, it's time to find out which types of people are most important for you to take the time to assess. If you know people with many of these traits and behaviors but they are only on the periphery of your life, it might not be a big deal because you do not have very much involvement with them. On the other hand, if someone is a close friend, family member, or a boss or coworker, it can be a much bigger problem.

As I mentioned earlier in the book, many of us are conditioned to fear and be wary of strangers, but strangers are not the only dangerous people in our lives. Often they may pose a much lower threat than people you feel closest to.

The following chart lists the "danger zones" for relationships we have with people on a regular basis. All of us have problems in at least one of these danger zones. If you are a city person, you might make great decisions when you are in zone 1 because you are well practiced at dealing with strangers and casual acquaintances. But how adept are you in the higher zones? How well do you make decisions about coworkers or friends or love interests? Have you trusted someone and allowed someone to get close to you only to later realize that you'd been manipulated or had? If so, then you have had trouble in the higher zones.

And it's in these higher zones where a bad decision can really put you in a very dangerous situation. As you get closer to the "intimate" category, it gets harder and harder to undo a bad decision. The person you've decided to trust has too much information. Too often I've seen that the biggest mistake a victim made was to put someone in the intimate category too soon.

As you look at each danger zone, think about the following questions: Where am I weakest? Where I am most at risk? Where is my family most vulnerable? Where are my finances most vulnerable?

Think about how successfully you are able to navigate each category. Which zone is most dangerous for you?

Zone 1: Strangers and quasi-strangers

This zone includes people you don't know at all (such as the person sitting next to you on the bus or on a flight) as well as people you know little about, such as someone you've met online or through a minor transaction. It includes the person who rings up your groceries, people who frequent the same coffee shop as you, the person who delivers your mail, and other peripheral people in your life who do not enter your comfort zone (your home, your car, your office, etc.).

Zone 2: Acquaintances

This zone includes people you know slightly or superficially. You have only a limited knowledge of them and vice versa. You are friendly with them, but you are not close enough to be considered friends. This might include your neighbors, the people who work in the same building as you do, and people you see occasionally at the gym, church, or your child's school.

Zone 3: Casual friends

This zone includes people you know virtually or see on a regular basis and who know some things about you and your patterns of behavior.

Zone 4: Close friends

This zone includes people you've known for a long time and who you know on a deeper level. It might include your close, long-term friends, your in-laws, your siblings, and some neighbors you feel very close to and who have lived near you for years.

Zone 5: Intimates

This zone includes the people you live with or are close to. It might include romantic partners, your best friend, and your children. It also can include people who know a lot about you—especially sensitive information that you would not want shared with others. For instance, your financial planner and accountant would be considered intimate since both have access to your Social Security number and other personal financial information. Similarly, your doctor would be considered intimate since he or she has access to your potentially sensitive medical information. A therapist or member of the clergy might be intimate if you've shared details about yourself that you would not want broadcast to the public. This zone could also include people who have access to your comfort zone, such as a cleaning person, landlord, contractor, or a computer expert.

When thinking about your danger zones, consider the following two pointers.

Don't spend too much time sorting the people in your life into these categories. It's not as important for you to understand which zone someone falls into as it is for you to understand that the threat someone poses to you goes up with each zone. Despite popular belief, people in zone 1 usually pose the least threat to you. Although the possibility of danger is present in each zone, you don't necessarily need to assess your dry cleaner, for instance, for dangerousness. It's very important to assess your new boyfriend, however, especially if you have young children at home and you are thinking of asking him to move in with you.

It's important to know when the people in your life are moving

from one zone to another. For instance, let's say a casual person you see occasionally at your gym takes an unusual interest in you. He or she fixates on you, posts things about you online, and seems to constantly be watching you and your home. Suddenly this zone 1 or 2 person has become a zone 3 or 4 person and a much greater threat to you.

How to Interview for Dangerousness

So now you know about the personality traits and behaviors that can be CTD, and about the danger zones that make it even more important for you to assess for those traits.

Now, let's talk about how to uncover the information you need to decide if someone manifests concerning, threatening, or dangerous behaviors. Your assessment might involve an interview with just one person, or it might involve gathering information from several people—others who know the person in question through various parts of his or her life.

We all show more of ourselves to some people and less to others, and the people around us do the same. There are five aspects of oneself that are important to understand and think about when trying to decide if someone is concerning, threatening, or dangerous to you. Once you understand these aspects of yourself, you will more easily be able to identify different people to talk to in order to obtain the information you seek.

Aspect 1: Public self

This is the part of yourself that you show to the public. Your acquaintances see this part of you. Your public self, for instance, is the persona you show to the checkout person who sees what you buy at the grocery store each week and gains insights from those products. The people who work at my grocery store, for instance, probably knew that I had a dog. They didn't know it because I'd shared this information with them. Rather, they knew it because I shopped there twice a week and purchased Frosty Paws each time.

Aspect 2: Professional self

This is the self you show at work. The people you work with probably know if you are married or single, a parent or not a parent, where you went to school and what you studied, and where you grew up. They might know your political views, if you've shared them. They are aware of casual information that you've been willing to share. They will also infer information about you during the eight hours a day that you spend with them. For example, they can draw conclusions about you based on whether you go out with "the group" for lunch, the friendships you form, what time you come to work and what time you leave, your interpersonal skills, your work habits, and so on. Some of these inferences might be right and some may be quite incorrect. But they can add up to how your coworkers view you.

Aspect 3: Personal self

This is the self that you normally would only show to friends. It's the part of yourself that you keep somewhat guarded and may include your personal schedule and activities, health problems, financial issues, and the location of the secret key you use to get into your house when you are locked out.

The Dangerous Truth

With the advent of social media such as Facebook, Myspace, and Twitter, details that were once considered "personal" are now often broadcast publicly to anyone who wants them. It's commonplace for people to post their current location, what they own and where they keep it in the house, their daily schedule, and other often very personal details. When you put private and personal details out in the public domain, you risk having strangers find something out about you that you wish they did not know. Putting this information on the Internet allows it to go out to thousands, and even millions, of people. You can never take it back.

Aspect 4: Private self

This is the area of your life and personality that you show only to your immediate family and very close friends. This might include serious health or mental-health issues, family problems, financial issues, legal issues, sexual issues, personal idiosyncrasies, and other details and information that you feel protective about and would not want broadcast to the general public.

Aspect 5: Secret self

This is the area of your life and personality that only you know about and that you do not share with anyone if you can help it, not even your spouse, partner, parent, or best friend. Your secret life might include behavior that embarrasses you, past dalliances, and behavior that would cause severe embarrassment or professional problems if others knew about it. It could include sexual fantasies or obsessions, suicidal fantasizes, or violent fantasies. It could include a shopping, alcohol, or gambling addiction. It might include an affinity for online porn.

You won't be able to find out everything about every single person you wish to assess. When assessing someone for CTD behaviors, think about the following questions.

1. How intimate is your relationship potentially going to become? The more intimate the relationship, the more you want to know about someone. The less intimate the relationship, the less you will likely need to know. For instance, you will want to do a thorough and complete assessment on someone you are planning to marry. Your assessment can be less thorough for peripheral people in your life.

2. What parts of this person's life could possibly affect you and your loved ones? For instance, you probably don't care about the online habits of someone you might hire to paint your house or repair your car. This behavior probably has no impact on how effectively your mechanic replaces your brake pads. On the other hand, if you are an employer, the significance of these habits becomes more important. And certainly if your relationship with someone becomes intimate, knowing a great deal more about these habits will be critical.

3. What's the risk level of this situation? In an extremely high-risk situation, you will want to know more about the person you are assessing than you would need to know in a low-risk situation. For instance, a school principal who is trying to assess whether a given student is planning to carry out an act of targeted violence will need to obtain a lot of information immediately. The school's behavioral intervention team will likely interview the student's parents and ask sensitive and uncomfortable questions such as "Has your child ever indicated that he has suicidal or homicidal thoughts?" "Does your child have access to weapons, including guns?" "What has your child recently posted on the Internet that might be indicative of plans to act out violently, including videos, photos, and violent rhetoric?"

Depending on how you answer the previous three questions, you might only need to find out a little bit. For instance, if you are interviewing someone you wish to hire to do some work in your home, you not only don't need to know about his or her secret side, you also would most likely offend that person by asking about it. It's really okay for your handyman to keep his private ideas and thoughts to himself.

On the other hand, if you are talking with a family member because you are worried that he or she has a drug problem or is entertaining thoughts of suicide, you will want to delve into his or her secret side and bring in mental-health experts to do an assessment. Similarly, if you are dating someone and thinking about becoming a lot more intimate, you will want to find out as much as you possibly can about every single area of that person's life. In these instances, not only do you absolutely need this information, you also will likely have an easier time accessing that information because your relationship puts you in a position to observe the person and the behaviors in question over a period of time and in different contexts and to ask a lot more personal questions.

There are no black-and-white rules about how deep to dig (see the next section), but you'll want to think about the different aspects of a person's life whenever you are dealing with someone you want to know more about. Whether it's a neighbor, a coworker, a friend, or someone else, think about which parts of that person's life might affect you and about what you want and need to know in order to make a decision about your next course of action.

How to Dig Deep

Depending on whom you are assessing and why, you might interview friends, coworkers, family members, and even consult with others such as clergypersons, mental-health professionals, or even a private investigator. And you may interview the person directly about their life, relationships with others, habits, practices, finances, and physical health.

These interviews do not have to be formal. For instance, if you are dating someone, you probably don't want to sit down with his or her mother and say, "Now, I'm trying to assess Jake to make sure he's a trustworthy guy and someone I would like to get close to. What can you tell me about him?"

But you do want to ask questions that will help you go beyond meaningless qualifiers like "She's nice" and "He's a good guy" that tell you little to nothing about someone's behavior or personality.

Ask questions designed to help you make sure the person will not cause problems for you. For instance, if you are planning on hiring someone who will be coming into your home to do work, you want to know if this person is likely to steal, damage your home, or act in a way that makes you feel uncomfortable or threatened. To determine this information, you will want to interview people who have hired this person in the past, and you want to go beyond questions like "What did you think of him?" and "What kind of a job did he do?" You will want to ask questions like these:

- Has this person caused any problems for you when he's worked in your home?
- Did he ever do or say anything that made you feel uncomfortable? If so, why?

- Did you ever find him roaming your home with no explanation as to why he was in a room he wasn't supposed to be in?
- Have you ever asked him to change some aspect of his work? If so, how did he respond to your feedback?
- Were you afraid to fire him?

You'll want to think of all the details you want to check out, and you'll want to write those details down. That way you'll be less likely to forget to ask an important question. You can look at your list as you interview people. To help you practice coming up with interview questions for various situations, I've included a number of sample assessments in the next chapter.

But first you need the final piece of the SMART model—how to use all of these techniques and information to make a decision. The next chapter will show you how.

CHAPTER 9 RAP SHEET

- CTD behaviors are the result of personality traits and characteristics that cluster together and can form a lifetime pattern of behavior.
- The people closest to you probably pose a greater threat to you than strangers.
- When assessing someone for CTD behaviors, think about the following aspects of your own, as well as his or her, life: public, professional, personal, private, and secret.

Chapter 10

How to Make a Decision

When criminal profilers like me go to a crime scene and attempt to draw a conclusion, we review all the information we can. We study witness statements, lists of all the evidence recovered from the scene, the forensic analysis of that evidence, police reports, investigative reports, neighborhood investigations, weather reports, crime scene photos, autopsy reports, the victimology (a study of the victim), and much more.

We look for the smallest details and nuances. We analyze how everything is interconnected, in order to look at the totality of the circumstances (see page 99). We do not identify one variable and give that piece disproportionate importance compared with all the other pieces. No, we look at how all the details interact, affect each other, connect, and evolve. And then we use those details to create a behavioral blueprint of the crime scene, a comprehensive understanding of the victim, the offender, and their interaction with one another.

For instance, we can frequently determine—from the totality of the circumstances—the unique personality of the offender, including their motivations, mental disorders, sexual disorders and habits, emotional versus chronological age (some people behave much younger than their physical age), gender, occupation, work history, social history, and much more.

We look for behavior that is present at the scene and, equally as important, behavior that is absent. For instance, if the victim in a bloody crime scene appears to have tried to fight off her attacker, we would expect to find evidence of their struggle with each other. This would include defensive injuries on the victim; body hairs from either the offender or the victim; fibers from clothing, carpets, and other items; DNA recovered from blood; semen; or contact DNA. When we don't find physical evidence indicative of such a struggle, we wonder why. Does it mean that someone tried to clean up the crime scene before he or she left? If so, what does that say about the attacker? It could mean the offender is evidence conscious and knows that if certain evidence is recovered it could lead to his being identified. It could also suggest that the person responsible is known to the victim, and will logically come up in an investigation, so he needs to destroy evidence that associates him with the crime.

When you make a decision, you'll go through a very similar process. Just like a profiler, you will gather lots of evidence and information. You will evaluate it. You will not allow one piece of information to overshadow another. You will look at the totality of everything you've been able to uncover.

The information a profiler uses to draw conclusions is based on a comprehensive review of a wide range of information. Your clues will be based on:

- information you've gathered through your interviews (see chapter 8)
- what you know about the situation (see chapter 7)
- what you know about yourself (see chapter 6)
- your own observations
- what you've learned through other resources, including a quick Internet search

You will take all that information and look at its *totality*. It helps to write it all down to make sure you are properly weighing all the clues. That is what I do. Once you have everything on paper, it will be easier for you to see where additional information or research is necessary. Writing it down also helps to ensure that you don't pay too much attention to isolated or sensational pieces of information and ignore other pieces altogether.

When analyzing your information, I would suggest the following approach.

Do not be swayed by superficial indicators of normalcy. As I wrote earlier, you cannot get an accurate read on someone by the way he or she looks or by how friendly he or she seems. Check yourself. Have you been swayed by any of the following faulty evaluations?

- The person you are evaluating seems "nice" or "friendly."
- The person you are evaluating is highly respected or comes from a good family.
- The person you are evaluating looks harmless.
- The person you are evaluating is religious, went to the same college as you, belongs to the same fraternal organization or charity, or in some other way shares something in common with you that lures you into a false sense of safety.
- The person you are evaluating has the trappings of a normal life: a house, a yard, a dog, a marriage, and one or more children.
- The person you are evaluating seems important: graduated from an important school, is wearing an expensive suit, is driving an expensive car, and otherwise lulls you with impressive titles or monikers.

Make sure you've screened for CTD behaviors. Make sure you have assessed whether the people involved in your particular situation have exhibited any of the dangerous or threatening behaviors described in chapter 9: anger problems, impulsive behavior, injustice collecting, signs of lack of empathy and callousness.

Depending on the type of decision you are making, you also might want to assess people for other characteristics that are important to that decision. For instance, you might not want to hire a financial planner who is a risk taker or a babysitter who is easily frustrated, exhibits poor coping behaviors, is emotionally immature, and shows a pattern of making poor decisions. In some hiring situations, you may not mind employees who are not team players. But in others it may be essential. Think about all the behavioral characteristics that are important for this particular decision and make sure you've gathered enough information to assess the various people involved.

Know the totality of the circumstances before making any decision: Don't make decisions based solely on one detail. Ask yourself some questions.

- Is there any information that I've overlooked or neglected to gather?
- Have I considered all the variables in the situation?
- Have I looked at all aspects of each person involved?
- Have I dug deep enough into their personal, family, work, private, and secret lives? Do I understand what makes them tick?
- What is the primary motivator for this behavior? What are the likely benefits and consequences?
- Is there something else I need to know but don't have time to find out?

Know when to stop digging and start deciding. Keep in mind that you probably won't be able to find out everything you want to know about a situation or person. Even in law enforcement, we have crime scenes where the physical evidence recovered yielded little if any forensic value. Similarly, you might find that you could not get as much information as you wanted about a person or that some information was too risky to gather.

You may never feel that you have everything you need, and you might have to make a decision when less is known than you would like.

Writing down the information you've gathered and comparing it to the information you wish you had will help you determine if you have enough information to make a thoughtful and prudent decision.

Consider your personal biases: Have you interpreted all this information correctly? Have your personal biases swayed you in one direction or another? Have you failed to gather key information because you are too timid, scared, or stressed?

Assuming you have all the information, know everything you need to know about the various people involved, and have interpreted the information correctly, then it's time for you to draw a conclusion based on what you know. When coming to a conclusion, think about the following:

- Does all of the information fit together? If not, why not?
- Am I seeing a pattern of behavior?
- Am I seeing one or more problems?
- Does my assessment tell me what to decide and how to prioritize the actions I will need to take to handle the situation?
- What are the risks? Where are the land mines?

Once you know the answers to some of these questions, you will be able to decide on a better, safer, and more effective course of action.

When forming a decision, remember to think about the possible benefits and negative ramifications of your decision not only today but a week from today, six months from today, a year from today, and three years from today. Ask yourself the following:

- Do I feel pressured to make this decision?
- Am I making this decision because I feel stressed, overwhelmed, rushed, frightened, bored, emotionally high, or in love?
- Am I making excuses in an attempt to justify my decision?
- What regrets might this decision lead to down the road?
- What potential problems might this decision cause for me six months from now, a year from now, and three years from now?
- What am I gaining by making this decision? What am I losing? What might I leave behind? What new problems will I encounter?

- How will my decision affect other people in my life who are important to me? How will it affect them in six months, one year, and three years?
- If others know about my decision or it becomes public, how would I feel and would it cause damage to me, my family, or others close to me?

Do a litmus test on your emotional state. If you are feeling shaky, emotional, or pressured, it might help to consult someone else. A therapist, arbitrator, friend, life coach, member of the clergy, or someone else you trust might help you sort through the decision and stay balanced.

Sample Assessments and Decisions

You are now familiar with every step in the SMART model. You know how to evaluate your judgment and avoid common pitfalls that could cloud it. You also know how to mitigate risk, conduct interviews, assess for CTD behaviors, and how to use all of that information to make a better decision.

Now let's get a little practice. It will help you to hone the process so you can better use it in real life.

In the following pages, I'm going to walk you through several situations and show you how I would complete the steps of this decision-making process. As we walk through each assessment and decision, I'll point out the factors that might cloud your judgment. I'll show you how I would weigh the pros and cons and take the potential long-term consequences into account. By doing so, I hope you will be able to see how the SMART model works in specific situations. It's also my hope that this will provide you with some practice and begin to sharpen your skills.

Sample Assessment

Is This Handyman Dangerous?

The situation: You are looking for someone to paint the inside of your house. You know the job will take almost a week. You want someone you can trust. What should you do to screen potential painters? What questions should you ask? What information will be important in making your decision?

Think about your answer, and then read on.

THE ASSESSMENT

Usually, when we hire anyone, we want to know "How much is it going to cost?" "Is he or she competent?" and "Have they done good work for other clients?" That's why typical interview questions are as follows:

- What do you charge?
- How long have you been doing this?
- Do you have any references?
- Are materials included in the price?
- How long will it take you to finish?

We usually want to hire someone who is nice and friendly too. So if the person smiles a lot and seems pleasant, we give them a high score in our assessment process. Yet, as you've already learned, how nice or how pleasant a person appears usually has little to do with how dangerous they really are.

Rarely if ever does anyone think to ask if the person has a criminal record. Yet whether he or she has been arrested may be the most important detail for you to know about the person who will be coming into your home. This is a high-risk decision, as your home is your comfort zone. Your home is where you go to feel safe.

You do not want to hire someone who will:

- be searching for the location where you hide your secret key
- be casing your house and looking for where you keep your valuables so he or she can break in later and steal them
- steal items that he or she thinks you won't miss until many weeks later
- give your information to someone else who is unsafe
- attack you

- disrespect your property
- behave inappropriately—for instance by making sexual advances toward you or a family member

You don't just want to know if he has a criminal record. You also want to know what that record was for. Just because a person has a criminal record does not mean that you can't trust them. Find out as much as you can about the crime and then think about how that crime applies to the job at hand. For instance, someone who was convicted of doing drugs twenty years ago, went to rehab, got clean, and has stayed clean since is probably not a threat to you and may well be capable of doing an excellent job of providing you a service. Someone who was convicted of stealing just a year ago, however, poses a much higher risk to you and your personal property. And someone who has convictions for assault should be screened very carefully. If the behavior is recent and/or reoccurring, this person could pose a threat to you if a situation arises where there is a dispute between you.

It's important to note that the absence of a criminal record does not necessarily mean that criminal or dangerous behavior is not present. You will need to find out more than just this information in order to assess the people you wish to hire.

Are you thinking that you could never be so rude as to ask someone if they have been arrested? Consider that a person without a criminal record won't mind being asked this question because she or he has nothing to hide. Think about how you would feel if someone asked you this question. Would you be put off, or would you empathize with the home owner who is worrying about his or her safety? I'm guessing that you would empathize, which is how any truly nonthreatening person will react.

You also might be thinking that it's so easy for people to lie and answer such a question with a no. That's true, but you learned how to detect deceit in chapter 8. Use those skills.

For instance, I recently interviewed a number of house painters. One painter came to me at the recommendation of a friend, someone who happened to also work in law enforcement. I asked this painter whether he would be bringing others into the house to help him paint. He answered that question by telling me how long he had been painting houses and how good he was at what he did. I noticed that he evaded my question. That made me suspicious.

I told him that I was a retired FBI agent, and I asked him if he or any of his coworkers had a criminal record. He stuttered, looked away, and then began talking quickly about the success of his business and about how he's never gotten any complaints. I hadn't asked him whether he'd gotten any complaints. Since he volunteered this, it made me assume that he had. More important, he had again evaded my question, making me even more suspicious. He never called me back with a quote.

I went with a different painter who did a wonderful job.

I ask everyone I wish to hire whether they have a record. I assure you that it would frighten you to know just how many times my "do you have a criminal record?" question has tipped me off that someone might not be so harmless after all.

In addition to asking about the criminal record, you might want to go even deeper, depending on the job you are hiring for. How thoroughly you screen your hired home help will depend on a few factors:

1. If they've already been prescreened. If the person you are hiring works for an established company, then a screening process may already be in place. For instance, if your insurance company sends someone to repair your roof, they will likely send a roofer they have used in the past. If this roofer were problematic, other home owners would likely have complained to your insurance company about him or her. As a result, it's likely that your insurance company would have filtered out any workers who have caused problems in the past.

2. How much access this worker will have to your home. If the person will be working outside the home or will be coming in and leaving while you are home, your screening process can be less intensive. On the other hand, if you are hiring someone who will have long-term unsupervised access to your home, you will want to screen more thoroughly. For instance, you'd want to screen a babysitter, nanny, or au pair much more thoroughly than the person who delivers and installs your satellite dish.

3. How regularly the person will have access to your home.
You will want to screen people more thoroughly if you are going to have an ongoing relationship with them, and maybe less thoroughly if it's just a short-term, quick, one-time-only job. For long-term, regular relationships, you'll want to continuously update your dangerousness assessment as you get to know more and more about the person. Keep in mind, however, that someone can come into your home just one time and acquire enough information about you and/or your family to hurt you, then or later on.

If the painter will have unsupervised access to your home, you'll want to screen thoroughly. That means you'll want to find out if your house painter exhibits one or more of the five dangerous behaviors (described on pages 182–186). To do so, you will want to ask questions that will give you information about whether they possess any of those dangerous qualities. You'll want to ask emotion-laden questions, most of which will start with phrases like "How did you feel when" and "How would you feel if." As various painters answer these questions, observe their comfort level. Do they struggle with the question? Do they provide evasive answers? Do they seem uncomfortable? If so, why?

Listen to the answers. Notice if a painter continually blames others, focuses on real or imagined slights that he mentions have victimized him over his lifetime, and fails to accept responsibility for problems in his life. Here are some questions you might ask:

- Can you tell me about conflicts you've had in the past with home owners or colleagues and how you've handled them?
- In the past, when a home owner experienced a problem that stalled a project—for instance a sudden financial stressor or a death in the family—how did you feel? How did you handle it?

You'll also want to talk with other people who know this person, and you'll want to ask questions designed to help you go beyond "He's a nice guy" and help you get at what you really want to know. Depending on the worker you are hiring, those questions might be:

- What issues came up on your job and how did Mr. X handle them?
- What were you most impressed with? Where could you recommend improvement?
- Have you or anyone in your family ever felt uncomfortable around him or her?
- What did your children say about him?
- How did he and his coworkers treat your pets?
- When you brought up issues or problems regarding his work, how did Mr. X take that criticism/feedback?
- How did you feel about Mr. X when the job was finally done?

Sample Decision

Should you go on this bargain cruise with some other women from church?

The situation: A woman you know from church is organizing a cruise and she's asked you to come along. You'll be spending five days and four nights in the Caribbean. This is enticing to you because it has been a hard, cold winter. A few days of warmth and sunshine are just what your mood needs. Plus, at only $450 for the whole trip, this is a bargain. The price even includes meals. You don't know the organizer that well, but she has always been nice, outgoing, and friendly to you in the past. If you decide to go, you will be traveling with her and five of her good friends and sharing a cabin with one other woman.

Think about how you would make this decision. Then read on.

THE DECISION

To make this decision, you'll want to counteract your excitement about the cruise. Remind yourself that this trip will have you traveling for a full week with a group of women you do not know very well at all—and you'll be sharing a room with one of them. You know little to nothing about the habits, values, personalities, or behaviors of this group of women and about your potential roommate in particular. What should you find out about these women? What unknown factors about them, their behaviors, and their personalities could cause problems for you on the cruise?

Think about all the potential negative consequences of going on this cruise. They might include the following:

- Since this cruise is being organized by another woman—who is potentially the leader of this circle of friends—you could easily find yourself outnumbered and feeling like an outsider. If you don't fit into the group or do not agree with their habits and values, this could potentially be a miserable experience for you.
- Will you and your roommate be going to sleep around the same time? What will you do if you are an early-to-bed person and she is a night owl?
- Will this group of women want to party when you prefer not to, and then try to coerce you into going along with their plans?
- Will they want you to go with them on expensive land excursions that you can't afford?
- Will you feel as if you must hang out with them the entire time, even if you would rather be alone or do your own thing?
- What will you do if they react to your personality or behavior in a negative way?
- What if your cabin mate is one of those people who takes over the cabin, causing you to feel uncomfortable and unwelcome there?
- What if one or more of the women tends to get out of control and needs you and others to keep her from getting herself into trouble when she drinks?
- Are any of the women demanding, controlling, moody, or sulky to the point that their problems could be significantly disruptive to the others?

Any of those factors could cause serious problems for you during this cruise—problems that will make this so-called vacation seem more like a nightmare.

If I were making this decision, I would not want this trip to be the first time I'd ever socialized with this group of women. I would create opportunities to go out with them socially so I could get to know them better and observe their behavior. I would also ask the person organizing the trip a lot of questions—questions designed to help me determine how likely any of the potential consequences are to arise. For instance, I would ask questions like these:

- Tell me about the woman I will be rooming with. What is she like? What are some of her unique habits?
- Tell me more about the other women going on the cruise. What are they like? Have you cruised with them before? If so, tell me about some of your experiences.
- Will we be hanging out as a group the entire time?
- Will we be meeting one another for meals or social time?
- What kinds of social activities do you think will be involved?
- What kinds of side trips might we be taking?
- How much drinking does the group like to do?
- What happens if, at the last minute, I decide not to go?
- Do you cruise a lot? If so, what have those experiences been like?

You also will want to assess this group of women. Find out more about the leader of the group and what she is like. Every group has a leader, even within friends. Does the same person generally lead the group at all times or does the leadership role shift from one woman to another depending on what is going on? Is the organizer of the cruise the leader of the group? Is there friction in the group? Are there historical problems in the group that will follow these women onto the cruise ship?

Once you determine who the leader is, you'll want to assess her leadership style and ability, her decision-making skills, and her ability to be a role model. Make sure she is the type of person you will feel comfortable traveling with. I know that this sounds like a lot of work just to decide whether to go on a short vacation, but even a little assessment of the people you will be traveling with can go a long way in helping you to make the best decision, and it is not just about the money. Remember, you will be away from home and your support group, living in very small quarters, and most likely outside of the United States or your home country in a place where the enforcement of laws will be very different. If you pick the wrong travel partners and there is a problem, or several problems, you will find yourself dependent on people you might not like or are even afraid of, and you will have limited options for making alternative plans. Do your homework.

Sample Decision

Is it the time right to introduce your new boyfriend to your children?

The situation: You are a single parent and have met someone you care about very much. You want to bring this man home and introduce him to your two young children. He is anxious to meet your children, and you are anxious to have someone in your life. Your goal is to get remarried.

Think about how you would make this decision, and then read on.

THE DECISION

You might have a tendency to want to rush into and solidify this new relationship, but this is a decision that you will want to take a lot of time and thought with, as you are not the only person affected by it. Your children will be affected as well.

Even though you care about this man and have come to feel close to him, it's important to remind yourself that you still do not know him in each of the six areas of his life (see chapter 9). You probably have not had ample time to observe his behavior in a wide range of circumstances. Early in a relationship, most people make an attempt to impress each other. They hide and downplay their unfavorable qualities. It will take time before you know this man fully enough to be able to answer important questions like these:

- How is he with children?
- Is he someone your children can respect and grow fond of?
- Will he respect your parenting style? What are his parenting style and philosophies?
- Does he have behaviors or habits that you would not want your children exposed to?
- What are his relationships like with others in his family, including his own children?
- Is he potentially dangerous? For instance, is he dating you to gain access to your children? What are his intentions regarding your children?

That last question is chilling, and it's also something that many women don't want to think about. Still, it happens, and it's something that you want to guard your children against.

Because this is a relationship that will, over time, potentially become more and more intimate, you will want to observe this boyfriend as much as possible and learn as much as you can about him, and you will want to do this in several different situations.

Before introducing him to your children, you will want to do a danger assessment on him—screening him for behaviors that could suggest long-term problems (see chapter 9).

Over time you might notice what he says about other people and about his place of employment. For instance, does he often blame others for his problems? (A sign of injustice collecting.)

Notice how he drives his car. Is he prone to road rage? (A sign of anger.) Does he run red lights, change lanes excessively, tailgate, drink and drive, or fill the car with cigarette smoke? (Possible signs of impulsiveness, anger problems, and immaturity.) How would you feel with your children in the car with him?

How does he talk to and about other people? Is he rude? Does he interrupt a lot? Does he talk down to people? Does he act like a bully? (Possible signs of arrogance, lack of empathy, and callousness.) Would you want your children on the receiving end of that kind of interpersonal communication style?

How well does he listen? Does he tend to dominate the conversation? How does he take criticism—real or imagined? Does he take responsibility for his own actions or blame others? (These could be signs of someone who can be dominating and controlling, as well as someone who is a blamer.)

Does he regularly sulk? Does he go through periods of time when his mood becomes dark and unresponsive or has he had outbursts of anger? (These are possible signs that he has problems with anger, injustice collecting, or serious mental-health issues.)

Is he jealous without cause, checking up on you, your whereabouts, and who you are with? Has he unexpectedly showed up at places where you have been? Is he becoming demanding of your time and attention to the exclusion of contact with your friends and family? Has he been unfaithful to you during your relationship? (These are possible signs of narcissism and of someone who is dangerously jealous, possessive, and suspicious.)

Who are his friends and what are they like? Are his friendships short term? Are his long-term friendships few or nonexistent? (If he has problems developing and maintaining friendships, this could be indicative of poor interpersonal communication and relationship skills.)

Does he ever cause you to feel unsafe or threatened? How does he treat your pets? (Signs of anger, impulsivity, or lack of empathy.)

Does he drink and drive? Use illegal drugs or abuse OTC drugs? (These are possible signs of impulsivity, a "rules don't apply" philosophy, immaturity, anger problems, and lack of empathy and/or concern for others and their welfare.)

You will also want to notice signs that he has a personality that is not compatible with long-term intimacy. For instance, does he lie, withhold information, or overstate claims? Has he boasted about getting away with lying to others? If he lies to others, what will stop him from lying to you?

Is he exceedingly frugal and does he expect you to pay most of the time? If so, what will stop him from moving in and becoming a parasite who lives off your paychecks?

Is he already talking about getting married, even though you've known each other for just a few months? An affirmative answer to this final question could be a big red flag. Many people assume that someone like this is a great catch. They might think, "Finally! I met a man who does not have a fear of commitment!" Yet you want to carefully consider why he is in such a hurry. Why is he pushing things forward? What is his main motivation? Is he really in love, or is some other reason motivating him to tie the knot?

Maybe he is a parasite who will do with you what he has done in his other relationships: move in with you, quit his job, and live off your paychecks. Worse, maybe he's a pedophile.

What do your friends think of him? Use the eyes and ears of others for feedback and include these details in your assessment.

Once you've done a danger assessment, you will want to introduce him to your children slowly and gradually. Try to avoid inadvertently sharing your opinions with your children up front, which will influence their own thinking or inhibit them from giving you their true opinion. For example, comments like "He's a great guy" or "I know you will love him—he is really nice" can communicate how you feel about him. It can be very intimidating to a child to attempt to form a different conclusion.

You might first introduce him to your children in a neutral location outside the home, and you might do it for a short period of time. During this first encounter, you will be watching what he does, listening to what he says, and noticing how he interacts with your kids and how they interact with him. Afterward, you'll want to ask your children what they thought, and you will want to spend time listening closely to what they say rather than talking to them about their experience with this new person. Here are some examples of some questions that might help you get started. Notice that these are open-ended questions rather than questions that require a yes-or-no answer. They are also questions that focus on your child's feelings, insights and experiences, and not on yours.

- What did you notice about him?
- What did you think about him?
- How did you feel about meeting him?
- Was there anything that made you feel uncomfortable?
- What are your feelings about him becoming more a part of this family?

Some children are likely to be resentful of a new man who comes into their mother's life, but be careful to not ignore the information your children give you about this man. If they are afraid of or intimidated by him, ask yourself what it is about him that caused their fear or concern. Was it something he said or did—something that is a sign of danger?

Sample Assessment

Is it too risky to open the front door?

The situation: It's 9:30 p.m. Your doorbell rings. You are at home with your small children, who are asleep. Your spouse is not home. You are not expecting anyone. You look through the peephole and do not recognize the person on the other side of the door. Do you answer the door?

Think about your answer, and then read on.

THE ASSESSMENT

This very situation happened to my coauthor as we were working on this book. She was fearful of answering the door because there had been a series of home invasions in her neighborhood, some of which had taken place while the homeowners were asleep. Yet she was afraid of not answering the door for precisely the same reason.

If she opened the door, she might allow a burglar to gain access to her home. If she didn't open the door, she might inadvertently cause a burglar to assume that the house was empty, causing him to look for a way to break in.

She quickly thought of ways she could mitigate the risk of a potential burglar breaking in and harming her and her daughter. She:

- called her husband and left a message asking him to come home
- turned on the porch light, so the person standing on the porch would know that someone was home
- dialed 911 on her phone and put her finger on the call button, ready to press it if need be

Then she opened the door. A Plexiglas storm door now separated her from the man on her porch. As it turned out, it was one of her neighbors. He was concerned about a strange car parked on the street.

My coauthor took a few actions to minimize her risk, but there is at least one more action she could have taken. She could have shouted through the door, without opening it, and asked the man on the other side who he was and what he wanted. This would have prevented her from having to open the door—and making herself and her daughter more vulnerable—to gain the same information.

When assessing whether to open your door, you will want to consider the following:

- The time of day. Is it late at night or the middle of the night? If it's dark, that raises the risk of danger.
- Who else is home with you? Is there someone there who could call 911 or help you defend yourself? That would lower the risk of danger. Are you home alone with small children that you would want to protect? This would raise the risk of danger.
- Whether you are expecting someone. If you are expecting someone, this lowers the risk. If you are not, it raises it.
- The purpose for the person being on the other side of the door. If you ask the person, through a shut door, who he is and what he wants and he doesn't give you a good reason or a logical or believable explanation, there's no reason for you to open your door.

Sample Assessment

What should you do if you suspect that your daughter's boyfriend is abusive?

The situation: You've overheard your college-age daughter's boyfriend talking down to her, ordering her around, and calling her what you think are derogatory names. You interpret his interpersonal style as abusive and you worry about physical abuse as well.

Think about how you would find out whether your suspicions are valid, and then read on.

THE ASSESSMENT

This is a delicate situation, one that will probably take every ounce of your self-control. If you are like most parents, you will be tempted to swoop in and unleash Armageddon on this boyfriend and/or to forbid your daughter from seeing him again. That might not result in a favorable outcome, however. First, it could trigger his abusive behavior to escalate. Second, it might cause your daughter to shut down and become evasive, sneaking around to see him and no longer confiding in you about what is going on. Even worse, it could result in your daughter putting emotional, even physical, distance between her and you and the rest of the family.

Here are some suggestions for how to learn as much as you can about what is going in with your daughter and her relationship and how to develop a course of action:

- Think about what you know and what you don't. You might be tempted to rush in and interpret what you overheard. Hold back. You don't know all the details just yet. To determine how much of a threat this young man poses to your daughter, you will need additional information, and some of it may not be easy to obtain. Some information about the boyfriend will have to come from your daughter, through her eyes.

- Think about your personal style and how that might cause her to react. How have conversations with your daughter gone in the past? When you've asked your daughter important, probing questions, has she shut down? Gotten defensive? Become argumentative? What about your interview style caused those reactions in her? It's very important to think about this now—before you ask a single question. You want to adjust your interview style so you can put her at ease and get her to open up. If your line of questioning has caused an undesirable result in the past, think about what triggered it and adjust accordingly.

Perhaps most important, think about whether you are the best person to gather this information. Will you become too emotional? Are you so enmeshed with your daughter that you will not be able to listen calmly? Does she usually confide in you? Or is she more likely to confide in someone else—perhaps a sibling or an aunt? Is your style or tendency to lecture, threaten, problem solve, or yell? If you answer yes, then understand that if you do not change this style it is likely it will impede your ability to get the information you critically need.

• Plan the interview. Where will you do it? Since she might become emotional, a crowded public venue is probably not the best location. Since she might be tempted to run, hide, and lock the door behind her, your home might not be ideal either. Perhaps a calming, sparsely populated neutral location would work best—such as a nearby park where you can talk while you walk. Think about the pros and cons of when, where, how, and who. When will you do it? Who else will be there? What is your strategy? Where will you talk with her? What is the best environment to help your daughter to open up?

• Conduct the interview. The toughest part will probably be the beginning, when you first bring up the topic. Try to stay away from a tension-provoking introduction like "I don't like him!" or "You need to break up with him!" That might come later, but it will kill your interview if you start with it. She may feel defensive of him and resentful, even embarrassed that you feel she is not capable of handling her own problems. To prevent her from shutting down, you'll want to ask open-ended questions that do not sound judgmental of him or her. You will also want to keep the focus on her, how she feels, and her overall safety, not on what you want. For instance, you might want to introduce the discussion by saying something like this:

> I am concerned about Joe because I heard how he spoke to you. It sounded scary to me. It's important for me to hear from you what you think of him and that behavior.

Then you might follow up with questions like these:

- Tell me about Joe. What is he like?
- Have you ever been frightened of him? Can you tell me about those times?
- Have there been times when you thought he could have hurt you or someone else?
- Have there been times when you and/or others have had to "talk him down" from his becoming angry with others?
- What would your friends tell me about him and his behavior?
- Are there times he has threatened you or been physical with you?

As she answers, look for signs of evasiveness. For instance, notice if she answers your yes-or-no questions with a "not really." You will want to follow up on all occurrences of "not really" and get to the bottom of what that means for her. Ask, "What do you mean you have 'not really' been frightened?" "Not really frightened" of him most likely means that she has been frightened at some time in the past.

As a mother you will probably want to rush in and protect her. You might be tempted to tell her what to do or to give her a lecture. Instead give her the opportunity to talk. Listen. You want to hear how she describes the situation and how she feels.

Be prepared, however, for her to shut down. This will be very difficult for her to talk about. In that case, you might say, "Just so you know, your not talking with me is not going to prevent me from making sure that you are safe. By not talking with me you may leave me no choice but to talk with others about this young man. I understand that you are embarrassed or not comfortable talking to me about this. I understand that. But I am worried about you, and I will find out about this in other ways if I have to because this is a situation where you could get hurt."

- Don't expect a one-time dump of information. Note that this might take several discussions. Try not to exhaust her with too many questions. She probably won't break down and tell you everything during just one talk. You might want to say, "We've talked enough for today. You can even set aside a day and time when you will talk again.

• Interpret the information you've gathered. Based on what she told you, do you think this is a one-time incident (not likely) or a disturbing pattern of behavior that will escalate (likely)? Use others, such as trustworthy friends or parents who have been through similar situations, to help you evaluate the information and the behavior. Although you might be able to call school officials and make them aware of a possible problem, note that most probably will not openly share information with you due to legal concerns about privacy.

• Decide on a course of action. This could be a dangerous situation, one that will likely get worse if you do nothing. And of course the age of your daughter will be a major factor in how aggressive you will want to be, should be, or can be. If your daughter is of legal age, by law she can make her own decisions, and you can only advise, unless she poses a danger to herself or others. Have a discussion with your daughter about what you plan to do. Your plans might include calling up the school and asking officials to help you ensure that he stays away from her. They might include getting law enforcement involved and getting a restraining order.

Often in cases like this, parents just want their daughters to be out of the relationship and for the young man to get help. More serious steps, like going to the school or law enforcement, are seen as too severe because of the negative consequences. However, if the behavior is egregious and dangerous enough, it may not be sufficient to handle it on your own. Getting professional help may be essential to keep him from revictimizing her or someone else.

• Be prepared for your daughter to stick up for him and to tell you that she doesn't want to get him in trouble. Be prepared for her to worry that he will become angry and really hurt her if you intervene. Be prepared for her to worry about other kids in school gossiping about her, teasing her, or worse.

Educate your daughter and help her get in front of her choices six months or even a year in the future, so she can realize the long-term consequences of her decisions on her life.

Sample Assessment

How do you assess a problem employee?

The situation: An employee has made veiled threats to another employee in his unit. This is an ongoing pattern of behavior that you have documented in your position as a human resources person. But you are concerned about retaliation if you terminate him. You have also had some incidents of anonymous nuisance situations on the job, including some vandalism and minor property damage. You have no evidence that this employee is responsible, but you suspect him. He has recently been passed over for a promotion that was given to a younger person with less time on the job. You are concerned about his behavior escalating.

Think about how you would go about addressing this problem, and then read on.

THE ASSESSMENT

When I was at the FBI BAU, I often got calls about individuals and their potential for workplace violence. I sometimes learned that the person had been a problem for a long time, his behavior had escalated, and now there were plans to terminate him because there was concern of his behavior becoming violent. I would then be asked for my assessment of the person and to factor in a strategy for terminating his or her employment.

These are some of the questions I would ask about the employee and the situation, and the answers I received.

You've been worried about this employee for a while?

Yes, we have.

So it's almost Christmas Eve (or some other holiday or significant date for the employee) and you want to let this employee go right away?

Yes, we do.

Several times I was tempted to respond, "You've got to be kidding me," but I didn't. The only way they could possibly make this situation any worse would be to make sure every single employee at the company was present on the day of the firing and then do the equivalent of a perp walk as they very publicly escorted the problem employee out of the building.

I knew they'd already made the decision to fire. They didn't want my opinion about whether to let the problem employee go. What they wanted to know was this: how best to handle the termination to minimize a negative response by the employee at that time or at some time in the future.

Let's walk through how you might decide to develop a strategy for the successful and safe termination of a problem employee.

  • Decide on your goal. In this case it's to safely terminate an employee while mitigating the risk of this employee harming the company or its employees now or in the future.

  • Know as much as possible about this employee, his job performance, and his personality, and problems he has had in the past with managers and coworkers. Be knowledgeable about the current precipitating issues.

You also want to find out everything you can about what might be going on in other areas of this person's life that might exacerbate how he views his termination. Does he go home to a loving family? Does he live alone? Did his wife just leave him? Has this employee talked to coworkers or his supervisor about stressful problems in his life? Is he an injustice collector? Has he ever acted out in the past? How important is his job to him? Is he quick to anger? Does he have access to weapons? What will his support network be like once he leaves the company?

Termination from one's job can be extremely stressful and embarrassing for a person. It is also mentally and emotionally debilitating, particularly for someone who is heavily or pathologically invested in his or her job. For someone whose coping skills are dysfunctional and/or weak, the loss of a job can have a devastating impact, particularly if his or her social or family network is weak or even nonexistent. Severing someone's ties to his or her employment or school might be severing the one social and interpersonal attachment he or she has left. As an employer, you need to know this. Losing that attachment can be extremely problematic for the person and result in a desperate response.

Decide who will terminate the employee. If you are planning on doing it, consider how you are viewed by this person. Does he consider you the source of his problems or blame you for his current situation? If he does view you in this light, you do not want to be the person in charge of terminating him. This could significantly increase his feelings of a personal vendetta.

Also, have you terminated employees in the past? How did those terminations go? Did they go well? Or did the employees become angry? If the employees became angry, are you sure you have the skills needed to terminate a problem employee who might become violent? If so, what will you do differently to prevent this problem employee from becoming angry? If not, who can you call on to help you terminate this employee? If you are a small business, is there an association or arbitration group you can call for assistance?

Think of ways you can mitigate the risk of this employee turning violent or destructive toward himself or others—both at the present time as well as in the future. First and foremost, you will want to give this person some dignity by showing appropriate empathy. The last thing you want to do is walk this employee out in front of his or her coworkers.

1. Do not do the firing when there is an audience or others around. Give the person some dignity.

2. If the employee is mad at or has a grudge against certain supervisors, they should not be present during the firing. Have a neutral person do the termination.

3. Make this employee feel cared for. Give him severance, even if it's not part of the company policy. Pay out all his vacation. Set him up with a job-finding service. Make it about how you will help him readjust.

4. When explaining the reasons for termination, do not blame the employee. Blame his behavior instead. For instance, you could word it like this: "Many employees are frightened. Some of the e-mails that you've sent have caused them to feel threatened." Remind him that your concern is not just for the company but for his welfare too.

5. Be willing to say, "I am sorry," if appropriate, and show appropriate empathy. For instance, say, "I'm sorry it turned out like this," and "I know this must be hard on you."

6. If the employee needs to gather up some possessions (and there is a concern over allowing him to return to his office and computer), have a neutral party (the head of security or human resources) deliver his personal belongings to him. This will also allow you to monitor his behavior and reaction to the termination.

7. Follow up with the employee, particularly if there is a concern for safety. If company policies permit, meet for coffee or lunch for some time after the termination. This will allow you to monitor the employee to find out how he is handling the termination. Always have neutral parties meet with the former employee and never anyone the employee held a grudge against. For safety, send two people rather than one and let the police know where and when the meeting is taking place, if warranted.

8. Stay in touch over a period of time. This not only causes the employee to feel cared for, it also allows you to see if his mood or behavior is deteriorating as result of the loss of his job and the potential for revenge or displaced violence is increasing.

Bonus Advice for Home Owners

If you are a home owner and you need to let go of hired help, you may be tempted to get it over with just to get them out of your life. You also might be tempted to unload on them about their awful work and creepy presence in your home. This, however, could easily backfire and result in the person having a vendetta against you.

Keep your goal in mind. It is to get this person out of your home and out of your life. To ensure that this happens, you will have to use a little psychology. Avoid arguing, insulting, or threatening them. Don't "hold on to" their tools or equipment to "teach them a lesson." Pay for the work that's been done to date, even if the job is half-finished and even if you will lose money and have to hire someone to fix mistakes. While in some extreme cases you may have no alternative but to withhold payment or even file a legal claim, realize that these actions will perpetuate a relationship with this person. If he or she is potentially dangerous, such actions can cause you and your family all types of problems.

To give you an example, I once hired someone to cut my grass. After finishing mowing my lawn, he drove over and crushed my yard ornaments. Then he broke my expensive landscape lights.

And then he committed the ultimate violation. He left my fence gate open. Buddy, my beloved new rescue dog, got out, which frightened me because I worried that he would get hit by a car. I eventually tracked down Buddy and got him home safe, but then I definitely wanted to let this guy have it for leaving the gate open. I thought about the condescending way he'd spoken to me in the past and how arrogant he'd been.

But then I took an emotional step back and thought about this man's personality. That arrogance and the anger that I found so off-putting were red flags—ones that I knew to pay attention to.

Instead of letting him have it, I telephoned him and casually said, "Look, the gate was open when I got home and my dog ran off. I am such a fanatic about this dog. I am just over-the-top about him. If anything happened to him, I don't know what I would do. I know I'm overly sensitive about the fence gate, and I'm sorry about that. But I'm thinking that it might be best if I cut the grass myself since I know I will always remember to keep the gate closed."

Then I wrote him a check for the work he'd done, along with a note thanking him. I even suggested that I would keep him in mind for future work. I have never had contact with him since.

Sample Decision

What should you do about the guy who pays too much attention to you at the gym?

The situation: You belong to an expensive gym and have paid for an entire year's membership in order to get a discount. Lately, however, you have not been enjoying your workouts because a man has been taking too much interest in you. Initially he just seemed to be politely chatting, but soon he was annoyingly pointing out what you were doing right and wrong. Eventually he began commenting on your choice of outfits, your makeup, and your hairstyle. At first you thought he must be harmless. After all, the gym is expensive and he's a lawyer. But it has reached the point where he seems to find you as soon as you walk in, and then dominates your time while you are there. He continually asks you questions about your personal life, especially about whether you are dating someone. Even when he's not right there talking to you, he stares at you and turns his head as you walk by.

He's made you so uncomfortable that you even stopped going to the gym for a while. Then when you showed up again, he seemed angry and made a snide comment about how you are slacking off on your workouts and it shows.

Think about how you would handle this situation, and then read on.

THE DECISION

Many factors might affect your judgment as you attempt to make this decision. Maybe you don't want to hurt the guy's feelings or you feel uncomfortable confronting the situation. Maybe you have been swayed by the fact that he's a lawyer who works out at a gym catering to successful professionals. Maybe you worry that you are not reading the situation correctly. Perhaps the guy is harmless and you are being overly sensitive.

Consider what you don't know about this situation. Do a behavior assessment on the man and consider how your risk level could go up or down depending on how you handle the situation.

It is important to keep the situation in perspective. Right now the man is a nuisance, and he has crossed a boundary with you by saying things that are inappropriate. At the moment, however, you have no evidence that he is either a stalker or a follower. Understand that incorrectly labeling people—even casually—is, at the very least, insensitive and, at the extreme, could be grounds for a defamation lawsuit. There are different types of stalkers, and it takes a great deal of expertise to do a professional threat assessment on one. A simple and reliable way to do a behavioral assessment for a novice, however, is to look at whether his behavior is escalating.

Nuisance behavior becomes concerning when it begins to escalate and becomes intrusive and more threatening. A behavior is escalating if it increases in frequency (he's attempting to contact you more often) or intensity (he's starting to threaten you or become highly critical or insulting). It's also escalating if he seems to be learning from his mistakes. For instance, if you start to go to the gym at a different time, he realizes what's going on, and he starts going to the gym at that time, too, he's escalating. The more aggressive he becomes and the more risks he is willing to take to make contact, the more worried you should be about his behavior.

To figure out what to do about this situation, consider the following:

- Think about your goal. What do you want? Many women would probably walk away from a situation like this. They'd give up an entire year's worth of membership dues in order to avoid feeling so uncomfortable and having to confront the situation. There's no absolute right or wrong here, but when you take the time to think about what you want, you will probably find that you want to be able to get in a workout in peace, without having some annoying man chatting you up the whole time. You also want to feel safe, and you want to know that this man hasn't somehow followed you home or otherwise taken his interest in you beyond the gym. Stopping going to the gym will not get you to any of those goals.

• Consider other possible options that might get you closer to what you want. You could try a few options incrementally:

1. Talk with a gym manager. Explain the situation. Ask if there have been other complaints about this man bothering women. Ask for the manager's advice or request that the manager handle the situation.

2. The next time this man comes over to you, explain that you feel uncomfortable. You might say, "Look, I am not comfortable with all of this attention. I really want to focus on my workout," and then make it very clear that you are not going to engage in a conversation.

3. Always come to the gym with a partner and work out with that person. This will make it more difficult for this man to intercede.

4. Ask a gym employee or another patron to walk you to your car.

5. If this man's behavior escalates (for instance, he starts leaving notes on your car), make a formal complaint to the gym. If that does not help, ask the gym for a refund.

6. If it still continues to escalate (he's calling you at home), consider contacting law enforcement and getting a restraining order. Make sure to find out what restraining orders are all about, how they can be enforced, and how they can be violated. Do not engage with him at all. Any type of communication—positive or negative—can encourage someone like this. Just answering the phone and telling

him to stop calling or to go away can cause him to continue or even escalate. Do not call him to give him a piece of your mind, and do not talk to him out of politeness. Ignore his every advance.

As I mentioned, there is no one right way to handle this. Once you weigh all your options, you may very well decide to stop going to this gym. You might walk away from the money and you might join a different gym or stop exercising altogether. That's your choice to make. But just know that you have options and that each option affects your risk level differently.

Sample Decision

You just learned that the father of your child's friend is a registered sex offender. What should you do?

The situation: You just found out through the rumor mill that the fifty-year-old father of your son's good friend is a registered sex offender. At first you didn't think it could possibly be true. After all, you've known this family for a long time. But then you checked the sex-offender registry for your county and found that he was convicted in federal court ten years ago for the possession of child pornography. Now this father is offering to give your son and other members of the team rides home from soccer practice.

Think about what you would do about this situation, and then read on.

THE DECISION

You have many unanswered questions. What does this conviction really mean? Is this just something harmless—something he got caught for many years ago and then never did again? If he never abused a child, does that make him less dangerous than someone who was actually charged and convicted of assaulting a child?

What are the important issues for you to consider as you make your assessment and subsequent decision?

To sort out what this conviction means, you might research reliable sites online (such as the frequently asked questions area of the sex-offender registry itself), or you may want to seek information from law enforcement.

Since I already know what information you need, I will fill you in. A federal conviction for this type of crime is a big deal. Federal prosecutors only take on a limited number of cases. When federal prosecutors decide to get involved, you can bet that a case is quite extensive. Otherwise the feds would likely defer the prosecution to the state.

The second critical and concerning issue is the conviction itself. If this father is looking at child pornography, that suggests he is fueling his own sexual fantasies about children. If these sexual fantasies began during his adolescence and continued into adulthood (he was forty when convicted), this increases the probability that his behavior is paraphiliac and not just harmless curiosity.

Paraphiliac behavior involves the need for unusual or bizarre imagery or acts for sexual arousal. Examples of some of the more common paraphiliac behaviors include pedophilia (sexual attraction to children), voyeurism (sexual attraction to watching unwitting people in the act of disrobing or naked or engaged in sexual activities), and exhibitionism (exposing one's genitals to unsuspecting strangers for the purpose of being sexually aroused). Most people who exhibit paraphiliac behavior tend to exhibit more than one of them. This is incredibly concerning.

The third major issue is this father's age. He is fifty. How likely is it that this man has been "satisfied" with only viewing child pornography over his lifetime? Is it likely that he has never attempted to act out sexually with a child? The absence of a criminal record for acting out against a child does not mean the behavior is absent. He may never have gotten caught or the child might never have told anyone. If a parent is the abuser, the child might never report it and the abuse can continue for years.

If this father has acted out or attempted to act out his sexual fantasies on a child, he could be classified as a pedophile. Pedophilia is difficult to treat and rarely cured.

You may never know for sure whether this father acted out his sexual fantasies involving children, but that is a gray area that I personally would not want my child caught up in. This is not a father you want around your son when other adults are not present.

Here are some other factors to keep in mind:

• You don't have all the information regarding this father's potential threat to your child, and you probably never will. Your assessment and decision of how to handle the situation must err on the side of extreme caution.

• You might feel empathy for the father and particularly for his son. You might feel the father has paid his dues and that his son, who apparently has done nothing wrong, should not be penalized because of his father's actions. Your assessment of the situation and your decision about how to handle matters can take into consideration your sensitivity toward both father and son. It is critical, however, that you understand the larger ramifications of what your son could go through for years and years were this father to abuse him under your watch. If you and your son want him to have an ongoing relationship with his friend, you will need to appreciate the potential for problems and be willing to be vigilant in monitoring your son's well-being.

• You or your spouse might be tempted to give this father a piece of your mind. Perhaps you want to tell him to stay away from your child if he knows what's good for him. Keep in mind that it's illegal to harass someone just because his name is listed on the sex-offender registry. If you do this, you very well might find yourself on the wrong side of the law.

• The whole situation might make you feel so uncomfortable that your initial reaction is to ignore it and try not to deal with it at all. Or you might be tempted to have some magical thinking. Perhaps your son has been under the care of this family before and nothing bad has happened. You might tell yourself that if nothing bad happened in the past, nothing bad will happen in the future. You also might tell yourself that the father is probably attracted to females, so the boys are probably "safe." Although some pedophiles do have gender preferences, it would be naive to think that one would never violate his own gender preference during a moment of opportunity. There is a definite possibility your son could be victimized by this father, so close and ongoing monitoring of his affiliation with the family is essential.

• Think about how you will protect your child. You obviously do not want a situation where your child might be alone with this father. To accomplish this goal, you need to politely decline his offer. You can say, "Thanks, but I enjoy watching soccer practice and don't mind driving him myself."

• Decide what you want to do with this information. Your child is not the only child at risk. Do other parents know that he's a registered sex offender? Is it up to you to tell them? Or is the responsibility of each parent to be vigilant about finding background information on their children's friends' parents?

• If this information gets out, what will happen to your son's friend? Will he become ostracized or bullied? And more distressing, is this boy being abused by his own father? You may or may not consider whether it's your moral responsibility to do something about these issues. You can consider talking to school officials. Let them know what you've learned and what you are worried about. Counseling and mental-health professionals at your child's school are trained and experienced in handling delicate situations like this in the most effective and sensitive ways. They are a great resource in this type of situation.

You are now well on your way to mastering the SMART model. You might even be finding that you are already thinking differently and changing the way you make decisions. You now know how to spot and outsmart dangerous people and how to avoid becoming one of their victims. In the final chapter of this book, you'll find out how to avoid becoming the object of their attention in the first place.

CHAPTER 10 RAP SHEET

- SMART decisions are not based on just one detail. They are based on the totality of the circumstances.
- Write down all the details to make sure you are weighing and interpreting them properly.
- Look for holes and blind spots. What might you have missed? What might you have overlooked?
- Before making any decision, carefully consider its long-term ramifications. Can you live with all the possible negative consequences of this decision?

Chapter 11

The *Dangerous Instincts* Safety Guide

I n the typical movie or television suspense thriller, a tiny woman wakes in the middle of the night. She hears noises and suspects someone is in her home. She gets out of bed, goes to the kitchen, grabs a knife, and slowly proceeds to tiptoe through the house, in search of the intruder, with an expression of horror and fear on her face.

Now that you've read most of this book, I'd like you to think about that scenario and about what's wrong with it. If you were awakened in the middle of the night, what would you do? Would you run to the kitchen to look for a knife? Would you grab a handgun you have never used before or practiced with? Or would you do something else?

It's my hope, after reading this book, that you would do something else. It's my hope that you would think about the best ways to mitigate your risk of being attacked by the person or people in your home. Will you be mitigating your risk of attack by grabbing a knife and walking through the house in search of the intruder? It's not likely. Here are some examples of what's more likely to occur in that scenario, and then some suggestions of what you might do instead:

1. You become startled by your teenager, who happens to be sneaking back in through his bedroom window, and possibly injure him or her in the process. (In other words, there

is no intruder. The strange noise you heard was made by a family member.)

2. You become startled by a real intruder, who probably knows how to handle a knife (or a gun) much better than you do. This person might also be bigger and stronger than you and have enough strength and adrenaline running through their body to get the knife away from you and use it against you.

You see, going for the knife and then in search of the intruder is actually one way to *increase* the risk. To decrease it you might do the following:

• Grab the phone and call for help. Okay, the phone line has been cut (as always seems to be the case in movies). So pick up your cell phone instead.

• If you and your family members can't run outside, lock your bedroom door. If you have small children in the house, get them all in the same room and lock and barricade the door.

• If someone tries to break down the locked bedroom door, climb out the window (if possible). Yell, scream, holler, and make noise to alert others around your home that you are in danger.

As I hope you can see, what you've already learned throughout this book is what to do to assess your situation, your thinking, and others in order to stay safe. I could provide you with a long list of tips to memorize. For instance, I could tell you what to do if you ever get tossed into the trunk of a car or what to do if someone tries to abduct you at gunpoint. But fortunately it's not likely you will ever find yourself in the trunk of a car, and it's not likely that you will ever find yourself staring down the barrel of a handgun either. What is likely are hundreds if not thousands of possible other scenarios—scenarios that cannot be navigated with an instruction manual because you'd never be able to memorize all the instructions.

You can't memorize how to avoid all the specific problems in life that involve dangerous situations and dangerous people. The possibilities are infinite. But you can do five things that will help you to avoid danger, minimize your risk, and make better decisions that can impact your life and the lives of your family members for years to come.

1. Fine-tune your decision-making skills (chapter 6).
2. Mitigate risks (chapter 7).
3. Identify the critical and relevant information you need and interpret that information based on the totality of the circumstances (chapters 5 and 8).
4. Develop your listening and interview skills to obtain critical and relevant information (chapter 8).
5. Assess for dangerousness and threatening behavior in others (chapter 9).

The skills you develop in these five areas will help you figure out your best course of action in nearly any situation that could be dangerous or threatening or concerning to you. You won't need someone like me to tell you what to do. You'll be able to stay safe on your own. It's for that reason that this chapter does not contain a list of ways to burglarproof your home, get free from bindings, or disarm an attacker. Instead, in this chapter you're going to learn a process to make yourself and your loved ones less vulnerable—so you will be less likely to get into a threatening situation in the first place.

What Makes You Vulnerable

Dangerous people often seek out vulnerable people—people who are most likely to fall for their schemes. Because of this, one of the ways you can make yourself and everyone around you safer is to think about your vulnerabilities. What would make you more likely to fall for a con? What would make you more likely to allow a dangerous person to get close to you? Where are your vulnerable areas? Think about these questions for yourself, and think about them for your family members.

For instance, at different times in your life you might be emotionally vulnerable. The following states are usually accompanied by emotional vulnerability:

- Low self-esteem
- Insecurity
- Loneliness
- Sadness
- Fear

Being emotionally vulnerable can cause most people to seek comfort, answers, and help. And it's during these times in our lives that many of us let down our guard or are too ready to trust someone we should not trust. If a dangerous person happens to walk into your life when you are experiencing a moment of desperation, he or she could seem like a savior to you. You might embrace this person and feel thankful that he or she has walked into your life at precisely the right time.

In reality, the dangerous person has probably read you much better than you read them. He may have even targeted you because he recognized your low self-esteem, insecurity, loneliness, neediness, or sadness and knew he could exploit or use you because of it. This dangerous person knew that you—more so than someone else—would respond to flattery, companionship, and easy fixes. He knew that you felt broken and that you were searching for a solution. All he had to do was make you think that he had the solution you wanted.

It's for these reasons that con artists prey on the elderly, particularly shut-ins or widows. They know they are lonely. So they call and offer them the antidote to loneliness. They chat with them over the phone and keep them company. Eventually they ask for money or something else.

It's also for these reasons that dangerous men prey on women who are getting over a breakup or divorce. It's why they prey on children whose parents have recently gone through a divorce.

And it's why they prey on people with chronic or terminal illnesses.

It's for all of these reasons that you will want to take steps to overcome these vulnerabilities, and you'll want to help your family members do the same.

You will also want to think about other factors that might make your family members vulnerable. If you have children, for instance, you'll want to remember that their ability to assess risk is not as good as that of most adults. They lack the judgment and experience of someone older. This is why you don't want to leave it up to them to decide, for instance, if they should answer the direct message they got on Facebook from a person who isn't in their inner circle of friends. This is why you don't want their computers in their rooms, where you cannot monitor their activities. It's why you want them in a common area, where you can see what they are doing and monitor who they are interacting with and what they are communicating about.

It's also why you want to do your own danger or threat assessments on their friends, and especially on the friend who emerges as the leader of the social circle. Is the leader domineering, a bully, impulsive, or someone with anger problems or who is likely to influence others to engage in behavior that is high risk, dangerous, or even illegal?

If your child is a more introverted and shy person who is more of a follower than a leader, he or she could be pulled along by such a person and end up getting involved in risky behavior, behavior that could result in long-term problems.

Your children are not yet capable of making these assessments. They need your help.

I recommend that you assess the following areas of your life and for your family members. Ask yourself if you have taken all available precautions to mitigate risk in these areas. Think about what problems could develop in these areas. How could you get hurt? What can you do to reduce the following?

- Professional risk
- Financial risk
- Physical risk
- Emotional risk

Don't wait until there's a crisis to reduce your vulnerabilities. Do it now, so you can avert a crisis in the future.

Make Yourself Less Attractive to Dangerous People

I just mentioned many ways people leave themselves emotionally open to being victimized. There are also a few ways that some people physically broadcast "I'm an easy mark."

The primary one: They are just too nice. Someone who is intent on harming you will probably watch you for a while without your knowledge. If you are unusually kind, this person will notice. If you tend to answer any question someone asks, this person will notice. If you have a hard time saying no, this person will notice.

I'm not suggesting that you turn yourself into a cold, heartless individual who never talks about herself and keeps all her information private. I am suggesting, however, that you pay close attention to what types of information you transmit and how someone with impure motives might interpret that information or possibly use it against you. Think twice before giving someone your address and other contact information. When someone pays too much attention to you, wonder why, especially if that person asks you personal questions about where you live and who you live with. If someone invades your personal space and causes you to feel uncomfortable, don't think, "I don't want to hurt his feelings." Take care of yourself and put up a boundary instead.

In the beginning this might feel foreign to you. Over time, as you pay more attention to your vulnerabilities, it will become second nature.

The same is true for the SMART model. Using it is a skill, one you

The Dangerous Truth

It's estimated that 35 percent of students have been threatened while they were online. Your professional reputation is also at risk. Anyone can find what you post, and what goes online stays online forever. As a general rule of thumb, if you wouldn't want it on a billboard in print large enough for random passing motorists to see, you don't want it online either.

can hone with practice. You are now familiar with the method. It's time to start putting it to work. Every time you use it, you will sharpen your skills. Keep practicing. Using the SMART model is a perishable skill. If you stop, you'll backslide.

The more you use and practice what you've learned in this book, the better you will get. To ensure that you put in that practice, I encourage you to find a *Dangerous Instincts* buddy or to form a group. Consult this friend or group of people regularly. Meet once a month or so and talk over what's going on in your lives and how the SMART model might apply. Whenever you are about to make an important decision, consult your friend or the group. You can go through the book together and consider what action is best for each situation that comes up in your lives.

You will know the SMART model is working because you will see the evidence in your decisions. You will feel more in control of your life, and you will experience a lot less regret. You will feel less insecure.

You will no longer feel conflicted, wondering, "What should I do?" You will know what to do. You'll make a SMART decision, and you'll feel more and more in control every time you do so.

CHAPTER 11 RAP SHEET

- Your SMART skills will help you make safer decisions in any situation you find yourself.
- Emotional vulnerabilities such as loneliness, grief, and low self-esteem can make you more likely to let down your guard at the wrong moment.
- Dangerous people know how to use your emotional vulnerabilities against you.
- It's important to do a danger assessment for your children, because they are not yet able to do this assessment on their own.
- Try to reduce your professional, financial, physical, and emotional vulnerabilities now so you are a less attractive target for someone trying to take advantage of you or your family.

Appendix

The *Dangerous Instincts* Resource List

Interviewing, decision making, and risk assessment all require a certain amount of information gathering. For instance, before interviewing someone you'll want to know as much as you can about that person. Before making a decision, you'll want to know all the potential consequences. To mitigate risk in any given situation, you'll want to fully understand all the circumstances involved.

You can't always find out what you need to know from other people. Some questions are too rude or too intrusive to ask. For instance, you probably don't feel comfortable knocking on your neighbor's door and asking, "Are there any dangerous people who reside in or visit your home?"

Fortunately a lot of the information you will need in order to make decisions and assessments and to conduct interviews can be gathered—at least in part—from public sources. In this chapter, you'll find a list of resources that will help you do just that.

How to Research Local Crime Problems

Go to the local police department and ask for summary crime reports and news and press releases about crime rates in neighborhoods. Archives of the local newspaper will also contain crime-related information. You can check any or all of the following Web resources too:

- The websites for local, regional, state, and federal law enforcement agencies: Many law enforcement agencies have their own websites where they post a variety of information, including crime activity and their responses to those problems.

- CrimeMapping.com: This free Web service allows you to click on a state and find the latest information on reported crimes in many of its areas.

- CrimeReports.com: Similar to CrimeMapping, this free service allows you to type in an address, and then it will show you on a map the reported crimes and sex-offender data for that area.

- Ucrdatatool.gov: The U.S. Department of Justice's Uniform Crime Reporting (UCR) Program allows you to see state and national crime statistics.

- FBI.gov/stats-services/crimestats/crime_statistics: Here you'll find reports you can download about specific crimes. You can also research the FBI's UCR database.

Information You Might Want to Know Before You Move

In addition to researching local crime problems (mentioned earlier), you might want to ask your Realtor about access to public transportation, possible traffic issues (when and where rush hour is an issue), the location of grocery stores and other types of essential shopping, whether there's a home owners' association and how effectively it functions, and whether you will be responsible for snow removal and street upkeep. You'll also want to find out about the municipality or incorporated area. What kinds of emergency services are available? Are the firefighters salaried professionals or volunteers? Must you pay dues to benefit from emergency services? How large are the local police and fire services, what geographic area do they cover, and how fast or slow is their usual response time? Are there hydrants in the neighborhood, or must water be pumped or trucked in to fight a fire? Can you register to get alerts by phone, text, or e-mail when there is a local Amber Alert or another emergency?

Here are some resources to check out:

• Access to food delivery: This could be important if you have a medical emergency. You can check to see if Meals On Wheels (mowaa .org) or MANNA (mannapa.org) operate in the area.

• The quality of the school system: Psk12.com, School Data Direct (schooldatadirect.org), SchoolMatters.com, and *U.S. News & World Report* offer rankings of public schools, high schools, and colleges. If you plan to homeschool or you have a child with special needs, you'll want to check with the state and local school district to find out about support, resources, and accreditation and registration requirements.

• The quality of local utilities: Ask your Realtor whether cable, DSL, and other utilities are available, especially if you are considering moving to a rural area. Find out what type of heating (natural gas, propane, electric) the house uses and whether the electricity is reliable (does it go out frequently during storms?).

• The quality of local hospitals: Various Internet sites offer hospital report cards and accreditation ratings. Examples include ipro.org/hospitals, ConsumerReportsHealth.org, and HealthGrades (healthgrades .com).

• Whether the home is in a flood zone: FloodSmart.gov is a site run by the National Flood Insurance Program that will help you determine whether a home is in a flood area. It also helps you find agents who sell supplemental flood insurance.

Information You Might Want to Know About Another Person

You can find out a lot about a person just by searching online. For instance, you can learn the following:

• If there's a dangerous dog in the house: Virginia has a dangerous-dog registry (virginia.gov/vdacs_dd/public/cgi-bin/public.cgi). Other states may follow Virginia's lead. Check to see if your state has.

• If any of your neighbors are convicted sex offenders: Every state has a sex-offender registry. You can find links to each of these registries through the FBI's site: fbi.gov/scams-safety/registry.

• If he or she has abused animals: Suffolk County, New York, started a registry of animal offenders, and some other states might follow suit. Check to see if your state has such as registry.

• What types of information someone has been posting online: Do an Internet search to see what someone has posted on Twitter, blogs, and other publicly accessible online forums.

Information You Might Want Before You Travel

Gathering the right knowledge before you travel can help you avoid certain types of problems and be better prepared to handle others. Here are some resources you might find particularly helpful:

• The U.S. Centers for Disease Control and Prevention (cdc.gov) offers information on flu outbreaks and other health issues. This information might allow you to avoid areas where certain diseases are common or severe, or to take steps to prevent catching them.

• The U.S. Department of Homeland Security (dhs.gov) has a security-advisory system on its site. This system gives you a color-coded national threat level and detailed and up-to-date information about what is and is not allowed on airlines.

• The U.S. Department of State (state.gov) issues travel warnings and alerts. It also lists helpful information such as the location of U.S. embassies in various countries. You can also find crime and security information on various countries and details about the quality of their medical systems. And you can register with them when you travel.

- You can find information on weather conditions (such as an approaching hurricane) at weather.com or, within the United States, at the National Weather Service site (weather.gov).

How to Be a Better Myth Buster

Throughout this book, you've learned about many common myths that tend to get people into trouble. The best way to avoid becoming a victim of misinformation is to arm yourself with credible information. I've listed some resources here to help you do just that:

- National Institutes of Health (nih.gov): For all types of health information, and specifically information about mental-health and personality disorders.
- Centers for Disease Control and Prevention (cdc.gov): For all types of health information.
- WebWiseKids.org: For information about cybersafety and Internet bullying.
- National Behavioral Intervention Team Association (nabita .org): For details on how to enroll your workplace, school, or campus in its program.
- National Center for Missing and Exploited Children (missing kids.com): For all types of information about missing children.
- America's Missing: Broadcast Emergency Response (amber alert.gov): For all types of information about missing children.

Notes

1. U.S. Department of Justice, Federal Bureau of Investigation. *Workplace Violence: Issues in Response*. Washington, D.C., 2004.
2. C. S. Nave, R. A. Sherman, D. C. Funder, S. E. Hampson, and L. R. Goldberg, "On the Contextual Independence of Personality: Teacher's Assessments Predict Directly Observed Behavior After Four Decades," *Social Psychological and Personality Science* 1 (2010): 327–34.
3. R. Hare, *Without Conscience: The Disturbing World of the Psychopaths Among Us*. New York: Guilford Press, 1999.
4. J. Reid Meloy, *Violent Attachments* (Northvale, NJ: Jason Aronson Inc., 1992).
5. Mental Health America, *American Opinions on Mental Health Issues* (Alexandria, VA: NMHA, 1999).
6. Reference approved by MSNBC, which taped this interview for use in *Criminal Mindscape*.
7. P. Babiak, C. Neumann, R. Hare, "Corporate Psychopathy: Talking the Walk," *Behavioral Science and the Law* 28 (2010): 174–93.
8. Paul Babiak, *Snakes in Suits* (New York: ReganBooks, 2006).
9. Mary Ellen O'Toole, *The School Shooter: A Threat Assessment Perspective* (Quantico, VA: FBI Academy, 2000).

Index